Ethics and Foreign Policy

The promotion of human rights, the punishment of crimes against humanity, the use of force with respect to humanitarian intervention: these are some of the complex issues facing governments in recent years. The contributors to this book offer a theoretical and empirical approach to these issues. Three leading normative theorists first explore what an 'ethical foreign policy' means. Four contributors then look at potential or actual instruments of ethical foreign policy-making: the export of democracy, non-governmental organisations, the International Criminal Court, and bottom-up public pressure on governments. Finally, three case studies examine more closely developments in the foreign policies of the United States, the United Kingdom, and the European Union, to assess the difficulties raised by the incorporation of ethical considerations into foreign policy.

KAREN E. SMITH is Lecturer in International Relations at the London School of Economics. Her recent publications include *The Making of EU Foreign Policy: The Case of Eastern Europe* (1999), and she is co-editor (with Christopher Hill) of *European Foreign Policy: Key Documents* (2000).

MARGOT LIGHT is Professor of International Relations at the London School of Economics. She is co-editor (with A. J. R. Groom) of *Contemporary International Relations: A Guide to Theory* (1994) and co-author (with Neil Malcolm, Alex Pravda and Roy Allison) of *Internal Factors in Russian Foreign Policy* (1996).

Ethics and Foreign Policy

edited by

Karen E. Smith and Margot Light

CAMBRIDGE
UNIVERSITY PRESS

PUBLISHED BY THE PRESS SYNDICATE OF THE UNIVERSITY OF CAMBRIDGE
The Pitt Building, Trumpington Street, Cambridge, United Kingdom

CAMBRIDGE UNIVERSITY PRESS
The Edinburgh Building, Cambridge CB2 2RU, UK
40 West 20th Street, New York, NY 10011-4211, USA
10 Stamford Road, Oakleigh, VIC 3166, Australia
Ruiz de Alarcón 13, 28014 Madrid, Spain
Dock House, The Waterfront, Cape Town 8001, South Africa

http://www.cambridge.org

First published 2001

Printed in the United Kingdom at the University Press, Cambridge

Typeface Plantin 10/12 pt.   *System* LaTeX 2$_\varepsilon$ [TB]

A catalogue record for this book is available from the British Library.

Library of Congress cataloguing in publication data
Ethics and foreign policy / edited by Karen E. Smith and Margot Light.
   p.   cm.
Includes bibliographical references and index.
ISBN 0 521 80415 9 (hb.) – ISBN 0 521 00930 8 (pb.)
1. International relations – Moral and ethical aspects.   2. Diplomacy – Moral
and ethical aspects.   I. Smith, Karen Elizabeth.   II. Light, Margot.
JZ1306 .E872   2001
172′.4 – dc21   2001025748

ISBN 0 521 80415 9 hardback
ISBN 0 521 00930 8 paperback

Contents

Notes on contributors   *page* ix

1 Introduction   1
   KAREN E. SMITH AND MARGOT LIGHT

Part I Theories

2 Ethics, interests and foreign policy   15
   CHRIS BROWN

3 The ethics of humanitarian intervention: protecting
   civilians to make democratic citizenship possible   33
   MERVYN FROST

4 A pragmatist perspective on ethical foreign policy   55
   MOLLY COCHRAN

Part II Instruments and policies

5 Exporting democracy   75
   MARGOT LIGHT

6 Ethical foreign policies and human rights: dilemmas
   for non-governmental organisations   93
   MARGO PICKEN

7 The international criminal court   112
   SPYROS ECONOMIDES

8 Constructing an ethical foreign policy: analysis
   and practice from below   129
   K. M. FIERKE

Part III Case studies

9   The United States and the ethics of post-modern war   147
    CHRISTOPHER COKER

10 Blair's Britain: a force for good in the world?   167
    TIM DUNNE AND NICHOLAS J. WHEELER

11 The EU, human rights and relations with third countries:
    'foreign policy' with an ethical dimension?   185
    KAREN E. SMITH

References   205
Index   219

Contributors

CHRIS BROWN is the author of *International Relations Theory: New Normative Approaches* (Columbia University Press, 1992), *Understanding International Relations* (Macmillan, 1997), and some two dozen articles and book chapters on international political theory; and the editor of *Political Restructuring in Europe* (Routledge, 1994). He is Professor of International Relations at the London School of Economics, and immediate past chair, and current president, of the British International Studies Association.

MOLLY COCHRAN is Assistant Professor in International Affairs at the Georgia Institute of Technology. She previously taught at the University of Bristol. She is the author of several journal articles in *Millennium* and *Review of International Studies*. Her book, *Normative Theory in International Relations: A Pragmatic Approach*, was recently published by Cambridge University Press.

CHRISTOPHER COKER is Reader in International Relations at the London School of Economics. He is the author of several books including *War and the Illiberal Conscience* (1998), *The Twilight of the West* (1998), and *War and the Twentieth Century* (1994). He has just completed a book on *Humane Warfare*.

TIM DUNNE is a Senior Lecturer in the Department of International Politics, University of Wales, Aberystwyth. His book *Inventing International Society: A History of the English School* was published by Macmillan in 1998, and he has co-edited a number of volumes including *Human Rights in Global Politics*. He is currently an Associate Editor of *The Review of International Studies*.

SPYROS ECONOMIDES is Lecturer in International Relations and European Politics at the London School of Economics. He is the author of 'Yugoslavia' (with Paul Taylor), in James Mayall, ed., *The New Interventionism 1994–1994: The UN Experience in Cambodia, Former Yugoslavia and Somalia* (Cambridge University Press, 1996), and of *The Balkans and International Order* (Routledge, forthcoming). In 1990–1991, he was a Research Associate at the Centre for Defence Studies at King's College, London.

K. M. FIERKE received her Ph.D. from the University of Minnesota in 1995. She was previously a Prize Research Fellow at Nuffield College, Oxford, where she wrote this chapter. She is presently a lecturer in the School of Politics, Queen's University of Belfast.

MERVYN FROST is Professor of International Relations at the University of Kent at Canterbury, England. He was previously Professor and Head of the Department of Politics at the University of Natal in Durban, South Africa. His work includes *Ethics in International Relations* (Cambridge University Press, 1996) and recent articles on 'A Turn Not Taken: Ethics in IR at the Millennium', in *Review of International Studies* (vol. 24, special issue, December 1998) and 'Putting the World to Rights: Britain's Ethical Foreign Policy', in *The Cambridge Review of International Affairs* (vol. 12/2, Spring/Summer 1999).

MARGOT LIGHT is Professor of International Relations at the London School of Economics. She is the co-editor (with A. J. R. Groom) of *Contemporary International Relations: A Guide to Theory* (Pinter Publishers, 1994), and co-author (with Neil Malcolm, Alex Pravda and Roy Allison) of *Internal Factors in Russian Foreign Policy* (Oxford University Press, 1996). Her most recent article, written with Stephen White and John Löwenhardt, is 'A Wider Europe: the view from Moscow and Kyiv', *International Affairs* (vol. 76, no. 1, 2000).

MARGO PICKEN was director of Amnesty International's office at UN headquarters, New York, and then the international human rights programme officer for the Ford Foundation. She has been an associate/visiting fellow at the Centre for International Studies at London School of Economics since 1996. She serves on the board of several non-governmental organisations working in the field of human rights and is presently advising London School of Economics on setting up a Centre for the Study of Human Rights.

KAREN E. SMITH is Lecturer in International Relations at the London School of Economics. She is the author of *The Making of EU Foreign Policy: The Case of Eastern Europe* (Macmillan, 1999), and several articles and chapters on the international relations of the European Union.

NICHOLAS J. WHEELER is a Senior Lecturer in the Department of International Politics, University of Wales, Aberystwyth. His book *Saving Strangers: Humanitarian Intervention in International Society* was published by Oxford University Press in 2000. He is the co-editor of *Human Rights in Global Politics*, and is currently an Associate Editor of the *International Journal of Human Rights*.

1 Introduction

Karen E. Smith and Margot Light

The genesis of this book lies in a conference held by the London School of Economics department of international relations in November 1998. The conference, for staff and students, takes place every year at Cumberland Lodge, near Windsor. The theme in 1998 was 'Ethics and Foreign Policy', and several contributors to this book presented the first versions of their chapters at the conference.

The theme was chosen to prompt reflection about the apparent proliferation of issues on foreign policy agendas that raise questions about how governments should act in international relations. The promotion of human rights, punishment of crimes against humanity, the prohibition of arms sales to unstable regions or to states which abuse human rights, and the use of force, particularly for the purpose of humanitarian intervention, are all issues which have recently been the subject of discussion among politicians and government officials. This is most evident in the 1997 proclamation by the new British Foreign Secretary, Robin Cook, that Britain would formulate and implement foreign policy 'with an ethical dimension'. He meant that the promotion of human rights would be a central concern of British foreign policy and that arms sales would be reviewed to ensure that British arms were not used by foreign governments to repress human rights. The European Union has also tried to incorporate human rights considerations into its relations with third countries, and has agreed on a Code of Conduct on Conventional Arms Sales. In President Clinton's State of the Union message in 1994 (*The New York Times*, 26 January 1994), he claimed that promoting democracy was an important goal of American foreign policy. Dozens of states approved a statute for an International Criminal Court in July 1997, which would prosecute individuals for war crimes and crimes against

We would like to thank the student participants in the Cumberland Lodge conference whose enthusiasm encouraged us to embark on this book; two anonymous reviewers, who provided extremely useful comments; and the editorial board of the London School of Economics and Cambridge University Press International Studies series and John Haslam of Cambridge University Press for their support for this publication.

humanity. Governments have frequently had to decide whether they should intervene militarily to protect the citizens of other states (for example, in Rwanda, Bosnia, Kosovo, East Timor or Iraq).

The starting point of the conference and of this book was that of the foreign policy analyst, not the normative theorist. But the general debate on an ethical foreign policy must perforce bring in normative theoretical considerations, primarily because the meaning of 'ethical' needs to be pinned down. International relations scholars have paid attention to normative theory in the past (Beitz, 1979; Brown, 1993; Hoffman, 1994; Frost, 1996). Policy-makers, steeped in realism, tended to scoff at normative theory, however, and at those who suggested that it should inform government policy.[1] National interest, they insisted, should be the basis of foreign policy; discussing ethics was inappropriate.[2] As a result, the normative theoretical debate was often quite separate from deliberations by government officials about policy. Now that governments and international organisations explicitly claim an ethical basis to their foreign policy, policy-makers can and should use the insights that normative theory can provide. As for theorists, they have new empirical material on which to test their concepts. Several leading theorists do so in this volume.

Conflicts can and do occur between perceived national interests and a government's ethical intentions. A simple example is the loss of jobs in the defence industry at home that may follow the cancellation of foreign arms sales because of concern about the use to which the arms will be put.[3] To realists, this proves that proclaiming an ethical foreign policy merely gives a hostage to fortune. To normative theorists, on the other hand, it indicates that decision-makers need a reliable method of choosing between contradictory claims. Policy-makers often deny that there is a problem. They tend to reiterate that their policy is ethical (as if repetition will make it so), and find some way of justifying their pursuit of national interest by insisting, for example, that they are simply fulfilling

---

[1] In the 1980s, for example, Alan Clark, a British government minister, made an entry in his diary complaining that, in briefing him for a visit to Chile, 'a creepy official' told him 'all crap about Human Rights. Not one word about the UK interest' (cited in *The Economist*, 12 April 1997).

[2] They did not mean that foreign policy should be consciously unethical, simply that it was amoral. Many of the chapters in this book, however, draw attention to the implicit and explicit role of ethics in foreign policy-making throughout the twentieth century.

[3] In the first two months of 2000 alone, the British government was criticised for approving arms exports to Pakistan (ruled by a military government), Indonesia (which had not yet punished human rights abusers in East Timor) and Zimbabwe (involved in the conflict in the Democratic Republic of Congo and accused of human rights abuses). In all three cases, the EU context was critical; the EU had decided to lift the arms exports ban on Indonesia. And critics of the government's policies with respect to Pakistan and Zimbabwe claimed that it was violating the EU Code of Conduct on Arms Exports (see Chapter 11).

commitments made prior to their adoption of an ethical dimension to their policy.

At one level, this example illustrates the long-standing debate between realism and idealism. Idealism is traditionally blamed for the rapidity with which the hopes for international peace collapsed after the First World War (Carr [1946] 1964). Realism was dominant in international relations theory and among practical policy-makers during the Cold War (Morgenthau, 1985). But idealism has deep roots, it seems, in human nature. Each time it appears to be defeated, it creeps back into theory and it also influences the way in which policy-makers wish to behave. Declarations of an ethical foreign policy are one manifestation of the revival it has enjoyed since the end of the Cold War. But does the arms sales example prove, as realists would argue, that it is as doomed now as it has always been?

At another level, the arms sales example epitomises a knotty problem with which policy-makers often have to grapple: how to choose between conflicting interests. Of course, balancing interests is always difficult, even when the issues have nothing to do with ethics. All governments have a number of foreign policy aims, and they frequently contradict one another. Ensuring that short-term needs do not undermine important and long-standing elements of the national interest, for example, is never easy. When ethical considerations enter the equation, however, the choice becomes more difficult. Should the duty to provide jobs at home override the responsibility to protect foreigners abroad? In essence, the problem centres on whether ethics cease at the water's edge, or whether the ethical standards applicable abroad are different from those that prevail at home.

A third problem that is highlighted by many aspects of an ethical foreign policy concerns the very basis of the international political system. Should the principles of sovereignty, inviolability and non-interference in the domestic affairs of other countries – the foundations upon which the international state system is built – take precedence over ethical concerns? In relation to arms sales, is it any business of governments that export arms how the weapons are used within the borders of another state? If the answer is affirmative, does that mean that sovereignty and non-interference have been replaced by new international rules of engagement, and if so, what are they? In fact, few policy-makers would reply that it *is*, invariably and always, their business. But if the response is that it is only sometimes their business, further questions arise: under what conditions is it their business, for example, and who decides what the conditions should be?

The question of 'who decides the conditions' leads to another of the problems that has dogged discussions about human rights and ethical foreign policy: are ethics universal, or do they differ from culture to culture? Cultural relativists claim that ethics are culturally bound, and that what we call universal human rights are simply Western norms that have been imposed on other countries and cultures. In normative theory there has long been a debate between cosmopolitans who believe that human rights derive from natural rights and an ability to reason and, therefore, are universal; and communitarians, who argue that individuals have rights by virtue of their community (Brown, 1992a). The debate is sometimes transposed into the question: are Asian or Islamic values different from Western norms, and if they are, should those who hold them be able to set their own standards of human rights?

The idea of a foreign policy with an ethical dimension, therefore, raises many complex problems of both a conceptual and a practical nature. The aim of this book is to examine some of the issues from a theoretical and empirical perspective. Three groups of key questions are investigated:

(1) What is an ethical foreign policy? How should conflicts between national interest and ethics be settled?
(2) What are the ethical issues facing foreign policy-makers? What instruments do they use to deal with them? How effectively do they use them?
(3) To what extent do particular international actors incorporate ethical concerns into foreign policy and what problems do they face in so doing?

In Part I, contributors explore what an ethical foreign policy means. Several different theoretical perspectives are offered which provide different approaches to this controversial question. Part II takes a thematic approach, looking at the key instruments used by foreign policy-makers and other international actors in their ethical foreign policy: the export of democracy; the promotion of human rights and its effect on the relationship between NGOs and governments; the attempt to create an institution which can hold governments and individuals accountable for international crimes; and grassroots efforts to put pressure on governments to improve their ethical practice. Part III consists of case studies which examine more closely developments in the foreign policies of three international actors, the United States (US), the United Kingdom (UK) and the European Union (EU), to assess their progress in, and the difficulties raised by, incorporating ethical considerations into foreign policy.

Inevitably there have been omissions: one book cannot do justice to all the issues surrounding the theory and practice of ethical foreign policy. On the theory side, for example, there is no chapter on the realist critique of ethical foreign policy. Partly this is because the realist view is fairly well known, but it is primarily because the editors wanted to address the key question, 'what is ethical foreign policy'? The realist answer, 'there is no such thing', would have closed the debate prematurely. Instead, the editors asked three normative international theorists to engage with this question. Readers may also lament the absence of important and related issues such as arms sales, international economic processes or environmental concerns. Some chapters do touch on the clash between economic interests (for example, selling arms abroad) or foreign economic policy (for example, promoting market economic reforms), and ethical concerns such as the promotion of human rights and democracy (see, for example, the contributions by Picken, Light, Smith, and Dunne and Wheeler). But space constraints prevented the inclusion of chapters dedicated to these issues, and to considering the clash between policies to foster the right to development and those to promote political rights, or whether ethics should extend to the physical world as well.

Lack of space, too, means that the policies of only three international actors are considered in this volume. The focus on the UK is explained by the fact that the proclamations of the new Labour government on ethical foreign policy rekindled a theoretical debate about ethics. On the other hand, the long history of the United States' ideologically driven foreign policy and the Clinton administration's humanitarian pretensions justify our choice of the US for one of our case studies. The EU offers an example of a collective actor incorporating ethical concerns into its foreign policy, with a wide impact on international relations due to its very nature as a collectivity of fifteen states (and many more, in the decade to come). Of course, the foreign policies of other international actors – such as Australia, South Africa and the Scandinavian countries – could have been explored here.[4] Since we could not cover everything, we tried to bring together theoretical reflections and empirical investigations of some issues and policies in the hope that our volume will encourage others to fill the lacunae left here.

What is ethical foreign policy?

Different theoretical perspectives provide different accounts of what constitutes an ethical foreign policy. The three contributors to Part I start from different positions, but they all agree that it is unreflective of actual practice to posit a dichotomy between an ethical foreign policy, on the one hand, and a non-ethical foreign policy, on the other. The issues are rather how governments act ethically, according to which criteria, and how they

[4] Some works have already done so: on the Australian case, see Keal, 1992; on South Africa, see Frost, 1996 and van Aardt, 1996.

balance competing ethical claims. All the authors, by and large, agree that governments have to be practical pragmatists. They cannot formulate foreign policy from a predetermined ethical standpoint, for down that road lies the tendency towards a superiority complex. All three authors emphasise that governments must be open to a variety of viewpoints, and engage in serious, open-minded dialogue with other actors, both governmental and non-governmental. Foreign policy-making must be open to scrutiny and must be reviewed constantly to ensure that governments live up to their own standards.

In the opening chapter, Chris Brown rejects the traditional (and widespread) idea that there is an antithesis between ethics and the foreign policy interests of a state, noting that this stems from a misreading of realist authors, none of whom discount the role of morality in international affairs. Brown argues that what is now proclaimed as ethical foreign policy is not new. States have always had to take into account the requirements of membership of the international society. As to the choices that policy-makers may have to make, in his view their primary duty is to pursue the interests of their own citizens, 'but in the context of a set of wider duties towards other states, and, through other states, the rest of humanity'. Their wider duties include: abstention from forcible intervention in the affairs of others, obedience to international law (and particularly the principle of *pacta sunt servanda*), cooperation with others wherever possible, and, arguably, humanitarian intervention to stop gross violations of human dignity. These norms mandate that governments take an enlightened, rather than a narrow, view of their self-interests. Brown admits that there can be a clash between the duties a government must assume towards its own citizens and those it owes to the wider world, but these can only be resolved by political argument directly on the issues.

One of the more controversial issues on foreign policy agendas in the 1990s has been humanitarian intervention. Do states have the right or even the duty to intervene to stop massive violations of human rights in other states? Mervyn Frost provides a moral justification for humanitarian intervention. He traces the development of two non-intervention norms in international relations. The first – the more familiar – demands that states do not intervene in the internal affairs of other states. The second, however, reflects the historical development of limitations on state power within the state: the state must allow freedom and space to civil society. Frost argues that observation of the non-intervention norm applicable to states in the international realm is dependent on states showing due respect for the non-intervention norm relating to civil society. When states do not respect it, the international non-intervention norm cannot hold. Humanitarian intervention should be directed at maintaining civil

society, at ensuring non-intervention by the state in civil society. He concludes by offering a series of guidelines and principles on how to decide and conduct such humanitarian intervention. Interestingly, in light
of the controversy surrounding the Kosovo crisis, Frost does not specify
that UN authorisation is necessary for humanitarian intervention.
Members of global society may make use of a state, many states, international organisations, or any other social power to prevent rights abuses
from taking place – as long as the actor chosen is constrained by the
norms of civil society.

Brown and Frost provide essentially pragmatic answers to the question 'what is ethical foreign policy?', and they do so from the perspective
of the dilemmas facing policy-makers today. Molly Cochran illustrates
that these dilemmas are by no means new. In Chapter 4 she argues that
pragmatism offered guidance as to what constitutes an ethical foreign
policy in the early part of the twentieth century, just as it does today. She
examines the writings of three pragmatists who wrote about US foreign
policy in the first half of the 1900s when ethical issues were prominent on
the US foreign policy agenda: John Dewey, Walter Lippmann and Jane
Addams. Cochran rejects the conventional view that foreign policy must
be either entirely ethical or unethical. Pragmatism, she suggests, provides
a middle path, in which progress towards 'growth' is the valued end; the
determinate content of ethical prescriptions is left no more precise than
this. This allows space for the search for creative solutions to specific
problems within international relations. For pragmatists, ethics must be
conceived democratically, through a deliberative, consensual and inclusive process. Foreign policy-makers must also be open to transnational
activity – to the voices of NGOs and social movements, a theme that
several other contributions raise as well.

The instruments used to pursue an ethical foreign policy

The contributors to Part II discuss some of the instruments states and
international actors attempt to use to implement the ethical aspects of
foreign policy and explore the difficulties that arise in the implementation.
The first contribution looks at a particular aspect of state policy, Picken
and Economides are concerned with international instruments, while
Fierke examines grassroots attempts to influence state policy.

Margot Light's chapter examines the challenges facing governments
who are trying to 'export' democracy. She argues that exporting democracy logically and chronologically predates most other aspects of ethical
foreign policy. Governments have three motives, she believes, for
exporting democracy: first, they think that like-minded governments are

easier to deal with, and second, they believe that economic development will be more successful where good democratic governance prevails.
The economic motive is not entirely disinterested – democracies provide
better markets and investment opportunities for the advanced industrialised states than non-democracies. The third reason why governments
export democracy is that they believe that democracy within states will be
accompanied by peace between them.

Light claims that the definition of democracy is not as simple as the
frequent use of the word seems to imply. Nor is it always easily and
successfully exported. She distinguishes between democratic procedures
(constitutional and electoral arrangements, voting procedures, laws and
institutions), and democratic processes (norms, expectations, agreements
between citizens and authorities on the mutual limits and obligations each
must observe). Procedures can be imported, while processes derive from
society itself. She argues that in many transition countries, the economic
reforms that were exported at the same time that democracy was being
established often served to undermine the processes on which democratic
consolidation depends.

Promoting human rights is one instrument of ethical foreign policy.
But should governments encourage respect for human rights abroad,
and with what means? Or is it illegitimate interference in the domestic
affairs of other states or the imposition of Western values on non-Western
states? What role should human rights advocates play in policy-making?
Margo Picken traces the history of human rights in post-1945 international relations, and highlights significant inconsistencies in aspects of
Western policies on human rights in the 1990s. She charges that 'much
of the decade came to be marked by "grandiloquent incantation" with
the risk of human rights falling victim to sloganism'. Picken stresses, as
do Cochran and Fierke, that governments must be monitored by vigilant citizens and independent institutions, and that NGOs have a role
to play in monitoring governments that claim to act for human rights,
as well as those that abuse them. But she also points to the dilemmas
that NGOs increasingly face: inclusion in policy-making, as well as the
increased channelling of government funding through NGOs, can compromise the independence that NGOs must have if they are to monitor governments adequately. She warns against the monopolisation of
human rights by governments (Brown makes a similar point). Picken
concludes by suggesting that Western NGOs should turn their attention to 'the anomalies that mark Western domestic and foreign policies
today in respect of human rights'. For example, Western governments
should ensure that their domestic policies and practices comply with their

international commitments, and strengthen the authority and power of international institutions to enforce those commitments. The need to get one's own house in order crops up in Part III as well, particularly with respect to the reluctance of governments to curb arms exports.

For several authors, such as Cochran, the signing of a statute that will establish an International Criminal Court (ICC) is a significant step, as individuals will be held to account for committing international crimes. Spyros Economides traces the history of the ICC (which can be considered to date back to the Nuremberg trials following the Second World War) and analyses the negotiations that led to the signing of the ICC statute. While he agrees that the establishment of individual responsibility is a significant step forward, Economides also illustrates that traditional state concerns dominated the negotiations. Many governments were unwilling to divest themselves of their traditional rights, and the ICC statute inevitably reflects a compromise among states. The issue of jurisdiction in particular makes manifest the extent to which states insisted on retaining control over the remit of the ICC. Yet individuals are now liable to be prosecuted for violating international criminal law, marking a step away from the traditional state-centrism of international relations.

The last chapter in this section takes a 'bottom-up' perspective, from below the level of the state. K. M. Fierke asserts that a foreign policy that is ethical requires 'that individuals and groups be ready to hold up a critical mirror to government action'. The power of a government to act is fundamentally dependent on being able to provide ethical justifications for its policies. The exposure of a discrepancy between the justification and a government's actual practice can prompt a government to align its practice with its words. As Brown, Picken, and Dunne and Wheeler all note, the Labour government is indeed, and rightly, under such pressure.

Fierke, like Cochran, argues that for a foreign policy to be ethical, the government proclaiming it must be willing to engage directly in dialogue with those most affected by it. She criticises the tendency of the UK and US governments in particular to dismiss the possibility of dialogue by arguing that actors such as Saddam Hussein or Slobodan Milosević only understand the language of force. Although she recognises that the use of force may be justified in some cases, Fierke argues that treating foreign leaders as if they were incapable of rational argument only ends up reproducing conflict. A dialogical form of analysis, in which a wider range of voices (including social movements) are allowed to speak, could open up a new space for thinking about how we can construct the future. The problems faced by governments in opting for dialogue or the use of force are elaborated in Part III.

How are international actors incorporating ethical concerns into foreign policy?

The three chapters in Part III on the foreign policies of the United States, the United Kingdom and the European Union illustrate that international actors that proclaim to be acting ethically can frequently be criticised for not living up to their own rhetoric. All three actors can be charged with inconsistency and selectivity in their approach to the ethical issues on their foreign policy agendas. The three contributors to Part III seek to explain the inconsistency. With respect to the preferences of many of the authors in Part I for a dialogical approach to foreign policy, it is interesting to note that both the UK and EU claim to use dialogue to promote human rights, but this is often judged to be a cover-up or excuse for not taking stronger action against human rights abusers.

Christopher Coker evaluates US foreign policy, particularly with regard to the use of force. He argues that although US foreign policy is no longer guided by a grand purpose, as it was until the Vietnam War, the US government has distinct ethical pretensions, namely 'humanitarianism'. President Clinton has proclaimed that the United States will only fight humanitarian wars in the future; in other words, it will only fight for the oppressed in other countries, not for its own self-interest. But Coker argues that American foreign policy is a great deal less ethical in a post-ideological age than it was during the Cold War. It is reactive and risk-aversive, and uses force essentially for its own safety (against 'terrorism', for example), rather than for the general good. The US government tries to manage crises, but it does so selectively, because it lacks a grand design to guide policy-making. Moreover, the means used by the United States have been disproportionately military, and the way in which it has used its military means (for example, in the air campaigns against Serbia and Iraq) has also been suspect ethically. Coker charges that although the United States uses the language of humanitarianism, it lacks the will to enforce it. And until it finds the will, 'its ethical pretensions will be open to challenge'.

Tim Dunne and Nicholas J. Wheeler analyse the foreign policy of the current Labour government in Britain in terms of whether it acts as a 'good international citizen': does it seek to strengthen international support for universal human rights standards, obey the rules of international society, and act multilaterally and with UN authorisation where possible? Dunne and Wheeler focus on three cases: policy towards China; policy towards Indonesia; and involvement in the Kosovo war. In the first two, they criticise the government. But they argue that the government's policy on Kosovo was based on humanitarian motives, gave diplomatic solutions and economic sanctions a chance, and committed itself to remain in Kosovo for the long term (although this has not prevented Serb civilians from being forced out of Kosovo). Thus use of force was in keeping with the requirements of good international citizenship – an evaluation that several other contributors to this volume (notably Fierke, Picken and Coker) would question. The one problem that Dunne and Wheeler highlight is the lack of UN authorisation for NATO's action. They suggest that Britain must contribute to a debate on the conditions that would legitimate unilateral humanitarian intervention in the absence of UN authorisation. Overall, however, they consider that the Labour government 'has created the context for the development of a robust human rights culture', and, while it might not have lived up to its own human rights standards, it has at least had the courage to strive for an ethical dimension to its foreign policy.

Karen E. Smith considers the extent to which the EU conducts foreign policy with an ethical dimension by examining how the EU fulfils its objective of enhancing respect for human rights in third countries. She reviews the evolution of the EU's commitment to human rights, and analyses how it pursues that aim. Inconsistency plagues the EU's external human rights policy. Third countries that violate human rights are treated very differently, depending on their importance to the EU and/or its member states. Smith argues that the very nature of the EU is to blame: it is difficult to reach consensus among the member states to treat all third countries similarly, and there are inter-pillar and intra-pillar problems of coordination. But, like Dunne and Wheeler, Smith is optimistic. It is significant that the EU has embraced human rights as a foreign policy objective to such a far-reaching extent, and that it is at the forefront of efforts to make it illegitimate to violate human rights and democratic principles.

The contributors to this volume do not, by any means, settle all the complex problems that are raised by attempting to implement an ethical foreign policy. But, in relation to some of the countries and international organisations that have explicitly adopted an ethical dimension to their foreign policy, they offer an evaluation that will serve as a benchmark for future assessments of progress. Moreover, setting out and discussing some of the theoretical and practical problems that arise in relation to ethics and foreign policy contributes to a debate that will, the editors and contributors are certain, continue to preoccupy international relations theorists and policy-makers for many years to come.

Part I

Theories

2 Ethics, interests and foreign policy

Chris Brown

Prologue: the Mission Statement

When, on 1 May 1997, a Labour government was returned to power in Britain after eighteen years in opposition, none of the ministers who were appointed to the Foreign and Commonwealth Office (FCO) by Prime Minister Tony Blair had had any prior experience of government office – indeed only the new foreign secretary, Robin Cook MP, had been in parliament when Labour had last held power. In the 1970s and early 1980s, Cook had been a critic of the underlying assumptions of British foreign policy shared by the Wilson, Callaghan and Thatcher administrations – assumptions such as the supreme importance of Britain's relationship with the United States and the value of British membership of the European Community – and although these criticisms had been more or less silenced by the emergence of 'New Labour', Cook was widely regarded as the most influential left-wing member of the new government. In the circumstances, there seemed good reason to expect at least some changes in the content of British foreign policy and in the foreign policy-making process.

One almost immediate symbol of change was the unveiling of a Mission Statement for the FCO. Although the imagery was very New Labour, the actual text of the Mission Statement was, for the most part, conventional. The summary reads 'The Mission of the Foreign and Commonwealth Office is to promote the national interests of the United Kingdom and contribute to a strong international community.' The statement goes on, 'We shall pursue that Mission to secure for Britain four benefits through our foreign policy', the four benefits being *security, prosperity, the quality of*

Earlier versions of parts of this chapter were presented at the International Studies Association (ISA) Annual Convention, Minneapolis, 1998, to the New Zealand Institute of International Affairs in Wellington, July 1998, at the British International Studies (BISA) Association Annual Conference in December 1998, and to the BISA Workshop 'Ethics and Foreign Policy' at the University of Bristol in June 1999. I am grateful to participants on these occasions for their comments, and especially to Michael Doyle, Tim Dunne, Mervyn Frost and Nick Wheeler.

life and *mutual respect*. 'We shall work though our international forums and bilateral relationships to spread the values of human rights, civil liberties and democracy which we demand for ourselves' (FCO, 1997a). This latter statement was reinforced by Mr Cook in his speech at the press launch of the Statement:

> The Labour Government does not accept that political values can be left behind when we check in our passports to travel on diplomatic business. Our foreign policy must have an ethical dimension and must support the demands of other peoples for the democratic rights on which we insist for ourselves. We will put human rights at the heart of our foreign policy. (FCO, 1997b)

This commitment, elaborated by the foreign secretary in a keynote speech of 17 July 1997, lay behind the claim that Britain was now to pursue what the media customarily refers to, sometimes ironically, as an 'ethical foreign policy' – although no official ever used that phrase, the term 'an ethical dimension' being considered much less likely to create unnecessary hostages to fortune. As part of the new policy, the FCO now produces an Annual Report on Human Rights – echoing in this, albeit on a much smaller scale, the US State Department; the Department for International Development has reshaped somewhat Britain's aid policy; and, in principle at least, the Department of Trade and Industry has re-tuned its policy on arms sales (FCO and DFID, 1998; US State Department, 1999). Overall, this new orientation has been considered by the government to be a key element in the 'rebranding' of Britain – the portrayal of Britain as a young, successful country no longer dominated by its past. Changing the emphasis of Britain's foreign policy has been seen as the international counterpart to the development at home of ideas of the 'third way' (Giddens, 1998).

Whatever else this reorientation has achieved – and the government itself is now (September 2000) unsure on this point and will not be stressing the ethical dimension in future – it has certainly sparked a great deal of academic commentary and debate.[1] Predictably, much of it has involved a hostile comparison of the government's record in office with its stated aspirations, both on the ground that the government itself chose – and in particular on issues such as the promotion of human rights and the sale of arms – and more generally in respect of, for example, its support for US action against alleged terrorist targets in Sudan and Afghanistan, and its

[1] There have been panels/roundtables on Ethics and Foreign Policy at BISA Annual Conferences in 1997 and 1998, as well as at ISA in 1998 and 1999, a Special Issue of *Millennium* on Ethics, the LSE Cumberland Lodge conference out of which this volume emerged, a BISA Workshop at Bristol in Spring 1999, meetings of BISA Working Groups and, of course, a great deal of press commentary. Some of the debate is summarised in Wheeler and Dunne, 1998.

participation in economic sanctions and military action directed against Iraq. In this chapter I will, eventually and briefly, address both these issues, but the bulk of my argument will be addressed to more fundamental questions about the ethical nature of foreign policy; in particular, I will suggest that the way in which these questions are generally posed – both by the government and by its critics – is misconceived, largely because of a misunderstanding about the nature of ethical behaviour, but also because of what I will term 'pop realist' ideas about the roots of state conduct. These fundamental questions will remain salient, even though the policy that occasioned them is no longer operative.

Interests and ethics

The FCO's Mission Statement refers to spreading Britain's 'values' in the world; Mr Cook glosses this as involving an 'ethical dimension' and placing human rights at the heart of our foreign policy. As is customary in official discourse, these positions involve envisaging the state as the possessor of legal personality (critical, of course, to any notion of international law), and as the kind of 'person' capable of possessing interests, as in the notion of the 'national interest' which it is the mission of the FCO to promote; to this is added, or made explicit, the notion that the state is also a person capable of acting in accordance with ethical principles. The Mission Statement assumes that these ethical principles are wholly consistent with the national interest – 'mutual respect' is simply one of the four benefits that will accrue to Britain as a result of the FCO's pursuit of Britain's interests and there is no suggestion that these benefits (security, prosperity, quality of life as well as mutual respect) are in conflict one with another. And there is no reason in principle why they should be; the four benefits are 'compossible' to use Hillel Steiner's useful, albeit slightly ugly, term – that is to say, there is no logical reason why the achievement of any one benefit should prevent the achievement of any of the others (Steiner, 1994).

The problem is that, nonetheless, it is not difficult to envisage circumstances in which there will be a conflict between two or more of the benefits. The benefit of national security might well be available only via close cooperative relations with undemocratic states that blatantly abuse the human rights of their citizens – such was the case, albeit in extreme circumstances, with Britain's alliance with the USSR from 1941 to 1945, while in the post-war world, membership of NATO (as opposed to the European Union) has never been restricted to democratic states. For example, NATO members Portugal (before the fall of Salazar) and Turkey (for much of the time since 1949) have been too important in security terms for their shortcomings in the realm of civil liberties and human rights to be of crucial significance. Again, achieving 'quality of life' becomes more difficult when the state which presents the biggest obstacle to solving the world's environmental problems – which is undoubtedly the United States – is also the state which underpins Britain's national security. And, of course, to save the obvious for last, there are many circumstances in which the prosperity of British citizens would be enhanced by selling arms to undemocratic regimes whose approach to civil liberties and human rights is inconsistent with the notion of mutual respect.

The potential conflict in this latter case is important for two reasons. First, British industry is particularly dependent on the arms trade. The armaments industry is the most successful remnant of Britain's old industrial, manufacturing base.[2] A small part of this trade is based on sales to other liberal democracies, but most is to regimes that have less than perfect human rights records, in particular to Indonesia and Arab regimes in the Gulf. Second, Mr Cook himself made the arms trade an issue. In his speech on 17 July 1997, Mr Cook made the following explicit commitment:

Britain will refuse to supply the equipment and weapons with which regimes deny the demands of their peoples for human rights. Last month, I announced a review of government criteria for the licensing of weapons for export. That review will give effect to Labour's policy commitment that we will not supply equipment or weapons that might be used for internal repression. (FCO, 1997c)

Although Cook did not make the point explicitly, it is clear that such a policy might well have consequences for British prosperity in general – and, of course, for workers in the arms trade in particular.

Here we have two benefits in conflict – 'prosperity' and 'mutual respect'. In the Mission Statement both are described as the product of the pursuit of national interests and therefore, on the face of it, one might think that there can be some kind of trade-off between the two benefits; to put the matter crudely for simplicity's sake, that it would be a matter for political decision how much of one benefit might be sacrificed in order to achieve an enhancement of the other. That, indeed, is how I believe

---

[2] In 1996/97 UK arms exporters had 22 per cent of the global market in arms, well behind the United States (with 42.6 per cent) but ahead of everyone else. UK arms exports amounted to over £5 billion by value, easily the largest sum earned by any sector of manufacturing. Some 75,000 workers are directly employed in arms manufacturing and a further 70,000 indirectly – and what is impressive is that these latter figures are much as they were in 1980/81, before the manufacturing slump of 1981/82, the only industrial sector in Britain of which this could be said (International Institute of Strategic Studies, 1997).

we should think of this problem – but the explicit emphasis on an 'ethical dimension' to foreign policy seems to point in another direction, drawing a distinction between 'interest' which is associated with prosperity, and 'ethics' which is associated with 'mutual respect' and thus causing a potential conflict between an interest-based foreign policy and an ethically driven foreign policy to emerge. This is certainly the way in which many critics have seen the matter and the FCO and the foreign secretary have themselves validated this perspective by the rhetoric they employed, which explicitly associated ethics with only one of the four benefits it is their mission to achieve. In any event, no matter who is responsible for posing the question in this way, the next step is to ask whether it is a sensible move; this involves investigating the relationship between ethics and self-interest.

The nature of ethical conduct

When we describe someone's behaviour as 'ethical', we are generally attempting to convey the idea that they are behaving in accordance with some kind of moral principle. Two possible problems have to be cleared away before we can examine what this might mean. First, there are, of course, social theories, most obviously Marxism, which deny the existence of moral principle and of ethical conduct altogether; the use of such terms is taken to be hypocritical or the product of 'false consciousness' – although it is possible to identify clusters of attitudes which might be termed, say, 'bourgeois morality', these amount to no more than a set of rationalisations – and therefore to characterise someone's behaviour as ethical would be either meaningless, or intended ironically (Lukes, 1985; Brown, 1992b). There is no way to show conclusively that this view is mistaken, but for the purpose of this chapter it is rejected out of hand and assumed that the notion of a moral principle *does* have content, if only because to do otherwise would close down the argument prematurely. Moral arguments are sometimes deployed tactically and with the intent to deceive, but I assume, first, that, in principle at least, we are capable of discerning when this is so, and, second, that sometimes individuals do act in accordance with moral principle.

The second problem is a little trickier. Is it really possible to assume that the 'person' of the state is such as to be capable of acting ethically, that is, in accordance with a moral principle – in other words of being a 'someone' in the sense used in the first sentence of this paragraph? I do not see a major problem here, but others do: it is noteworthy and paradoxical that some of those who argue most strongly for an 'ethical foreign policy' also argue against state-centric views of the world and, in other contexts, are suspicious of the very notion of foreign policy. For the time being this problem will be noted and set aside.

What constitutes a moral principle (and therefore ethical behaviour) is, of course, a matter of dispute. For some, ethical behaviour means behaviour in accordance with a set of moral rules ('deontology'); such rules might be accessible by reason alone, on the basis of an account of what is required for human flourishing (natural law); or they might be, as it were, wired into the way in which we think about the world (the case for Kant's 'Categorical Imperative', which tells us to act in such a way that our behaviour could form the basis for a universal law, and to avoid treating human beings solely as means rather than as ends); or they might be the product of divine revelation (such as the Ten Commandments); or produced by convention, for example via a (fictional) contract (Foot, 1967; Norman, 1983). Others judge conduct ethically in terms of its consequences, the most obvious example being the various forms of utilitarianism, with its 'greatest happiness' principle – the two main variants being 'act-utilitarianism' which argues that the contribution of particular deeds to the greatest happiness is central, and 'rule-utilitarianism' which justifies rules rather than specific acts by reference to this criterion (Scheffler, 1988). Modern moral philosophy is dominated by deontology and 'consequentialism', but recently there has been somewhat of a revival of an older way of looking at ethical issues, via the 'virtues' (Anscombe, 1958; Crisp, 1996). Here the focus is not so much on what people ought to do when faced with characteristic moral dilemmas, but rather what sort of lives they ought to live, what sort of people they ought to be, on the principle that the virtuous individual will, by definition, know what to do when presented with a moral dilemma. Meanwhile, the 'Continental' strand of contemporary moral philosophy focuses more closely on interpersonal relationships and an ethic of responsibility towards the Other, which cross-references to feminist ethical theory (Critchley, 1992; Held, 1995).

This is simply a selection of the available moral codes at the end of the twentieth century, but it provides enough information to tell against the notion that we can, in some simple minded way, work out what it means to act in accordance with a moral principle without specifying which account of the nature of moral principles is intended. Some of the doctrines mentioned above clearly pull us in different directions in quite common circumstances, including circumstances faced by states. Thus, in a not-altogether- hypothetical example, an 'act-utilitarian' might well sanction the covert supply of arms and expertise to a legitimate government-in-exile to allow it to effect the overthrow of military usupers, even if such an act breached a UN resolution, while a Kantian would be altogether unwilling to allow that the end justified the means. More, to refer to another issue at the heart of Britain's mission, some ethical principles are 'universalist' and endorse the idea of human rights, while others are, for a variety of reasons, suspicious of this notion – Bentham famously referred to the idea of natural rights as nonsense on stilts, while, from a very different perspective, Alasdair MacIntyre, at the time moving from a heterodox Catholic-Marxism to more orthodox Neo-Thomism, characterised a belief in rights as akin to a belief in unicorns and fairies (MacIntyre, 1981:67).

Given the existence of so many accounts of what it means to be-have ethically, it might be doubted whether it is possible to say any-thing in general about the relationship between 'interests' and 'ethics'.[3] In fact, there is more agreement here than one might expect. All serious approaches to ethics reject the notion that behaviour based on naked, short-run self-interest, with no regard for the interests of others, could be regarded as moral. However, virtually no ethical theory man-dates a totally other-regarding approach to moral problems. Some the-ories are based directly on the self-interest of individuals, as in David Gauthier's Hobbesian account of 'morals by agreement', while others, such as Christianity (and, indeed, most religious systems of ethics) and Kantianism, refuse to see any possible *long-term* contradiction between one's own interests and the demands of morality (Gauthier, 1986). Theories which *do* envisage a potential contradiction between the moral point of view and one's personal self-interest do not, as a rule, suggest that individuals should entirely submerge their interests in the interests of humanity; some very strict utilitarians suggest that we have no reason to treat our own interests as more compelling that those of any other human being, but they generally concede that the general good/happiness will usually be advanced if we assume that we do have such reasons (Smart and Williams, 1973). In the same way, even strict 'impartialists' and util-itarians will agree that we have at least some obligations towards our fellow citizens which are different from, go deeper than, those we have towards humanity taken as a whole – and most other ethical theorists would have no difficulty in accepting that this is so (Barry, 1995; *Ethics*, 1988).

To summarise: on all counts naked egoism is wrong – behaving ethically involves being aware of, and sensitive to, the interests of others – but self-abnegation is not mandatory. There are circumstances where individuals might feel drawn to self-sacrifice, but such behaviour is, according to most

---

[3] It should be noted that there are almost as many ways of characterising the idea of 'interest' as there are of characterising 'ethics'; some distinctions will emerge in this chapter but, for the most part, if only for reasons of space, this issue will not be pursued.

ethical codes, 'supererogatory', that is, something which it would be good to do, but not wrong not to do. The right thing to do will often, perhaps usually, involve not pursuing one's interests to extremes, but it will not, except in most unusual circumstances, involve ignoring those interests altogether. Unless expressly invented for the purpose, moral dilemmas very rarely involve a stark choice between one's own interests and one's moral principles; more usually they involve striking a balance between different conceptions of the good for oneself and others, and between short-, medium- and long-term conceptions of one's own interests. In short, the notion that there is a stark divide between 'interests' and 'ethics' does not make a great deal of sense. How is it, then, that the notion of an ethical dimension to foreign policy is so often framed in these terms?

Moral absolutism and 'pop realism'

Two factors, which feed off and reinforce each other, are important here. First, the extraordinarily absolutist terms in which a great deal of moral thinking about international relations is conducted should be noted. States are rarely allowed to have mixed motives for their actions. The best illustration of this mind-set was provided by the Gulf War of 1990/91. Critics of the war invariably accused the United States and its coalition partners of acting out of the purest self-interest. This was a 'war for oil', or, in a slightly more sophisticated variant, a war to demonstrate US hegemony after the fall of Soviet communism. Supporters – including officials on both sides of the Atlantic – generally grounded their moral position on international law and the need to oppose naked aggression. In fact, of course, *both* material self-interests *and* legal principles were involved. Critics were right to say that if Kuwait's main export had been bananas Operation Desert Storm would not have taken place – but if the preservation of oil supplies had been the only issue, then Desert Storm would not have taken place for another reason, because the United States and its allies would have had no difficulty in striking a bargain with the Iraqi regime. As for the broader argument about US hegemony, in the 1980s Saddam Hussein had frequently been described as a useful counter to Iran's religiously fuelled ambitions and his behaviour condoned accordingly – indeed, there is some reason to think that he thought that this was what would happen on this occasion. On the other hand, if the only issue had been international law, critics would have been justified in pointing to the occasions in the past when the UN Charter has been broken without provoking such a strong response.

It was the combination of economic and strategic interests with a wider interest in resisting such a clear defiance of international law that made the war both possible and necessary – and there is no reason why such a combination should be regarded as immoral or unethical. The notion that action can only be described as ethical if motives are absolutely pure and untainted by self-interest is bizarre, and unsupported by any plausible moral philosophy. The traditional doctrine of Just War certainly stresses that there must be 'right intention' (those who act should do so in order to right a wrong) but it would be strange to suggest that this precludes the existence of other reasons for action. Some writers have interpreted the notion in this way, but usually with perverse results; thus, for example, the Roman Catholic moral philosopher G. E. M. Anscombe opposed war in 1939 on the principle that Britain and France were too tainted by self-interest to be allowed to resist Hitler, a position that makes sense – if it does – only if one assumes that God will somehow prevent the long-term triumph of evil (Anscombe, 1981). Kant is certainly concerned that we should not allow self-interest to dominate our actions, and argues that we should inspect our motives very carefully when self-interest and the requirements of the categorical imperative seem to point in the same direction, but if we are satisfied that we are not deceiving ourselves, it would be absurd to suggest we should not act and this is not Kant's position – and, it should be noted that the categorical imperative does *not* tell us that we should never treat others as means rather than ends; rather, it tells us that we should never treat others *solely* as means.

It is difficult to see why there is such a tendency towards moral absolutism when it comes to international affairs. Possibly it is merely a symptom of a wider difficulty with post-Christian moral discourse in the West – certainly, amongst students of International Relations there is resistance to the idea that we can think systematically and logically about ethical issues, and moral principles are often regarded almost as judgements of taste which it would be somehow improper to ask those who claim to hold them to defend. At the same time, most people do not have much difficulty in understanding that their own motives are frequently mixed. In any event, the consequences of this absolutism are clear. If it is the case that the merest hint of self-interest is sufficient to undermine any claim that a state might be behaving ethically, then states never do behave ethically, because there is always some element of self-interest involved in state action. If being partly motivated by self-interest becomes morally equivalent to being wholly motivated by self-interest, states then do indeed come to be seen as the kind of nakedly egoistic beings that virtually all ethical theories condemn. Those who think this way and are familiar with the academic discourse of International Relations assume that this rampant egoism on the part of states is sanctioned by both the theory and practice of conventional international relations – the theory in question being 'realism', the doctrine that the underlying basis of world politics is that states pursue interests defined in terms of power. Conventional wisdom tends to agree, without, of course, reference to the theory. The result is either cynical indifference or a kind of pacifist globalism. Either way, an attempt to introduce an ethical dimension to foreign policy is seen as an heroic but doomed attempt to upset the status quo – which is more or less a self-fulfilling prophecy, since from this perspective the first time a decision which incorporates a degree of self-interest is taken on a sensitive issue, ethics will be assumed to have been abandoned.

In order to think clearly about ethics and foreign policy it is necessary to undermine this kind of 'pop realism'. I use this term partly in recognition of the degree to which the pop realist perspective is genuinely widely held, but also because it bears very little relationship to the actual doctrines that realist international relations theorists have propounded over the past half-century.[4] The egoistic, narrowly self-interested state is neither entailed by realist international theory, nor sanctioned by the practices of international society. All variants of realism may agree that states are, in the last resort, egoists, but nearly all also agree that, although enlightened self-interest is difficult to achieve in conditions of international anarchy, it is still morally desirable to think long rather than short term, and that a focus upon one's own interests is not necessarily incompatible with a concern with the common good and broader principle. The kind of 'blood-and-iron' statements of a pure *Machtpolitik* are not characteristic of contemporary realist thinkers; the work of Alastair Murray and Joel Rosenthal has demonstrated how thinkers such as Hans Morgenthau and George Kennan were far more interested in the interplay between general moral principles and the contingencies of international politics than the pop realist account suggests (Rosenthal, 1991; Murray, 1997). Contemporary neo-realists are less burdened with Augustinian doubts than their predecessors, and agree that states tend towards a quite narrowly egoistic approach to the world, but only a hyper-realist such as John Mearsheimer comes close to arguing that normative principles have no purchase at all on state action.

Could it be said that the practices of international society – diplomacy and international law in particular – are either completely ineffective or actually endorse a narrow pop realist account of self-interest? In the twentieth century we have certainly seen no-holds-barred ideological struggles in which notions of the common good have gone by the board, although it should be noted that the participants in these clashes believed themselves to be driven by moral principles and behaving ethically – indeed,

---

[4] The 'pop' formulation is borrowed with thanks but without permission from Paul Krugman's excellent *Pop Internationalism* (Krugman, 1996).

they often justified breaches of international law in terms of, for example, the need to defend the Socialist Commonwealth in Czechoslovakia in 1968, or the promotion of 'freedom' in Nicaragua in the 1980s. We have also seen in the post-1945 era the emergence of a distressing number of gangster states, states whose rulers are, in effect, out to maximise their own power and wealth with no consideration for anyone other than themselves – President Mobutu's 'Zaire' can serve as an extreme example of the gangster state, but less extreme examples can be found in most parts of the globe. Motivated by the purest kind of selfishness, these rulers exploit and oppress their own people and anyone else who comes within range. Nonetheless, the pop realist dismissal of the notion of international relations as norm-governed is too pessimistic. Most of the time international law is effective; the underlying institutional fabric of international life holds together in ways that would be impossible if power and interest were the only concerns of states – one of the strongest reasons for thinking that hyper-realists such as Mearsheimer are wrong about the 'false promise of international institutions' is simply the continued existence and extraordinary growth in the number of such bodies (Mearsheimer, 1994/5).

And what of the content of the norms of international society? Speaking of another age, but in words which, suitably amended, can be applied today, A. J. P. Taylor put the matter well in his magisterial survey of *The Struggle for Mastery in Europe*:

the world of diplomacy was much like the world of business, in which respect for the sanctity of contract does not prevent the most startling reversals of fortune. Many diplomatists were ambitious, some vain or stupid, but they had something like a common aim – to preserve the peace of Europe without endangering the interests or security of their country. (Taylor, 1954:xxiii)

The norms and practices of international society mandate enlightened, rather than narrow, self-interest; they call upon states to abstain from forcible intervention in the affairs of others, to obey international law (in particular the principle of *pacta sunt servanda*) and to cooperate with others wherever possible, which in the post-1945 world involves a commitment to global institutions such as the United Nations. Further, even in the old European international society the principle of non-intervention did not apply in situations where gross violations of human dignity were taking place (Wight, 1966). In the modern era, the evolving human rights regime means that the internal political arrangements of states are increasingly under scrutiny, and the possibility of humanitarian interventions directed towards changing the behaviour of states towards their own citizens arises – certainly humanitarian motives were present when a zone of safety was established for the Kurds in northern Iraq in 1991, and lay behind the NATO action against Yugoslavia in 1999.

It would obviously be a mistake to suggest that these various norms and practices present no moral problems or are universally observed. The potential ethnocentrism of the present human rights regime is a problem that will persist, and the contradiction between the principle of humanitarian intervention and the 'domestic jurisdiction' provision of the UN Charter remains unresolved. Moreover, many weaker states cling to a strict definition of the principle of non-intervention because they are aware that any kind of intervention, humanitarian or not, reflects power as well as moral principle (Brown, 1999; Forbes and Hoffman, 1993). Clearly states are selective in their response to the new norms of international society, although – with the obvious exception of the 'gangsters' – they adhere quite strongly to the older norms, which Mervyn Frost is right to regard as 'settled', in the sense that virtually no state denies their existence or force, even when, on occasion, violating them (Frost, 1996).

Putting all this together, an 'ethical dimension to foreign policy' far from being a novel idea is actually part of what is involved in the very idea of membership in international society. States have a primary duty to pursue the interests of their peoples but in the context of a set of wider duties towards other states, and, through other states, the rest of humanity. Both of these sets of duties involve moral obligations and it is a mistake to think of the first as simply interest-based, while the second constitutes the 'ethical dimension' of foreign policy. Both sets of duties involve both interests and ethics. On occasion the (ethical) duties states have towards their own citizens may seem to conflict with the (ethical) duties they have to the wider world. There is no reason to be surprised by this, any more than one is surprised by the common observation that sometimes a short-run view of foreign policy objectives conflicts with a longer-run perspective. Clashes between duties to fellow-citizens and duties to foreigners cannot be resolved by reference to some calculus drawn from moral philosophy but only by a political argument that engages the issues directly. Clearly the terms of that political argument will often involve an appeal to the narrow, materialist, self-interest of compatriots, but there is no reason to think that such an appeal will always be successful – indeed, part of the job description of successful, progressively minded, politicians refers to their capacity to get ordinary people to define their own interests in less narrowly materialist terms, and to come to understand that acknowledging obligations to others is not incompatible with a healthy concern for one's own interests. This is the very stuff of politics, whether foreign or domestic issues are at stake.

One final point is worth making before proceeding to a few brief comments on the record of the Labour government. As noted above, pop realism can lead to cynicism but it can also lead to a kind of pacific globalism or revolutionary universalism – figures like Noam Chomsky or (in a minor key) John Pilger come to mind here. Such writers are pop realist in so far as they absolutely deny the possibility that state conduct can be influenced by moral concerns, but they react to this diagnosis by rejecting statism altogether. From this perspective it is not accepted that states have a primary duty to pursue the interests of their people even if this duty is seen in the context of a wider set of obligations. Rather, the argument is that no element of self-interest is morally acceptable, at least in so far as the 'self' in question is identified as the state, or any other institution that stands between the individual and the claims of a wider humanity. There are deep issues here, but it is clear that going down this cosmopolitan path (whether in a liberal or a revolutionary Marxian direction) takes one away from a consideration of ethics and foreign policy. From the cosmopolitan point of view, *all* foreign policy is, by definition, immoral and unethical, simply because it is the policy of the state, an entity that is by its very nature immoral and unethical, even if it accurately represents the values and interests of its citizens. From a cosmopolitan perspective only a world government (or perhaps a world revolution) could provide the basis for an ethical politics. Those who reject this perspective argue that given the enormous practical problems involved in establishing world government – not least the absence of global consensus on substantive norms and political procedures – the present political division of the world is both practically necessary and morally desirable, and so issues of ethics and foreign policy do arise; pacific globalists and revolutionary universalists will, inevitably, find this position unacceptably statist. It is difficult to see what could bridge this difference of perspective.

Human rights and 'mutual respect'

One of the points that ought to be clear from the above discussion is that an assessment of the effect of the present government's stated goal of developing the ethical dimension of Britain's foreign policy cannot simply be based on policy in the area of human rights – a more rounded judgement must be made. Nonetheless, before proceeding to such a judgement it may be useful to make one or two general comments about this area, if only because it is the ground upon which the government has staked its claim to be different from its predecessors – other essays in this volume will address the government's record in more detail.

First, the terms of the Mission Statement in this area, and subsequent official commentary, are worthy of examination. The Mission Statement promised Britain the benefit of 'Mutual Respect' which would follow from the government's promotion of 'the values of human rights, civil liberties and democracy which *we demand for ourselves*' (emphasis added). Mr Cook fleshed out further what was involved in this commitment in a keynote speech of 17 July 1997. After offering a fairly conventional list of rights and dismissing the speculations of philosophers about the grounding for these rights, he added: 'These are rights which we claim for ourselves and which we therefore have a right to demand for those who do not yet enjoy them . . . The right to enjoy our freedom comes with the obligation to support the human rights of others' (FCO, 1997c).

It is worth thinking about these statements and, in particular, examining the grammar and vocabulary in which they are expressed. 'We' claim certain rights and declare them to be unproblematically desirable. Because we want them we need have no hesitation in assuming that everyone else wants them. We show our respect for others by acting on that assumption, that is, by inviting them to become more like us – more, we are obliged to demand that they become like us. In fact, of course, we do not put it quite so bluntly. Instead we define what we are like by reference to abstract universals – rights, civil liberties and democracy – and it is to these abstractions that we ask others to conform. The interesting point is whether this is actually much different from urging others to conform to our standards.

I will not here go into all the debates about universalism and particularism with respect to human rights because by now this is very familiar ground, but underlying much of the rhetoric of 'Asian Values' and the like is precisely the idea that in its present form the international human rights regime constitutes a kind of Western cultural imperialism.[5] Quite possibly these arguments are often used to serve the interests of authoritarian rulers, but even if this is so, it seems unwise to sustain their plausibility by using the kind of language employed by the Foreign Secretary. If a practising Muslim Foreign Minister were to make a speech declaring that because he and his co-religionists valued most highly submission to God and recognition of the Prophet as his Messenger, they therefore had the right to *demand* that all the peoples of the world make a similar profession of faith, I doubt very much whether this would be taken seriously by Western Christians or secular humanists. Certainly such an attitude would hardly be taken as indicative of 'mutual respect'; on the contrary, it would be regarded as showing great disrespect for the beliefs of others. Indeed,

---

[5] In Brown (2000) I offer a more extended commentary on these ideas.

Muslim leaders are quite frequently accused of displaying just such disrespect, by, for example, taking advantage of liberal Christian gestures towards ecumenicism without reciprocating. Mr Cook would doubtless insist that his 'demand' was based on the requirements of the current international human rights regime and thus different – but it is precisely the nature of this regime that critics of Western universalism contest.

Second, accepting for the sake of argument that the current international human rights regime can be defended in its own terms, what ought to be the role of the state, as opposed to non-state actors, in the promotion of human rights? The point I want to make here is nicely epitomised – albeit in the negative – by a pronouncement of Clare Short, Britain's International Development minister, last year. Ms Short has been attempting to reorient aid policy towards the promotion of human rights, but, as Amnesty International (AI) had pointed out, British policy still involves practical support for some regimes with a less than savoury record on human rights. Responding forcibly, Ms Short remarked: 'The discourse of human rights has got stuck in a denunciation of abuses of civil and political rights. While this is important, it is very carping and does not see human rights as work in progress' (*The Guardian*, 4 June 1998).

This is, I think, quite wrong. It is precisely the role of AI and similar bodies to 'carp' and 'denounce' without taking on board all the reasons, often quite compelling in nature, for failings in the area of human rights. It is the role of government to make the kind of rounded judgement that takes into account such reasons. Because the goals of foreign policy are multidimensional, governments are never able to judge relations *solely* on the basis of human rights, and it would be wrong to expect them to do so. They inevitably find themselves having to make judgements in the round, and explicitly human-rights-oriented bodies will criticise these judgements. To criticise the latter for doing so is to misunderstand the politics of the situation. In effect, by attempting to take over the task of promoting human rights and feeling obliged to defend its actions in these terms, the government ends up trying to take over the task of defining what promoting human rights ought to involve. This is particularly damaging because bodies such as AI, which do not possess direct coercive power, can attempt to promote human rights in a way that is less tied up with Western interests, and are less liable to charges of hypocrisy.

Ethics and the pursuit of security, prosperity and the quality of life

Any judgement about the ethical status of a particular foreign policy programme has to be made in the round, and not simply in one area.

If, for example, and perhaps a little implausibly, a government were to have an outstanding record on the promotion of human rights, but to combine this with wholesale and flagrant breaches of international law in other areas it would be perverse to suggest that it was behaving ethically. Rather, as noted above, states have a primary duty to pursue the interests of their peoples – a duty which is, itself, ethical – but in the context of a set of wider moral obligations, and our moral judgements ought to be based on the way in which, in general, a government manages to reconcile this duty and those obligations. Has the government adopted enlightened, long-term, or selfish, short-term, definitions of self-interest? Is Britain a 'good citizen' internationally, in the sense of being a law-abiding member of international society, meeting its specific obligations and willing to pull its weight on international projects devoted to the common good? These are the relevant questions.

Unfortunately, to answer this kind of question – as opposed to the more specifically ethical questions that arise over human rights – requires a very wide assessment of matters of substance beyond the scope of this chapter. It requires a view to be taken on Britain's stance *vis-à-vis* the European Union and NATO and the UN family of organisations, relations with Eastern Europe and the successors of the former Soviet Union, with the Commonwealth and the rest of the Third World, and so on. In short, it requires an assessment of British foreign policy taken as a whole; as an inadequate substitute for such an assessment, it may be worth finishing with a few general points about British foreign policy over the last few years.

First, it might well be thought that this government, like the last, has rather too high an opinion of what Britain's proper standing in the world is and ought to be – the tendency to try to 'punch above our weight' remains. New Labour in office has endorsed the nuclear weapons programme of its predecessor and its much-heralded defence review has failed to make the kind of cuts that would reduce Britain's defence spending to something like that of its peers in Europe. There has been no sign of a willingness to give up Britain's seat on the Security Council (or to turn it into a European seat). The rather nominal British contribution to the recent air war in Kosovo was talked up by British leaders in ways that were clearly resented by some of those making a greater effort, especially, in this case, in France – although it should be noted that Tony Blair deserves considerable credit for putting his personal reputation on the line in this instance, and arguing very forcibly, and surely correctly, that it was necessary to back up the air campaign by the plausible threat of a land invasion. Moreover, Blair's 'Doctrine of the International Community' speech in Chicago on 22 April 1999 played an important role in defining the moral issues involved in the conflict for US public opinion at a time when the American president was in no position to make moral arguments of any kind, so perhaps in this particular case, the British foreign policy elite is entitled to consider itself at the centre of events.[6] Nonetheless, in general, British politicians continue to act on the world's stage as though their deeds were taken rather more seriously than they are. To aspire to exercise power that one does not actually possess cannot be consistent in the longer run with a truly ethical foreign policy.

Second, and not unconnected to its delusions of grandeur, New Labour's devotion to the American Alliance seems excessive even by the standards of the previous government. John Major's administration might have felt constrained not to oppose such actions as the US cruise-missile bombing of an apparently harmless pharmaceutical factory in the Sudan, but it seems doubtful that it would have been prepared to support this blatantly illegal act with quite as much enthusiasm as that shown by the Blair government. Again, the willingness of the British government to join the United States in its air campaigns in Iraq does not stand to its credit. Obviously the American Alliance is important to Britain, but if the British government feels that it is obliged to support with enthusiasm every step taken by the US in the strategic area then it is, in effect, putting the ethical status of its foreign policy in the hands of the President of the United States, which is not a desirable policy at any time, but is particularly undesirable at the present, when US policy is so frequently oriented to short-run domestic concerns. Doubtless defenders of the government's record in this respect would point to the benign use of the influence gained with the United States at the time of the Kosovo Crisis, but it is not clear that supporting the United States when they are wrong is necessarily the best way to persuade them to do the right thing on other occasions. A true friend should be prepared to give honest, even if sometimes unwanted, advice.

On a much more positive note, New Labour deserves credit for changing the atmosphere in which foreign policy is conducted and debated. Even in areas where the government's policy has attracted a great deal of criticism, the 'mood music' has changed. For example, under the previous government it was not uncommon for arms sales to be defended by the argument that if we do not do it, someone else will – the logic of which could, of course, be extended to anything from drug dealing to the slave trade. Centrist Tories such as John Major, Kenneth Clarke, Douglas Hurd and Malcolm Rifkind had a proper respect for the opinions of mankind, but their right-wing and 'Eurosceptic' colleagues – taking a

[6] I owe this point to Michael Doyle.

lead from Major's predecessor, Margaret Thatcher – seemed to take a perverse pleasure in standing alone in Europe and the Commonwealth. Their underlying assumption seemed to be that international isolation was in some strange way an indicator that Britain's national interest was being served, while the efforts of British diplomats to reach agreements acceptable to all was regarded as a sign of weakness.

Perhaps the single most important result of the arrival of New Labour has been to de-legitimise such blustering. The present government clearly believes in the importance of international law and international cooperation. Its stance in the European Union has been broadly positive; when unable to reach agreement it has taken no pleasure in this fact and has avoided making idle threats, and when it has achieved a successful outcome, there has been no vainglorious boasting. European governments have been treated as partners rather than potential enemies. There is no evidence that this has produced fewer selfish benefits for Britain than the Thatcherite policy of confrontation, but plenty of evidence that the changed atmosphere of relations between Britain and Europe will work in favour of all – the only sour note is struck when British subservience to US foreign policy angers its European associates, and on that issue the latter are right to be angered. Much the same might be said about Britain's improved relations with the United Nations and other multilateral bodies. It is in terms of this kind of international civility as an expression of a willingness to reconcile the national interest with the norms of international society that the true ethical dimension of foreign policy is to be found – and on its record in this area the new government passes, if not with flying colours, then at least with some merit.

3   The ethics of humanitarian intervention:
     protecting civilians to make democratic
     citizenship possible

Mervyn Frost

Preamble

This is neither a survey, nor a guide to the literature on the ethics of intervention in general or humanitarian intervention in particular. It does not track the twists and turns of the debate on this topic within the domains of International Law, International Relations (IR) or Political Ethics. Instead, it presents a self-contained argument, making extensive use of examples and analogies taken from fields other than IR, suggesting how we might tackle the ethical issues that arise when considering humanitarian intervention.

Introduction

Is it ethical for individuals, non-governmental organisations, states and international organisations to intervene in the domestic affairs of other states on humanitarian grounds? More specifically when, if ever, is the use of force ethically justified for humanitarian purposes? Since the Cold War ended these questions have been posed with increasing frequency and urgency, for example with regard to events in Kurdistan, Iraq, Rwanda, Sierra Leone, Haiti, Bosnia, Kosovo, Angola and East Timor. Intervention is bound to become an issue in many other places, too.

Several circumstances have brought questions about the ethics of intervention to the fore. The rigid bipolar Cold War balance of power has gone. Powerful states can now intervene without fear of triggering a superpower conflict that might escalate into nuclear conflict. Many states are weak and bedevilled with internal strife in which the suffering of civilians seems to call for some kind of intervention. Modern communications make the suffering of people in far-flung places immediately apparent to a global audience, provoking the public into believing that something ought to be done. A global discourse of human rights has emerged which, in turn, is reflected in a large number of international legal instruments. This discourse seems to warrant intervention where rights are being abused on a large scale. There is also a global climate of opinion in favour of democracy. Calls for intervention to support democracy are now commonplace, most recently in East Timor. Finally, since the Cold War ended, there has been a resurgence of national liberation struggles, most notably in the former USSR and the former Yugoslavia. Where such struggles are responses to oppression, or where they have led to war and suffering for civilian populations, a case is often made for intervention on humanitarian grounds.

How might we set about determining, in a general way, whether and when humanitarian intervention (including armed intervention) is ethically justifiable? A useful way to start is to dispose of the familiar answer, that in making foreign policy governments ought not to concern themselves with ethical considerations at all.

The ethical dimension inherent in human conduct

It is wrong to suggest, as many did when the 'New Labour' British government announced that it would pursue a foreign policy with an ethical dimension, that it is possible to make foreign policy without an ethical dimension. Clearly this belief influenced columnists like Simon Jenkins to write 'When foreign ministers turn to philosophy, decent citizens should run for cover' (*The Times*, 14 May 1997) and Peter Riddel to entitle an article 'Wrestling with Demons: Moral Crusades Do Not Make the World a Safer Place' (*The Times*, 24 November 1997). Their underlying supposition is that ethics is to policy what sugar is to tea; something that may be added or not according to taste. They suppose that in considering foreign policy, we confront the following sequence of choices:

- Is this a foreign policy with an ethical dimension?
- If 'yes', then we may proceed to ask: What ethical code is being used in this case?
- If the answer is 'The code which provides the ethical dimension to this foreign policy is x (where 'x' might stand for 'a rights based theory', 'a utilitarian theory', 'a Kantian deontological theory', 'a Christian ethic', 'an Islamic ethic', to mention but a few of the possibilities), then we may proceed to ask 'Is x a good, defensible, reasonable, justifiable, ethical code?'

The following guiding ideas underpin these questions: first, that some policies are guided by ethical considerations, while others are not. Second, that when policy-makers are guided by ethical considerations, they have to choose what ethical considerations they take into account. They can choose whether to be guided by human rights considerations, utilitarianism, Islamic or Kantian ethics, or they can choose to be guided by no ethical considerations. This line of thinking can lead to a lengthy discussion comparing the merits of different ethical codes. But the first of these guiding ideas is fundamentally wrong. It is wrong to suppose that foreign policy-makers have an initial choice whether or not to be ethical. *We are ethically constrained in everything we do.* Policy-making necessarily has an ethical dimension. Let me elucidate.

To act, or to do something, is to make a move within a practice that gives the doing of that deed its sense. Consider what I am doing at present. I am writing this chapter. In doing so, I am making a well-recognised move within that very wide form of life which we might call the practice of scholars. What I am doing only makes sense to me and to my readers because we understand this practice. It is a practice that includes within it the sub-practices of primary schooling, secondary schooling and the educating which takes place in tertiary institutions such as universities. The wide practice of scholars includes traditions nurtured for centuries by theologians within churches, practices kept going by libraries and carried forward by academics who maintain scholarly facilities on the internet. It includes the complex traditions maintained by publishers and booksellers and the practice of organising the production of edited works like this one. What I am doing only makes sense to me and you, the reader, because we are both participants in the practice.

It is easy to see how I might write at length about the other things I do, from cross-country running to participating in strikes organised by my union, and the practices within which they are done. In each case we understand what I do only in so far as we understand the rules, principles, maxims, folkways, conventions, and so on, of the practices within which these deeds are located.

When I come to understand a practice and to participate within it, I am constituted as an actor within that practice, just as you who are reading this chapter are constituted as scholars within the practice of scholars.[1]

The social practices within which we are constituted as actors have ethical components embedded in them. Thus, for example, the practice of scholars has built into it ethical norms to do with the pursuit of truth, a commitment to wide reading, a norm against plagiarism, a commitment to freedom of speech, freedom of conscience, academic freedom and many other values. They are not norms which scholars may or may not decide

---

[1] On constitutive theory generally, see Frost, 1996, Part II. On social practices, see Schatzki, 1996, ch. 4.

to take up. They are fundamental to the practice. Adhering to them is a precondition for participation. Were I to flout all of them all the time, I would no longer be accepted by my fellow scholars as a scholar. I would be labelled a charlatan. I would no longer be constituted as an actor within that practice.[2]

I could write at length about the ethical components embedded in the many other practices within which we are constituted as actors. Embedded in the practice of marriage are ethical norms which marriage partners understand and are expected to advance. Similarly, members of established churches have clear rules of participation and sets of values embedded in those rules.

The key point is that participants in these practices – those who are constituted as actors in good standing within them – do not have to decide whether or not to be ethical. *Through their day-to-day participation in such practices, the actors in them uphold and endorse the ethics embodied in the practices in question.* Participation in these practices requires adherence to the ethical codes embedded in them. In short, ethical conduct is not an 'add-on' to normal non-ethical or amoral conduct.

Let me drive the point home with reference to the practice of scholars. I have not made a conscious decision to pursue an ethical policy in writing this chapter. I am simply doing what is required of me as a scholar. I seek to use premises that I believe to be true. In linking my statements up to form an argument, I adhere to the canon of formal and informal logic as best I can. Where I refer to the work of others, I am committed to acknowledging my sources and to avoiding plagiarism. In short, my very participation in this practice requires that I uphold the ethical canon embedded in it. For participants, like me and you, the reader, who are well versed in the conventions of the practice and its underlying values, it would require a conscious decision to be unethical.

In the light of this analysis, it is clear that in any practice, including the practices of international relations, ethical conduct is not the exception – something which calls for comment by newspaper columnists – it is the norm. Ethical behaviour is, for the most part, commonplace and unremarkable. It is only in exceptional cases that actors make explicit the ethical dimension of a course of conduct.

---

[2] Of course, there are grey areas here. In all practices the possibility of cheating exists and in most practices some people cheat. Similarly, in all practices some participants may adhere to some or all of the norms in a hypocritical fashion. But cheating and hypocrisy are exceptional. They are only possible against a background state of affairs in which participants do not cheat and are not hypocrites. No sense can be made of a practice in which everyone cheats all the time or is hypocritical all the time.

Questions about the ethicality of a given course of action become prominent in two types of circumstances. First, when an act patently flouts accepted standards of ethical conduct within a given practice, as happens, for example, when it becomes known that a professor is guilty of plagiarism, or, where it becomes known that a minister of trade and industry accepted bribes in return for issuing licences for arms sales to human rights abusing states. Second, when it is not clear what counts as ethical conduct in a given situation.

The international practices within which we are all participants are no different from the ones I have discussed. Ethical features are embedded in them. Participation in them requires that we uphold the ethical codes internal to these practices. Consider the following: as a participant in global civil society I cannot but play my part in advancing the ethical code embedded in this practice. Most of us (most of humankind) today are in some measure participants in this practice. Global civil society is that very large practice (which includes within its compass the global market) within which we claim individual rights for ourselves and recognise them in others. When I participate in the global market by, for example, buying an object made abroad, by donating money to an international charity, through being a tourist, or by investing in a unit trust growth fund with foreign holdings, I am upholding and adhering to the ethical norms woven into that practice, norms which recognise individuals' rights to own property, to move about freely, to form associations, to make contracts (which itself requires a right to speak freely) and so on. In normal day-to-day practice in global civil society I am hardly conscious of my participation in ethical conduct. I simply buy the book printed in the United States, make my contribution to Oxfam, take a travel package to Morocco, invest in the Global Growth Fund, etc. I do these things without going through any ethical agony.

Similarly, when we act within that practice which we know as the democratic state, we do what we are entitled to do as citizens within such states. By so doing, we uphold and make real the values embedded in this practice, values that have to do with the realisation of autonomy. When I use my right as a citizen to harangue my MP or to write to the newspaper praising or criticising my government, I uphold the democratic ethic which the democratic institutions were designed to advance. Being ethical is not something I might bring in as a supplement to my everyday conduct as citizen. It is built into the activity of being a citizen. Citizens in established democracies are usually ethical as a matter of course. Questions about a failure to be ethical arise only in unusual cases where someone has flouted one of the underlying norms, or where it is not clear, under the circumstances, what ethical conduct would be; in other words, in cases which we might refer to as 'hard cases'.[3]

A similar account may be given of normal conduct within the practice of sovereign democratic and democratising states. I shall not describe this highly complex practice in detail here. In the international domain, democratic and democratising states interact each day in thousands of different ways.[4] They trade, negotiate about how to deal with international crime, participate in international organisations, negotiate arms control treaties and so on. In doing these things there is very little self-conscious theorising about whether or not to behave ethically. Their conduct is largely undertaken as 'a matter of course'. But like all practices, the international practice of sovereign states has built into it a normative component. Participants know the basic conventions that govern relations between sovereign states. States are accorded sovereignty which, in general, is protected by the non-intervention rule which, in turn, is reflected and honoured in international laws, treaties and organisations. A primary value which is achieved through people constituting one another as citizens within democratic states is a form of autonomy not achievable by other means. The states within which citizens achieve autonomy are themselves recognised as autonomous by other democratic states.[5] Citizens of one state who, through their government, recognise the autonomy of other states are engaged in upholding the morality embedded in the practice of states. Similarly, states (and citizens in them) who generally recognise and abide by international law are upholding the values implicit in that legal order. As always, then, participation in this international practice is an activity with a large ethical dimension. Limited cheating and limited bouts of hypocrisy are possible, but a complete ethical 'opt out' is not an option.

It follows that we learn how to be ethical when we learn how to participate in those many practices which, taken together, form the structure within which we are constituted as the persons we are, and within which

[3] A good example of the flouting of ethical constraints was provided by CREEP (the Campaign to Re-elect the President) when President Nixon's henchmen sought to pervert the democratic process by tampering with ballot boxes in intra-party elections, or by wrecking their political opponents' election meetings by changing the date on the posters so that voters arrived at closed venues on the wrong night. Here they had clearly taken a conscious decision to be unethical. In contrast, under normal circumstances, party political workers, in advertising meetings, organising ballots and so on, do not consciously decide to be ethical. They simply know what normal democratic practice is, and they get on with the business of fighting the election.

[4] Most states fall into this category. Many states that are not fully democratic claim to be heading towards democracy. Few profess themselves opposed to democracy.

[5] Put negatively, in the system of sovereign states the values to be avoided are domination, colonialism and empire (which are different words referring to much the same thing).

we lead our lives. I learn the ethics of family life as I am inculcated into its ways as a child, the ethics of scholarship at school, those of the market through participation in the market, those of citizenship through participation in the state, and so on, right up to my participation in the international practice of sovereign democratic and democratising states.

Ethical argument

In our day-to-day activities we act ethically without conscious deliberation or discussion. However, from time to time hard cases arise. This happens, *inter alia*, when it is not clear to us, as a matter of course, how we ought to act. It happens, for example, when new technologies present us with options we have not had before. Thus the invention of machines that can prolong life raises questions about how they ought to be used and when it would be appropriate to switch them off; the possibility of cloning human DNA chains raises questions about ethically acceptable uses for this technology; and the invention of nuclear weapons raised questions about the circumstances under which such weapons might justifiably be used.

A second way in which hard cases emerge is when unexpected events bring them into existence. For example, the break-up of the Soviet Union spawned a host of vigorous nationalist movements which posed new choices for international actors; recent events in the global economy put into motion thousands of economic refugees – the sheer scale of this movement created new, hitherto unanticipated, problems.

A third way in which hard cases come into existence is when what is required of us in one evolving practice contradicts what is required of us in another. A graphic example occurred when what was required of people within the practice of modern science came into conflict with what was required of them within traditional religious practices. Science required that they question many things which they were required to accept as settled within their traditional religious orders.

When new technologies, new circumstances or inter-practice developments throw up hard cases – cases in which it is not immediately clear to participants what is an appropriate response – ethical argument is likely to ensue. Whenever there is a lively discussion about business ethics, medical ethics, professional ethics and international ethics, this indicates that hard cases have emerged in those practices. *It does not indicate that the participants have suddenly decided to take ethics into account after having previously been content to behave in an unethical (or amoral) manner.* It means rather that the settled ethical norms within a practice have been disturbed by the emergence of hard cases. The process of confronting and dealing with such hard cases may lead over time to fundamental change in the practices within which we are constituted as actors.

Solving hard cases

How do we set about solving hard cases? Let me illustrate with an example of a settled practice being disturbed by the occurrence of a hard case. The invention of steroid drugs presented sportsmen and women with a set of hard ethical choices. On the one hand, steroids made improved performance possible, which, after all, is what competitive sport is all about. Yet, steroids posed unknown health risks to those taking them (thus undercutting what I assume is a value for all forms of sport, which is that they improve the health of participants), and they also opened up a huge domain for allegations of unfair competition (if drugs were available to some, should they not be available to all?). Participants, spectators and administrators were all faced with the question: should they permit or prohibit the taking of performance-enhancing drugs?

When it is no longer clear what we ought to do under the circumstances, we, who are participants in the practice, customarily engage in an exercise of collective introspection. We look at the relevant practice in the round. We question ourselves about the practice, and about the values embedded in it; questions which, in the normal course of events, it is not necessary for us to pose. The general question we ask is: what are the major values embedded in this practice? So with regard to the use of steroids in athletics, we ask whether athletic competitions are held to see who can get his or her chemically unmodified body to perform best. Some might conclude that they are. Others might suggest that, on the contrary, athletes seek to determine the limits to which the human body can be pushed by whatever available means. Where differences of opinion like this arise we seek to settle the dispute by showing how the value which we picked out as fundamental, coheres or fails to cohere with the other core values embedded in the practice. In short, we seek to make explicit, in a comprehensive and coherent background theory, the whole web of values which underpin the practice.

In seeking to construct a coherent and comprehensive background theory, we might attempt to strengthen our case that our preferred background theory is the best one by referring to the ways in which it links in with, and is supported by, other practices in which athletes, and those who watch athletics, participate. For example, we might point out that most schools run athletic meetings, that parents support them because they promote a value which is crucial to another important social practice, the family. We might point out that a goal of family life is to promote the physical wellbeing of family members. Families seek to promote this goal by encouraging their members to take part in athletics. We might argue that steroids are unhealthy and thus inimical to the values inhering in family life.

I have not spelled out the details of arguments for and against the use of steroids in athletics here. I have used the example in a general way to show what kinds of argumentative manoeuvres we attempt in order to resolve hard cases. I wish to highlight how important we deem it, in seeking answers to hard cases, to find an ethical theory which *brings into coherence all those values which are embedded in the practice (or practices) under consideration.*

Foreign policy-making and ethics

Making foreign policy is one of the things governments do.[6] From the previous argument it is clear that making foreign policy has an ethical dimension to it. It takes place in a particular social practice, that of the system of sovereign states, and, like all social practices, it has embedded in it certain value commitments – a certain ethic. For most of the time making foreign policy does not call these ethical elements into question. Thus, for example, British foreign policy-making takes place within the practice of the British democratic state which is itself situated within the wider practice of democratic and democratising states. Like foreign policy-makers in other states, British foreign policy-makers normally take for granted a commitment to international law, to protecting state sovereignty, to upholding domestic law, to promoting the policies and values professed by the governing political party, etc. The rules of the game demand that the British government must not advance the interests of foreign states at the cost of British interests. The ethical underpinnings of the practice are normally taken for granted. No discussion is offered and none is called for. These considerations apply to the normal conduct of other states in the system, too.

As we have seen above, when explicit and widespread discussion of ethical matters arises, this indicates that a hard case (or several hard cases) has appeared. The obvious questions to ask are: why has the matter of ethical foreign policy-making come to the fore? Why is there so much literature devoted to ethics in IR now? My answer is that all three of the factors that I mentioned earlier have given rise to hard-case reasoning with regard to contemporary foreign policy-making, not only in Britain but also within the society of states in general.

---

[6] Indirectly, as citizens, we are also involved in foreign policy-making in so far as we put forward, advocate or oppose certain policy positions.

First, new technologies have produced new circumstances in which states, their governments and their citizens have to act. In these new circumstances, it is no longer clear, as a matter of course, what is to count as appropriate foreign policy behaviour. New communication technologies enable us to know what is happening elsewhere in the world minute by minute. Worldwide audiences now know about natural and man-made disasters as they happen. As a result, and given that we now have the means to do so, we are called upon to respond almost immediately. Modern modes of transportation make it possible for many states to intervene in distant places in ways that were impossible before. The new technologies make it possible for people to call upon others who are far away to help them in the face of famine, to defend them against genocide, to protect them from tyranny, etc. In earlier times, non-intervention was, in large part, dictated by the lack of appropriate means to do anything about distant events. This technological impediment no longer exists. The new technologies require government decisions on matters that were not traditionally on the agenda. Many of these matters are difficult; they are hard cases. One example will suffice. When the government of Somalia was too weak to protect food supplies to its starving citizens and when other states had the resources to provide this protection, the resource-rich states faced the stark question of whether or not to act to protect the food supplies.

The second factor which is evoking hard cases in the domain of foreign policy is the occurrence of unexpected events, such as the collapse of the Soviet Union and Yugoslavia. Where formerly one superpower faced another in a remarkably stable balance of power, there is now a single superpower and, in place of the other, a whole range of different states, many of them no more than quasi-states. Virulent nationalist movements have arisen, each demanding self-determination within its own territory. These newly unleashed political forces have presented the foreign policy-making establishments of older settled states with new and knotty questions which they have not had to answer before. For many years states had operated on the understanding that existing state boundaries were fixed. Now many nationalist movements are actively seeking to change them by creating new states or enlarging existing ones. Should their aspirations be supported or opposed? These questions are nowhere more apparent than in the area of the former Yugoslavia. Similarly, the collapse of the USSR left treaty-based organisations of states, such as NATO (a classic collective security arrangement), bereft of their traditional role. NATO member states face the hard choice of what to do with their organisation or, to put it differently, what to have it do for them.

The third new factor is that there may be a clash between the underlying ethic embedded in one of our major international practices, global civil society, on the one hand, and the ethic inherent in another of these practices, the society of democratic and democratising states.[7] The former – the practice within which many human beings recognise one another as first-generation rights holders – requires that we not do anything that would damage the rights of other rights holders wherever they happen to be, and that we do what we can to protect their rights. The latter requires that we protect the state within which we enjoy citizenship rights, and that we respect the autonomy of states elsewhere (states within which other people enjoy their citizenship rights). Respect for states' rights and the non-intervention rule, however, sometimes seem to require that we turn a blind eye to human rights abuses in other states. It is at this point that the tension between our practices emerges. Should we intervene in Yugoslavia to protect people from human rights abuses, or should we respect that state's right to non-intervention in its internal affairs? Modern technology gives us the means to intervene. But should we do so? If we are called upon to do so in Yugoslavia, should we also intervene in Algeria, Afghanistan, Pakistan, Iraq, Israel, Sudan, Somalia, Rwanda, Burundi, Burma and Indonesia, to mention but a few places where human rights abuses are taking place? This apparent clash between the ethical codes underpinning two major practices within which we participate, presents us with a series of hard cases where it is not obvious what we ought to do under the circumstances.

To summarise briefly: we are constituted as actors within social practices, all of which have within them an embedded ethical component that, for the most part, we take for granted. Hard cases, those cases where ethical issues come to the fore, arise, *inter alia*, when we, who are constituted as actors within given practices, confront new technologies, or changed circumstances, or when a tension emerges between what is required within one practice, and what is required within another. The recent interest in, and discussion about, ethical foreign policy is the result of our encountering all three of these conditions in both civil society and in the society of democratic and democratising states. At the heart of much of the concern with ethical foreign policy is the issue of humanitarian intervention in the domestic affairs of foreign states.

Humanitarian intervention: where two non-intervention norms clash?

As civilians (members of civil society) and as citizens (in the society of democratic and democratising states), we normally take two sets of

---

[7] Global civil society could also be called 'the global discourse on human rights'. The participants are those who claim rights for themselves and recognise such claims coming from others.

non-intervention norms for granted. In the normal course of events, abiding by both non-intervention norms, each embedded within its own practice, is unproblematic. However, circumstances have brought us to a point where this is no longer straightforward. A hard case has emerged, most dramatically with regard to the issue of humanitarian intervention. I shall consider each of the non-intervention norms in turn, first, the non-intervention norm in civil society, and, second, the non-intervention norm in the society of states.

Non-intervention in civil society

As civilians, that is, as rights holders in civil society, we consider ourselves to have a set of fundamental rights that secure us freedom against intervention by others.[8] Within civil society my first-generation rights (such as the right not to be killed, assaulted, tortured; the rights to freedom of speech, movement, assembly, contract, conscience, and to own property), secure for me a zone of action which is protected against intervention by the mafia, a state, a set of states, an international organisation or any other actor.[9] Civil society is a practice within which our rights protect us from wrongful intervention. This is a statement of the norms embedded within civil society. Of course, individuals, groups or states, sometimes attempt to infringe our rights (and often they succeed). But the civilians who comprise civil society condemn such acts and may (and often do) set about mobilising themselves to oppose the wrongdoers. In civil society, then, the non-intervention norm protects an area of freedom around every individual and this protection is provided by a set of first-generation rights, also known as negative liberties.

There are two features of the practice of civil society to which I wish to draw attention here. First, it is a society without borders. Specifically, civil society pays no heed to the borders of states. Civilians recognise the rights

---

[8] I use the term 'civilian' in an unorthodox way here to refer to participants in civil society. The defining feature of civilians is that they claim first-generation rights for themselves and respect such claims from others. The rights people have as civilians are distinct from those that they have as citizens within democratic states. Rights of citizenship are logically connected to membership of a state. A citizen is always a citizen of a particular state. In contrast, civilians claim their basic rights against one another whether or not they find themselves in functioning states, weak states, collapsed states, quasi-states or no state at all.

[9] Rights 'secure' these things in the sense of providing an argument widely accepted as decisively ending any argument in favour of intervening in the domain protected by the right in question. To have a right is to have an argument that the rights holder may deploy in justification for a certain course of action (or inaction) in a prescribed set of circumstances. In the practice of rights, in civil society, the other participants in that practice recognise such arguments as valid.

of fellow civilians wherever they may be. They see these rights as universal. Similarly, they consider that they have a right to non-intervention in their private affairs wherever they happen to be. Civilians do not give up their basic rights as they cross state borders from one country to another. Second, in civil society we claim our rights whether or not we have the means to enforce them. Often it is precisely where civilians are most persecuted that they claim their rights most vociferously (as happens in Iraq, Algeria, Burma, Indonesia, Yugoslavia and so on), and it is in those cases that our recognition of their claims is most important. The non-intervention norm in civil society is a depoliticising norm. Through the norm as embodied in our set of basic rights, civilians in civil society have taken a whole set of items off the political agenda – off the list of rules which can be changed (whether the contemplated change involves modifying the rules or eradicating them). Rights holders in civil society, by acknowledging one another as rights holders, have established an arrangement within which they may engage in all kinds of political bargaining, wheeling and dealing, pressure group politics, etc., subject to the constraint that their basic rights are not up for negotiation. Thus, as long as we respect this constraint, we are free to trade, to form political associations (such as political pressure groups, parties, states, confederations or federations, consociations, international organisations), commercial arrangements (partnerships, firms, corporations, multinational corporations), social formations (clubs, teams, churches), educational enterprises (schools, colleges and universities), in an ongoing flux of social rearranging, as we think fit.

Another way of stating what has been achieved within civil society is that civil society establishes a strong private/public distinction. In civil society the non-intervention norm embodied in our basic rights establishes a private domain within which individuals are free to make decisions as they think fit. My right to freedom of speech protects a private domain within which it is my choice whether or not to speak, the right to freedom of conscience establishes a private domain in which I may choose whom and how to worship, what I do with my property is my affair, and so on, through the list of rights.

It is important to realise that the creation of civil society, the society of rights holders, was the outcome of a complex history of political struggle, most of which took place within the territories of specific states. For long periods of history many people were not considered to have rights (for example, slaves, serfs, women and blacks, to mention but a few of the many categories of humans who were denied rights in the past). The outcome of the struggle was the formation of a practice in which the participants, by recognising one another as rights holders, took a whole set of items out of the political domain (both in general and in the context of individual states). For civilians, it is no longer a political issue whether blacks ought to be accorded the same autonomy as whites, women the same as men, the poor the same as the rich, homosexuals the same as heterosexuals, Christians the same as Islamic people, and so on through the categories of difference that were once the subject of fierce political disputes. At the end of this political struggle, key issues had been privatised, depoliticised and universalised. In civil society we have constituted one another in a way that secures for each one of us a secure domain of autonomy. In this society autonomy is constituted by the non-intervention norm embodied in civil liberties.[10] I must stress that I am describing the practice of claim and counter claim which exists between civilians. It is, of course, true that the people involved in this practice do not always adhere to these norms in their daily round. Many civilians turn out to be abusers of human rights. That some people flout the norms of the practice within which they profess themselves to be participating is not proof that the practice does not exist.

Non-intervention in the society of democratic and democratising states

In the previous section I discussed how we constitute one another as rights holders in the global practice known as civil society. Civil society is a practice which includes in it all those many millions worldwide who claim that they have basic human rights. It excludes only those who deny that they have such rights.[11] Let me now turn to the second great contemporary global practice, the society of democratic and democratising sovereign states within which we constitute one another as citizens. In recognising one another's right to citizenship, we constitute one another as people who have the right, in association with others, to form self-governing political communities – to form democratic states. This society includes within it both those who currently enjoy citizenship status within functioning democracies, and the many people who seek to realise democratic citizenship for themselves in sovereign democratic states. They include

---

[10] Within civil society there are constant disputes about what basic rights civilians ought to accord to one another. I do not intend entering this fray here. I have simply highlighted some central features of what is involved in making rights claims in the context of civil society.

[11] Few people positively deny that they have a right to life, a right not to be assaulted or tortured, a right to own property, a right to speak, assemble, move, contract and so on. Many millions claim that their rights are being denied them, but this, of course, is to affirm their claim to basic rights.

those who seek to reform their existing state in a democratic direction and those who seek to break away from their existing political formation in order to form new democratic states.[12]

In the society of states, we claim (and in many cases also enjoy) citizenship rights. These rights include, amongst others, the right to form political parties, the right to stand for public offices, the right to participate in elections, the right to hold elected officers accountable during their term of office, the right to lobby elected representatives, and so on. Like all rights, we may use (or not) these rights at our discretion.

Just as the non-intervention norm in civil society creates a private and depoliticised space within which individuals can exercise their autonomy, so too the non-intervention norm in the society of states constitutes states as actors, each with a private and depoliticised domain of action within which citizens may exercise their autonomy through their constitutional structures. In civil society the non-intervention norm protects a space for individual actors; in the society of states it protects a space for a collective actor, the state. The state is the collective actor constituted by citizens and in which citizenship is constituted. In the society of states, as in civil society, the non-intervention norm takes a host of items off the political agenda. For example, how a state, through its citizens and their government, decides to arrange religious affairs internally is a matter for it alone to determine, no other state (or set of states) has a right to interfere. Similarly, how each state chooses to develop its constitutional structure, organise its legislative programme and arrange its administration, and its social services, is, like many other matters, the private affair of the individual state. The non-intervention norm takes these issues out of the realm of international politics and stresses that they are the private concern of the state in question. Importantly, the non-intervention norm precludes one state using military means to intervene in the internal affairs of another state.

We who are citizens in autonomous democratic states (or who aspire to bring such a state into being) value the non-intervention norm because we deem it important that people are constituted with that form of autonomy, that form of self-governing status and capacity, that only citizens

---

[12] At the inception of the Westphalian system of sovereign states, the non-intervention norm protected the jurisdiction of sovereign monarchs without reference to the form of government they practised. The right to self-government was normally given a religious justification. In our current global practice, the right to self-government is understood to be the right of citizens in a state to govern themselves through democratic forms of self-government. The adoption of appropriate forms of democratic government is a precondition nowadays which new polities must meet before being granted recognition as sovereign states.

in democracies enjoy. We deem it important that a whole host of choices are left exclusively to citizens. These choices are private to the state in question.

As with civil society, this practice, the society of states constituted around the non-intervention norm, only came into being after a long history of political struggle. For long periods ordinary men and women were not constituted as citizens with citizenship rights which allowed them to be self-governing in sovereign democracies. Instead, as often as not, they were subject people, subject to the authority of kings, emperors, suzerains, despots and conquerors of one kind or another. More recently, colonial people were subject to the authority of distant imperial governments and tribes in South Africa were coerced into systems of 'self-rule' in Bantustans that were far from free. The struggle to destroy, undermine and transform practices within which people were constituted as subjects rather than citizens took a long time (indeed, it is not yet complete), but the pay-off was the establishment of a practice within which, through the non-intervention norm, certain courses of action were ruled out of bounds to international politics, and were made the private affair of individual states.

Civilians and citizens: harmonising the non-intervention norms

Is being a civilian in civil society compatible with being a citizen in the society of democratic states? This is arguably the central hard case for ethical theory in the contemporary practices of world politics. To put it another way, is the domain of individual autonomy which is secured around individuals in civil society through the operation of the non-intervention norm (encapsulated in our basic rights), compatible with the domain of autonomy which the non-intervention norm in the society of democratic states secures for us as citizens within such states? On the face of it, the two non-intervention norms may seem to contradict one another. Consider the case of a single individual, Eve. As a civilian, Eve is entitled to have her basic first-generation rights secured, but it may seem that, as a citizen, she is bound to accept whatever decision her democratically elected government makes. This might include a decision to require of her that she forfeits a part of her wealth for the benefit of the poor, or that she puts her life at risk to protect the polity, and so on. Similarly, when Eve goes abroad, making use of her right to freedom of movement amongst other civilians, wherever they may be, she may encounter a state in which the citizens have decided that someone with her skin colour, religious affiliation, ethnic background, gender or lack of wealth must be prohibited from entering their territory. It appears, then, that both in our own states and in the states of others, citizens exercising their rights to self-government may override our rights as civilians. It seems as if we have to choose between the two practices: we can opt for the practice of autonomous individuals protected by one non-intervention rule, or, for the practice of autonomous states protected by a different non-intervention rule, but we cannot choose both.

This way of understanding the relationship between the two practices is, however, fundamentally flawed. It rests on a misunderstanding of the relationship between civil society and the society of democratic states. We are not required to choose whether we want to be civilians or citizens, because civil society and the society of democratic states are not rivals, but complementary practices. *Only those who enjoy the rights of civilians can be constituted as citizens – as holders of citizenship rights.*

Citizenship is worthless unless citizens are simultaneously constituted as civilians, as holders of first-generation rights within the global practice of civil society. To be a citizen is to enjoy the kind of autonomy we have when we are equal participants with our fellow citizens in the processes of electing, influencing and holding to account the governments under which we live in the sovereign states in which we live. But we could not enjoy these citizenship rights were we not initially constituted as holders of first-generation rights in civil society. What use would the right to vote be, if there were no freedom of speech to discuss the merits of different candidates and policies? What use would the right to stand for office be, without the prior rights which protect us from being killed, assaulted or tortured? What use would rights entitling us to participate in the processes of self-government be if we did not, in the first place, enjoy freedom of conscience and academic freedom, those rights which allow us to consider and investigate different forms of life before deciding how to deploy our political rights?[13] Internationally, too, our citizenship in one state would not establish us as autonomous people *vis-à-vis* people outside our state if outsiders did not respect our basic civilian liberties – the basic first-generation rights that we enjoy in global civil society. Were, for example, South African citizens to recognise Mozambicans as citizens in their state without at the same time recognising their civil liberties, this recognition would hardly amount to much. It is difficult to think what sense could be made of the notion of citizenship in the absence of civil liberties.[14]

---

[13] The Soviet Union is an example of what happens when people have 'citizenship rights' without civil liberties.

[14] The muddle that accompanies any attempt to confer citizenship on those to whom civilian liberties have been denied was well demonstrated in South Africa between 1948 and 1989. During this period, the white minority government attempted to create forms of citizenship for black South Africans within separate ethnic 'Bantustans', while at the

Citizens in democracies can, and usually do, use the machinery of state to protect their first-generation civilian rights, either through the device of entrenching a bill of rights in the constitution, or through the operation of common law. It is crucial to note, however, that in doing this, they are not creating civilian rights, but merely using the machinery of government to protect pre-existing civil society rights in that portion of civil society covered by their state.[15] If the states which have used the machinery of government to protect civilian rights were to become weak or to collapse altogether (as has happened in many places recently), we would still regard the civilians there as having their first-generation rights. Their state has collapsed but they are still members of civil society. When people in such places make rights claims, the validity of their claims is not dependent on the existence of a functioning state.

Thus, our autonomy depends both on our being constituted as civilians in global civil society and on our enjoying the status of citizen in the practice of democratic states. On this reading of contemporary global practices, states that deny to their own citizens (or to people elsewhere) their basic civilian rights bring their own ethical standing into question. For in our contemporary global practice of states, the moral standing of states derives from there being the institution within which democratic citizenship is established. Citizenship itself, however, can only be established amongst people who enjoy basic rights in global civil society.

Returning to the non-intervention norms, it follows from my argument that a state's claim to non-intervention in its domestic affairs derives its force from the rights of its citizens to participate in the self-government of that state. But democratic citizenship itself depends on the people concerned enjoying the prior status of being rights holders in civil society, the key feature of which is a non-intervention norm surrounding a domain of autonomy for the individual rights holder. *In sum, the non-intervention norm applicable to states depends on states (and the citizens within them) showing due respect for the non-intervention norm of civil society.* The

same time denying to them their basic rights within global civil society. The recognition by white South Africans of the 'citizenship' rights of black South Africans within ethnically defined Bantustans was hollow because the blacks were not given prior recognition as holders of basic rights such as the right to safety of the person, freedom of speech, assembly, movement, conscience and the right to own property. On this analysis, separate development failed not because what might have been a workable policy was poorly executed. Its failure flowed from a fundamental incoherence in the minority government's thinking about what is ethically required for the establishment of citizenship, democracy and self-government.

[15] This point can be illustrated with an analogy from academic life. When a specific university makes a set of regulations prohibiting plagiarism, it is not creating *de novo* the academic crime of plagiarism; it is merely using its machinery to enforce the anti-plagiarism rule that is a constitutive component of the worldwide practice of scholarship.

non-intervention norm of the one undergirds the moral force of the non-intervention norm of the other.

Humanitarian intervention

Humanitarian intervention is sometimes portrayed as a breach of the non-intervention norm that holds between sovereign states. This is wrong. Using the preceding analysis, I shall argue that humanitarian intervention is best understood as an act directed towards upholding the non-intervention norm of civil society, which protects an area of freedom for individuals. Respect for this norm, far from undermining the non-intervention norm of the system of sovereign democratic states, is a prerequisite for the establishment of the practice of democratic and dem-ocratising states with its own non-intervention norm prohibiting intervention in the domestic affairs of sovereign states. Only people whose basic rights are recognised (that is, only people who are constituted as civilians) may come together to establish themselves as citizens within democratic states, and those states will then have rights to non-intervention in their domestic affairs.[16]

This analysis suggests that whether or not to engage in humanitarian intervention must be understood in the context of global civil society. It arises in response to allegations of wrongful intervention into the domain of autonomy of individual rights holders. So, in order to answer the question, 'is humanitarian intervention justified in this case?', we must enquire whether the non-intervention norm of civil society has been breached – whether human rights violations have taken place. What kind of intervention would be justified depends on the severity of the infringement of basic rights. Gross human rights violations might require military intervention, lesser violations, lighter forms of political intervention. Making such ethical judgements is often difficult, and disagreements are likely to be frequent. What will aid the process is the gradual embodiment of agreed ethical judgements which have become established in international law. Establishing them may require the creation of new specialised institutions which are widely recognised as legitimate and which have built-in procedures and training programmes to ensure consistency and fairness.

---

[16] This is nicely illustrated in recent South African history. Black South Africans had to be accorded a basic set of civilian rights before they could embark upon the process of negotiating the formation of a new state within which all South Africans could enjoy equal citizenship rights. Negotiations would not have been possible if they had been forced to remain in their previous rights-less position. As *apartheid* came to an end, granting civilian rights was a precondition for the establishment of a democratic constitutional state.

My argument is that in the contemporary practices of world politics, humanitarian intervention must be understood as directed at maintaining civil society – the global society of rights holders which has no borders.[17] Metaphorically speaking, humanitarian intervention is the darning of a hole in the fabric of civil society.

There is no room here for a detailed delineation of the circumstances in which humanitarian intervention would be justified. Instead, I shall close with a few suggestive remarks about the implications of my analysis.

- Humanitarian intervention is not best understood as an action which fits into theories of just warfare, as they do not involve war between states. The concerns of just war theory about proper authority, just cause and just means are not readily applicable to humanitarian interventions.
- Humanitarian intervention is best understood as being undertaken on behalf of, or in the name of, civilians. It is undertaken by rights holders seeking to protect fellow rights holders from abuses of their rights. Where the actors are states, they are acting on behalf of global civil society which is the foundation on which the legitimacy of states themselves is built. Humanitarian intervention is not undertaken by states acting in the national interest, where this interest is understood as existing independently of the rights of civilians.
- It follows that the civilians in the region concerned must request intervention. The aim is to actualise the rights that they claim for themselves.[18]
- Members of global civil society seeking to intervene to protect rights holders, may use a state, many states, international organisations, private companies or any other social power which they believe may be effective as the mechanism for preventing rights abuses taking place. Whatever actor is chosen, it will have to be constrained by the norms of civil society.
- Interveners act for civil society as a whole. Thus care should be taken in setting up the intervention apparatus to demonstrate that this is the case. Every effort should be made to avoid any suggestion that an imperial power is intervening to impose its will on the weak.

[17] This must be the basis upon which the society of democratic and democratising states can be built.

[18] In some cases the victims of rights abuse may be so oppressed that they literally cannot (or are too frightened to) request help in realising their rights. In that case, those contemplating intervention must take whatever steps are necessary to determine whether, in the absence of such oppression, the people concerned might request intervention. This might require holding clandestine meetings with the oppressed, or talking to those living in the relevant diaspora and so on.

- The aim of humanitarian intervention is to protect and repair a rights-respecting order, which is civil society. The aim is not conquest. Any talk of 'the enemy' and 'victory' is out of place in such actions.[19]
- Humanitarian intervention is short term and instrumental. The interveners do not seek to rule in the area concerned, but to nurture a rights-respecting order and then to withdraw. The language of war is inappropriate in this context.
- Members of civil society intervening where rights abuses have taken place are required by the norms of civil society to respect the rights of all civilians in the area in which they have intervened. This includes respecting the rights of the wrongdoers. The wrongdoers are rights holders who are to be prevented from committing crimes, they are not enemies to be vanquished.
- During the conduct of a humanitarian intervention care should be taken to ensure that all the people involved are accorded their civilian rights of freedom of speech. The press should not report only the views of one side in the interests of scoring propaganda victories over the 'enemy'. An intervention in the name of civil society should be scrupulous in upholding the norms of civil society, especially those that pertain to freedom of speech and freedom of the press.
- In every such intervention care should be taken to specify precisely which individuals are guilty of rights abuses. Civil society is a society of individuals. Care should be taken not to label the entire people or ethnic groups as the enemy, but only specific, named people. If this is not possible, the organisation most closely associated with wrongdoing should be specified. In civil society wrongdoers are always ultimately individuals.
- Intervention should be understood as police action within 'our' global civil society, rather than as a military campaign against 'their' enemy state. The aim is not to defeat an enemy, but to prevent aggression against the domains of freedom of individuals.
- Civilians only become fully free once they have established themselves as citizens in democracies. Interveners must, therefore, always aim to facilitate the creation of democracies. How many democracies there are to be in a given area is for the civilians themselves to decide, not the intervening actors. Facilitating the emergence of a democracy is quite different to imposing a democratic form on an unwilling people.[20]

[19] In this regard, much of the rhetoric surrounding the intervention in Yugoslavia during the Kosovo crisis was misplaced.

[20] Referring again to Kosovo, it is not for the intervening powers to stipulate the future status of Kosovo. Whether one, two or more democracies are formed in the region is for the civilians in the region to decide.

Concluding remarks

My overriding goal here has been to situate our ethical understanding of humanitarian intervention in a holist analysis of the two major global practices within which we are presently constituted as ethical actors. I have argued that we are constituted as civilians, as holders of first-generation rights, in global civil society, and that this is a precondition for our achieving the higher order status of citizen within the practice of democratic and democratising states to which most of humankind presently aspires. Humanitarian intervention is not properly understood as wrongful intervention in the domestic affairs of a sovereign state, but as an act aimed at a region of civil society where it has broken down. The aim is to repair civil society so that the people there might proceed to build democracies for themselves within which they may enjoy the rights of citizenship.

4   A pragmatist perspective on ethical foreign policy

Molly Cochran

In 1898 the United States engaged Spain in war with imperial gain its objective. The United States had already annexed the Hawaiian Islands; in defeating the Spanish, it forced that country to relinquish Cuba and Puerto Rico, and to negotiate the status of the Philippine islands. However, American troops, unaware of the armistice, took Manila Bay. Spain accepted the US acquisition of the Philippines in the Treaty of Paris in November 1898, but by 4 February 1899, the United States was engaged in war again, this time with the Filipinos who were fighting a war of independence.

Until this time, America had thought of itself as a country 'opposed to militarism, conquest, standing armies and all the other bad habits associated with the monarchies of the old world' (Tuchman, 1996: 137) that is, the aspects of the war system perpetuated by the European powers. America was to serve as the example of the democratic ideal abroad: a new world not bent on foreign dominion and conquest. According to this ideal, legitimate authority or power comes from the consent of the governed. Now the United States was fighting a war to suppress the will of Filipinos to rule themselves.

At roughly the same time, American philosophy was taking its own decisive turn. A tradition of thought which is understood to have had its beginnings in the writings of Ralph Waldo Emerson and its first expression in philosophy in the work of Charles Peirce was labelled as 'pragmatism' by William James in 1898 and advanced by him and John Dewey before and after the turn of the century (West, 1989). Its approach to ethics and truth in philosophy rejected absolutisms of all kinds, recognised the fallibility of any principle or proposition, and vigorously attacked dualisms like mind/body, object/subject, fact/value that permeated continental philosophy. For James, these ideas were not unconnected to foreign policy. He understood pragmatism to be a way of thinking that worked against, and was critical of, the imperialist tendencies he saw growing within American sentiment and action at this time. He and another influential pragmatist, Jane Addams, were members of the Anti-Imperialist

League, founded in 1898, which viewed this kind of activity as antithetical to democracy, and the origins of American democracy in particular. Indeed, James wrote to a friend at the time saying, '[t]he way the country puked up its ancient principles at the first touch of temptation was sickening' (Tuchman, 1996: 161).

This chapter asks what general guidance pragmatism might offer to policy-makers and analysts regarding an ethical foreign policy. The answer that I will offer is that pragmatism finds that ethics must be conceived *democratically*. Pragmatism works from the assumption that all persons are capable of, and should have opportunities for, self-development and growth, and this requires that activity which affects them in their day-to-day lives should be subject to their consent. Applied to foreign policy, this ethical imperative suggests that a state must seek to ensure, as best as possible, that persons affected by transnational activity have *access to decision-making* in regard to the regulation of that activity. Consequently, it is important that states are responsive to the collective will of international publics articulated in a growing number of new institutions as informal as social movements and as formal as NGOs and transnational networks.

Such a proposition is not altogether recognisable as foreign policy traditionally conceived. Where is the reference more specifically to *our* citizens or to national interest? Is this just ethics divorced from the realities of legitimate foreign policy interests related to security or to the economy? My two main tasks are to examine whether ethical foreign policy, pragmatically conceived, has any empirical relevance for the challenges states face today, and to offer normative justifications of the ethical guidance pragmatism lends.

In order to proceed, it is important to demonstrate that pragmatism is not a 'head in the clouds' approach to ethics with little practical interest in lived experience and the real dilemmas faced in foreign policy decision-making. Thus, it may be useful to look back to a period in which pragmatist philosophy was at the height of its powers, a time which also is notorious for the world taking heart in the possibilities for the ethical and peaceful conduct of foreign relations: the first three decades of the twentieth century. Since this time, political scientists have rebuked those – policy-makers, commentators and academics alike – who were caught up in normative and emotional appeals for a world free of war, guided by international organisation.

In *The Twenty Years' Crisis*, E. H. Carr argues that this period could not do what the nineteenth century, in its historical particularlity, was uniquely able to do: manage a sort of utopian compromise between idealistic appeals for respectful conduct between states and the necessities of power in dealing with aggressive, expansionist states (1964 [1946]: 27, 60–2). Interestingly, in relation to the mistakenly characterised idealist/realist spectrum, which has an immeasurable impact on the discipline of IR and for which Carr's book is largely responsible (Wilson, 1998), pragmatism sits at each end of that spectrum as well as in the middle. For example, one writer influenced by pragmatism, Walter Lippmann, was harsh in his assessment of US isolationist attitudes and lack of foreign policy and military preparedness from the turn of the century until 1945. Another, John Dewey, the most influential and prolific pragmatist philosopher of the twentieth century, wavered in the middle of this spectrum, since he ultimately supported US entry in both wars, yet keenly advocated the Outlawry of War Movement. Jane Addams, on the other hand, despite harsh criticism from the public as well as some of her fellow progressives, maintained a pacifist stance during US involvement in the First World War.

What explains this variation within pragmatism? More crucially, what guidance can a philosophical approach offer which is capable of generating such diverse opinions? In response to these questions and the tasks of this chapter, I shall begin with a brief synopsis of the key elements of pragmatism as an ethical approach. Next, I shall trace the positions of each of these writers, Lippmann, Dewey and Addams, on their pragmatism and views on the conduct of American foreign affairs in the first three decades of the twentieth century. I shall thus make two related points. The first supports the opinion that the idealism/realism dualism is misconceived and has impeded consideration of ethics and foreign policy for too long. None of these writers were oblivious to the 'realities' of world politics. Indeed, the variation in their stances was due primarily to differing interpretations of the facts of the world situation and prospects for order in it. My second point is that while the realities of a new kind of international politics, as Dewey and Addams perceived them, proved to be less than well entrenched in their day, Dewey and Addams identified the beginning of trends towards forms of post-sovereignty and global governance which today are both better established and entrenched in ways with which we are ill-prepared to cope. Thus, this chapter considers whether the vision of a new world politics that Dewey and Addams shared, one in which the pragmatist democratic ethic is deeply embedded, is not only a defensible normative agenda, but one that has a good grasp on the ways in which the nature of peace and security is changing today, and therefore, how foreign policy decision-making must change.

Pragmatism as an ethical approach

As a philosophical approach, pragmatism is characterised by Peirce's work on semiotics and James' work in psychology, but Dewey was largely responsible for exploring in a more systematic manner the significance of pragmatism for ethics and politics (Thayer, 1981: 383). Dewey understood inquiry into how we could better solve the problems of persons in their day-to-day lives and help them find not only workable solutions, but ones they found meaningful, to be an *ethical* responsibility. For Dewey, the failure of philosophy was that it was more interested in abstract speculation about universal truths and absolutes than in the real social problems that individuals faced in their everyday worlds (Dewey, 1948). The ultimate goal of inquiry is to promote an ever-widening sense of community, of persons working in cooperative effort towards the development of our capacities of intelligence and the ways that we manage activity that affects us. Dewey called this ethical imperative growth and he saw it as the only end (1948: 177). Inquiry into experience through cooperative effort with others in the acts of identifying problematic situations, seeking solutions and experimenting with possible solutions leads to growth. This idea of growth as an end is vague, but that is its intended effect. To suggest anything more than that would narrow inquiry, limiting the possibilities, avenues and endeavours of inquiry, and thus, solutions tried. Growth requires openness and an assumption of fallibility in all of these endeavours which absolute moral principles close off.

What exactly is the democratic character of this pragmatism? An idea which is at the core of democratic thought regarding who we are as persons is also central to an ethical concern with inquiry and growth. Pragmatism works from the assumption that all persons are capable of intelligence and should have opportunities to direct their lives, and this requires that persons should have a say in human activity which affects them. The idea that consent should guide human relationships is an assumption common to democratic thought. In pragmatism, this basic assumption drives inquiry towards growth.

However, the democratic imperative within pragmatism is not limited to this. Democracy is required by pragmatism methodologically as well. Democracy is needed both as a context for, and the way in which, inquiry and the method of intelligence are pursued. If we think about the conduct of an experiment into the resolution of a problematic social situation, pragmatism assumes that this work is best carried out in a context open to the exchange of ideas. Where there is freedom of expression, where persons can voice critical opinions, where the flow of information is free, a democratic culture is in place. As for the method in which inquiry is pursued, there are several elements that call for democracy. First, pragmatism assumes the more critical minds at work the better. Solutions are better tested, arrived at and more workable when all those involved are participant in its deliberation. Second, inquiry must be conducted as widely as possible, not only in terms of the numbers involved, but in the imagination and creativity with which solutions, truth, are sought. This is exactly why the end of inquiry, defined as growth, should not be any more specific than calling for sensitivity, diligence and a balance of interests in the pursuit of inquiry. A third and final democratic consideration in regard to method is that balancing ends and means is very important. Problematic situations arise in the real world. In order to provide for a workable solution, the means employed must not only be realistic in regard to what is available, but well suited to the end. In particular, if the end in view is growth in human capacities and welfare, then any means chosen which undermine this end, even in part, undermine the solution reached. In sum, democratic ends require democratic means.

To summarise what might be drawn from this as guidance in the consideration of ethical foreign policy, I suggest the following. First, pragmatism sees that truth is not out there, discoverable by abstract philosophical speculation, but instead, rests in the degree to which it accords with human experience and our inquiry into that experience. Second, pragmatism rejects dogmatism of all kinds, because inquiries into experience which are genuinely open and sensitive to that experience will reflect its contingent nature. Thus, all conclusions regarding the truth must be understood to be fallible; that is, they are subject to revision. Third, the focus of pragmatism is on problem-solving in regard to indeterminate situations; it understands each situation to be unique in character, requiring its own particular solution. Fourth, there is a crucial inter-relationship between means and ends such that pragmatists talk of a means–ends continuum. Finally, an open or democratic community is indispensable to inquiry into indeterminate situations and to the widest potential development of human capacities.

Let us turn to Walter Lippmann, John Dewey and Jane Addams to illustrate how these notions find expression in their particular assessments of the problematic situations raised by American foreign relations in the first part of the twentieth century. I will consolidate these ideas into three themes, drawing attention in the work of each to: (1) attacks on dogmatisms and/or abstractions ungrounded in experience; (2) means-ends analysis; and (3) arguments for democratic consent and the need for wider forms of association based on consent.

Pragmatism in practice: Lippmann, Dewey and Addams

Lippmann

Bringing Lippmann into the pragmatist fold here may seem puzzling. Not typically associated with pragmatism, he was often categorised in International Relations as a realist along with George Kennan or Hans Morgenthau. Lippmann frequently sparred with Dewey in print; the two disagreed over many issues – from the real problem behind the eclipse of the public in American politics, to questions like support for the League of Nations or the Outlawry of War Movement. The First World War left Lippmann convinced of the intellectual chasm between common people and natural elites and experts; thus, he saw the need for elite leadership in the conduct of human affairs (Kaplan, 1956: 357–9). He did not share the faith of Deweyan pragmatism in all persons having the capacity for intelligence and conducting their lives by using their intelligence. As a result, his democratic concerns had a different character to those of Dewey. Nonetheless, he maintained a democratic ethic based on consent, even in his writings on foreign affairs, and he took away from his weekly invitations to tea with James, occasions he valued greatly while studying at Harvard (Steel, 1980: 17–18), several key pragmatist themes which appear in his writings, including his 1943 book, *US Foreign Policy: Shield of the Republic*.

Recently, Lippmann's book, *US Foreign Policy*, was included in a list, compiled for the 75th Anniversary Issue of *Foreign Affairs*, of the most influential books in the field in the last seventy-five years. Its nominator attributed the book's significance to this idea at the heart of Lippmann's argument: '[w]ithout the controlling principle that the nation must maintain its objectives and its power in equilibrium, its purposes within its means and its means equal to its purposes ... it is impossible to think at all about foreign affairs' (Lippmann, 1943: 7). For Lippmann, the great mistake of US policy since the Spanish–American war was that it had significantly expanded its commitments with the occupation of the Philippines, demanded rights and proclaimed ideals for which it was ill-prepared to fight (Lippmann, 1943: 8). Lippmann regarded this as a national failure which resulted in dire consequences. For not balancing its late nineteenth-century commitments, the United States was compelled to fight two great and unexpected wars for which it was not ready (Lippmann, 1943: 26). This argument is a very good illustration of the pragmatist understanding of the means-ends continuum applied to foreign policy. The *means* the United States had at its disposal (with regard to armaments, alliances and so on) did not match or suit its *ends* (outside recognition of its claims to extended dominion). An argument regarding the close inter-relationship between means and ends, a pragmatist argument, was the basis for Lippmann's call for the United States to build up its military capacities.

Another pragmatist theme that emerges in Lippmann's work is in his critique of Woodrow Wilson for leading the country into war under the banner of 'making the world safe for democracy'. For Lippmann, such abstractions lacked the precision required for diagnosing the real nature of the problem, namely that the resumption of submarine warfare could cut off and starve Britain and that Europe would be dominated by Germany, so that the United States would have to live in a constant state of military preparedness (Lippmann, 1943: 33). This kind of vague moralising had negative consequences, according to Lippmann, because if Americans had been made aware of the true nature of the US security problem, they would have backed the League of Nations, which would have been strengthened through US participation in a powerful alliance with France and Britain, all steering the League (Lippmann, 1943: 37). Here, we see a pragmatist focus on the kind of misguidance abstractions can generate, since they are not grounded in the particularities of the concrete situation at hand.

Finally, and perhaps most interestingly considering his realist credentials, Lippmann, in pragmatist fashion, saw the need to build a form of wider association based on consent in order to promote human welfare which, in his case, was centrally conceived in terms of security. The new order to be constructed from the aftermath of the Second World War rested for Lippmann on the consolidation and maintenance of an alliance of great powers, the United States, United Kingdom, Soviet Union and China. This alliance would lead a new order in which 'the other peoples find that their liberties are recognised by laws that the great powers respect and that all peoples are compelled to observe' (Lippmann, 1943: 175). He recognised that such an order might be regarded as illiberal, since it would be governed by the principles that a few, the great powers, could live with. However, Lippmann insisted that this would not be the case, because for the alliance to endure, it would *have to be liberal* in its policy. This is what he called the 'inexorable logic' of the alliance: that its members had no choice but to recognise the liberties of the peoples outside it (Lippmann, 1943: 173). Otherwise, they would become rivals for the domination of those peoples, and consequently, would not be able to garner consent and support for the continuation of their alliance. There was no alternative but to support a 'world-wide system of liberty' (Lippmann, 1943: 173). He acknowledged the diversity of opinions about what liberty is, but maintained that 'what can prevail everywhere, if the alliance holds together, is the universal law that force must not be arbitrary, but must be exercised in accordance with laws that are open to discussion and are subject to orderly revision' (Lippmann, 1943: 174).

What Lippmann is suggesting is a form of global governance conducted by great power elites on the basis of discussion, consent and law. He supported the League because he saw it as an organisation that could facilitate the formation and maintenance of this kind of alliance and governance. I think there are two key assessments that shape the reality of the problem of international order for Lippmann and influence the character of his suggestion for its resolution. The first derives from his experience of the First World War: his deep conviction that both domestic and international problems should be addressed by elites. Thus, his efforts towards the development of democracy were directed at helping the public understand that its interests were better kept in the hands of elites. The second assessment from his experience of these war years was that human welfare in the first instance must be thought of in terms of survival, in particular, the survival of US citizens, and that the means towards this end was to form a unified foreign policy based on an understanding of the needs of security and the capacities it required.

Therefore, the problem at hand for Lippmann was American security; its means of resolution was military preparedness and a wider association which was realistically based on a recognition of the power capacities of states. However, that same realism required the acknowledgement of the need for governance by an alliance of great power elites and a leap of faith that US interests might be best placed in their hands, since, to endure, such an alliance would have to construct a wider association based on consent and the recognition of liberties. This is where his pragmatist-like commitment to democracy comes through, even in the international realm, but it is a commitment tempered by the realities of a state system that regulates itself through the instrument of war and thus takes a great power or elitist, state-based form. In this instance, Lippmann's position resembles pragmatism because of its orientation to a wider democratic community based on consent. However, it does not resonate fully with pragmatism because his democratic concerns are constrained, limited by his willingness only to trust elites in the resolution of problematic situations.

Dewey

Although Dewey never wrote a book on American foreign policy, from 1916 to 1935 he contributed regularly to the *New Republic* and other periodicals and commented on America's role in the world, the League of Nations, international law and the World Court, the Outlawry of War Movement, and the international politics of the Far East. Despite the differences between him and Lippmann, Dewey agreed in 1917 that the US had little choice but to enter the war in Europe. For Dewey, the situation was clear: force would have to be used in order to ensure a democratic reordering of international politics. But the reordering he envisioned was quite radical in its democratic intent, far beyond that suggested by Lippmann. It would not be a great power alliance, or even state-based leadership, that would determine the new basis of foreign relations. Instead, this war was a means to a world organisation that would be 'the beginnings of a public control [by peoples, not governments] which crosses nationalistic boundaries and interests' (Dewey, 1929: 565). In other words, his support for the war arose from the idea that force was a means that could be executed intelligently in a way so as to further the end of the public control of transnational activity. Alas, neither the peace, which he regarded as unjust, nor the League of Nations, constituted the democratic reorganisation he envisioned. Ultimately, this led him to reconsider his position on war as an adequate means for any kind of democratic or peaceful end. He turned his energies towards the Outlawry of War Movement, writing numerous articles in the hope of uniting American public opinion in support of the cause (Dewey, 1929: 666–90). However, according to Dewey, the Kellogg–Briand Pact which outlawed the use of force among its signatories in 1928 was premature, since the outlawry sentiment had to be held and articulated by democratic publics in order to gather the moral force required for it to work, and it was not in place before the private interests of diplomats shaped this pact (Westbrook, 1991: 269). When war loomed once again in Europe, Dewey urged that the United States stay out, since he was concerned that it would undermine the democratic achievements of the New Deal era and was doubtful that it would achieve any significant democratic reordering of foreign relations (Dewey, 1939: 364).

What was Dewey's position on the three pragmatist themes that I have isolated in Lippmann's work? Like Lippmann, Dewey was contemptuous of the vague sentiments exhibited in the statements of leaders and the public which he found to be isolated from the realities of the dilemmas of world order. As Steven Rockefeller notes, Dewey sought 'a commonsense middle way between extreme pacifists and those who glorified war without regard to consequences' (Rockefeller, 1991: 291). Dewey's efforts were concentrated more upon the pacifists, who, he felt, entertained a misguided hostility to the use of force. For Dewey, their hostility took the form of a moral absolute which limited their capacities to see and consider all the means available to achieve their ends. After the war, Dewey attacked the absolutes in the determinism which characterised current views of human nature: that war and conflict were inevitable because of something inherent in men, making militarism, and thus military preparedness, inevitable as well. Dewey understood that there is no proof that war may be abolished at some date. However, he saw that '[a]lready the forces that once caused wars have found other outlets for themselves; while new provocations, based on new economic and political conditions, have come into being. War is thus seen to be a function of social institutions, not of what is natively fixed in human constitution' (Dewey, 1922: 81).

The ends–means continuum was a theme to which Dewey returned again and again. He wrote, '[t]o be interested in ends and to have contempt for the means which alone secure them is the last stage of intellectual demoralization' (Dewey, 1929: 638–9). This was the pacifists' central failing, according to Dewey. He criticised their '[f]ailure to recognize the immense impetus to reorganization afforded by this war; failure to recognize the closeness and extent of true international combinations which it necessitates, is a stupidity equaled only by the militarist's conception of war as a noble blessing in disguise' (Dewey, 1929: 584). He shared the pacifist vision of a world better organised for democracy and peace, but felt that the pacifists had wrongly closed themselves off from considering the proper means equal to effecting it. Ideals without force are hopelessly discredited for Dewey. But, as I have mentioned, when that reorganisation did not take shape, he saw the war as a failure. Dewey did not explicitly acknowledge a turnaround in his assessment of the suitability of force as a means, but soon after the war he began to look for alternative forms of force, means beyond war, to effect the end of a democratic reorganisation of international politics (Westbrook, 1991: 196n2, 231).

What exactly was the reordering that Dewey found necessary? This brings us to the third theme: the democratic ethic that is at the base of pragmatism, which requires the seeking of a wider form of association in which human welfare can be better promoted. The First World War brought home to Dewey the extent to which transnational activity had not only increased, but was drawing people together in ways that were compromising the sovereign state. The state was no longer a forum in which peoples could effectively have some say over the activity that affected them. The scope of that activity was changing radically and linking them with diverse peoples across state boundaries. And foreign relations – anarchic as they were, conducted in private by states and their officials with little regard for the need to publicise their deliberations or concern for the peoples affected by their activity – represented a practice which impeded effectual social change that might meet the welfare needs of persons. Instead, the sovereign state system perpetuated a war system that only affected change through military conflict. Therefore, what was needed was world organisation, but not of the shape the League of Nations took. Dewey saw the League's main purpose as enforcing the peace through legal mechanisms that would work in more stable periods, but that would break down when confronted with problems of national expansion and attempts to redistribute power. For Dewey, the League simply worked to consecrate the balance of power at that particular time (Dewey, 1929:

620–35). What was needed was a league of peoples, not governments, that might grow out of, and operate in order to meet, the commonplace needs of everyday life with respect to food, labour, securing raw materials and so on (Dewey, 1929: 610–14). Dewey's preferred end was a people-directed, not a state-directed, organisation that provided a forum for discussion, the facilitation of consensual politics, and the regulation of transnational activity by those involved.

In contrast to Lippmann, Dewey looked to the welfare needs not just of Americans, but of all individuals; and he perceived welfare needs more broadly to mean enhancing the capacities of individuals for self-development, rather than merely insuring their security. But like Lippmann, survival was the first priority as evidenced by his reluctant support of US entry into the Second World War after the attack on Pearl Harbour. The reality of the problem of international order for Dewey, however, was the need to get to the sources of war and meet them head-on with the appropriate means. His views on the appropriate means or forces evolved in line with his experience of those years, but the end in view – a democratic reordering of world politics – remained the same. Lippmann's solution, a wider association of states governed by elite great powers, did not represent a liberal or democratic order for Dewey, since it would only perpetuate the status quo. International order could only be achieved through a radical democratic restructuring of international relations, through education and great human effort towards a post-sovereign world, in which states would not necessarily disappear, but in which they would be responsive to international publics that might form around realms of transnational activity for the purpose of deliberation and regulation among persons affected.

Addams

Jane Addams does not immediately come to mind when thinking about international politics at the beginning of the twentieth century, yet she was awarded the Nobel Prize for Peace in 1931. She led the formation of the Women's Peace Party in America in 1915 and, later that year, went to The Hague to chair the International Congress of Women for Peace, which later became a permanent organisation called the Women's International League for Peace and Freedom (WILPF). She served as its president, and in working to bring about a conference of neutrals to work out terms on which to stop the First World War, she met with the foreign ministers of many of the belligerent states. Although widely known across America prior to the war for her social work in Chicago with immigrant communities, and often labelled in the press as a heroine for that work,

Addams was persecuted during the war for maintaining her pacifist stance (Davis, 1973: 232–50). In part as a response to that criticism, she also directed her efforts towards more positive channels, speaking on behalf of Hoover's Department of Food Administration about the world's food supply crisis and the need for international organisation and cooperation to prevent starvation (Davis, 1973: 247–50). Addams believed that one has to put oneself actively into social processes. What her experience suggested to her in relation to the three pragmatist themes I have been examining ran along the following lines.

Since Addams maintained her pacifist views throughout the war, it may seem odd to suggest that she opposed absolutism in belief. However, she maintained that her opposition to war was not a form of dogmatism, but was based on an assessment of means and ends. On the basis of this assessment she held that war was not the way to effect positive change in foreign relations – a position that Dewey later came to of his own accord. Her attacks on absolutism were directed elsewhere. First, she spoke out against and treated as an absolute anything that limited human welfare, the sovereign state system which bred enmity, competition and conflict and blinded us to the life experiences of other people. She saw that the state system imposed a form of order that was no order at all, since it limited our intercourse with others, generated contempt and limited the scope of our ethics. Second, she also treated *man's reason* as another form of absolutism that limited freedom of thought and possibility. As she said in her Presidential Address to the International Congress of Women at The Hague (Addams, 1976: 70–1):

[i]t is possible that the appeals for the organization of the world upon peaceful lines have been made too exclusively to man's reason and sense of justice quite as the eighteenth century enthusiasm for humanity was prematurely founded on intellectual sentiment. Reason is only a part of the human endowment, emotion and deep-set radical impulses must be utilized as well, those primitive urgings to foster life and to protect the helpless, of which women were the earliest custodians, and even the social and gregarious instincts that we share with the animals themselves. These universal desires must be given opportunities to expand and the most highly trained intellects must serve them rather than the technique of war and diplomacy.

Returning to ends and means, pacifism and not war was the most appropriate means to what Addams regarded as the necessary end of foreign relations: international organisation. In 1917 she wrote, 'we pacificists, so far from passively wishing nothing to be done, contended on the contrary that this world crisis should be utilized for the creation of an international government able to make the necessary political and economic changes when they are due' (Addams, 1976: 141). She added that far from pacifists being isolationist, they wanted the United States to lead the push internationally towards 'a wider life of co-ordinated political activity' out of the recognition that 'the vital political problems of our time have become as intrinsically international in character as have the commercial and social problems so closely connected with them' (Addams, 1976: 143). For Addams, the experience of this 'world crisis' served to confirm a position she had come to years before the war: intersocietal development is only as good as the means that individuals use to establish it.

In regard to the third theme, the need for wider association, Addams felt that human welfare could only be enhanced if the world was made more inclusive, if democracy and social ethics were extended to the world scene. In fact, working among immigrant communities, and seeing the nascent social morality emerging among diverse groups working cooperatively to sustain themselves, entrenched her belief that if this development were encouraged and directed on a larger scale, then the need for war would gradually disappear (Linn, 1935: 292–3). Extending democracy in this way would mean that we have to interact with others to see for ourselves how they live. Diversified human experience and the resultant sympathy which follows from this kind of interaction is the base of democracy. Addams felt that she could see it growing internationally, particularly in the work of an increasing number of transnational organisations like the ones in which she was active. This was the kind of activity that brought about the democratisation of world politics. On this, she and Dewey, who later questioned force as a means of change, were like-minded. Through WILPF, she was bringing to fruition the kind of publics that Dewey felt the Outlawry movement required in order for it to be successful: groups of like-minded people driving politics by the force of their collective opinion. In WILPF, women came together out of concern over transnational activity which affected them, and worked to have some say or control over it, by meeting with statesmen; delivering to the Paris Conference a resolution on how the peace should be shaped; filing reports; sending missions to far-flung places; and generally trying to influence the policies of governments and other peace organisations through publicity.

Like Dewey, Addams perceived welfare needs more broadly than Lippmann. In fact, Dewey and Addams agreed that human welfare requires more democracy, not just within states, but in a realm which had been untouched by it: the international. Also, for them democracy had a qualitative dimension: democracy should run deep, beyond civil and political rights to meeting the basic needs of persons. They agreed that the greatest obstacle to the end of this democratic ethic is the state system that limits our imagination in thinking about the ways in which the new trends in transnational activity can be harnessed so as to fulfil a more complete sense of human development.

Addams and Dewey differed, however, on the uses of war. They also diverged in their respective beliefs as to whether international organisation could indeed emerge that might facilitate this kind of human development and, if it did, whether it could ever provide a level of security that would end war. Addams, who died in 1935 and did not witness the Second World War, thought that both were possible. She participated in forms of international organisation already working in that fashion, albeit not in a coordinated, overarching way, and she remained convinced that this kind of social activity and ethic could provide an alternative to war. Dewey, on the other hand, who lived to see the Cold War entrenched, was less convinced on both counts. He found the conduct of both superpowers to be irresponsible for the instability it bred and did not see any countervailing international public discovering itself and challenging the order shaped by this rivalry. Yet he remained convinced of the power of intelligence and would not rule out either possibility, because there was always the chance that intelligence would be dutifully and methodically applied to social activity and the ways of growth.

Conclusion

What guidance does pragmatism offer those who wish to implement an ethical foreign policy today? First, it is clear that pragmatism not only breaks down the realist/idealist dichotomy, but it shares to a significant degree Carr's aim of balancing the realities of world politics with normative visions of how it should be conducted. Ultimately, this balance is a good way to begin thinking about what an ethical foreign policy has to do. The means–ends continuum emphasised within pragmatism operates as a 'reality check' on its ethics of democratic inclusion. It is an approach to ethics that starts from experience. That is, what kicks ethical consideration into gear is the recognition of empirical situations which are problematic, and attention to such facts – in combination with the pragmatist requirement that in seeking solutions, one must maintain an awareness of the interrelationship between ends and means – suggests that pragmatism does not resemble a caricature of idealism. However, its method operates in a way that is not exactly resonant with Carr's 'utopian compromise', and this perhaps results in a different impression of how pragmatism fits with the idealist caricature than what I am suggesting here.

The difference is one of emphasis in which pragmatism stresses the need for a utopian's *responsibility*, rather than the need for compromise.

That responsibility entails a positive choice to engage one's critical intelligence to free up more democracy where possible; that is, to critically interrogate absolutisms, authorities and entrenched customs that potentially constrain our capacities for thought in solving problematic situations, thus limiting our possibilities for self-development and growth. It is a choice to think in untraditional ways, to use our imaginations to explore alternative possibilities, which can mean projecting solutions that seem fanciful because of the extent to which they challenge present modes of thinking or present perceptions of 'reality'. Therefore, the balance sought is one that works as a form of reflective equilibrium between the need to project alternative, perhaps idealistic or even seemingly irresponsible, visions and then checking their fit with what the public can consent to and what institutional arrangements can stretch to meet and still find workable. So, while I think Carr's idea of balance is on the whole right, I want to emphasise that to be truly ethical in character, foreign policy has to be guided by this understanding of a utopian's responsibility to project alternative futures, and not start with a lasso of 'reality' before creative thought is allowed to run.

As I have said, reality is an important check, but the problems in allowing it to compromise thought before it gets off the ground include the questions of 'whose reality are we to believe?', and 'how do we pin down reality if it is constantly in flux?' What is 'real' for the pragmatist is always open to question, since the reality or truth of a situation is what people can agree to be true at a particular point in time. Reality is an important check not simply for the objective purpose of getting things right and finding workable solutions, but for the idea that what is workable or right is that which people can agree to. So reality serves a normative, democratic purpose as well. Reality or truth is a consensual process within communities that draw from their collective experience. Lippmann, Dewey and Addams discussed different interpretations of the problematic realities of peace and security that they faced in their day, which produced varied ideas of the means and solutions required of an ethic of democratic inclusion, pragmatism's central end.

What can be said by way of a conclusion about these three interpretations of the realities foreign policy decision-makers faced, and the guidance that pragmatism as an ethical approach can offer? My own view is that Lippmann shared Carr's emphasis: that attention to the means–end continuum meant seeking a utopian compromise. Thus it is appropriate that Lippmann is more often associated with realism than with American pragmatism. However, Dewey and Addams possessed a sense of the utopian's responsibility. That is, Lippmann sought solutions within the parameters of the status quo, the sovereign state system and power politics. Dewey and Addams, on the other hand, projected alternative futures, the seeds of which they saw in increased transnational activity and forms of organisation across state boundaries in the shape of social movements and non-governmental actors. This was their interpretation of a budding reality on which we could build social change through human effort towards the pragmatist end.

With hindsight, it is clear that the sovereign state system was too well entrenched in those decades, and many after, for human effort to have much success in achieving the projected future of a more democratic international politics. Dewey himself recognised this. Has the 'reality' of the situation changed? Is the alternative future suggested by Dewey and Addams coming to pass? I believe that the pragmatist democratic insight, in the form that Dewey and Addams suggested, is key for thinking about ethical foreign policy in a landscape today in which transnational activity and the problems it presents are more readily recognisable, as are the needs for transnational solutions. Principally, the guidance that pragmatism offers entails that all of those affected – not just states and their representatives, who may not be all that representative, but the peoples affected – should be included within international processes which must be deliberative and consensual if democratic and workable solutions are to be found. I want to give some brief illustrations of the new processes which suggest that international publics are organising world politics in ways that are enabling recognition on the parts of both states and individuals of transnational problems and the need for democratically derived transnational solutions.

States have been forced to acknowledge across many issues areas and fora the normative power that non-governmental organisations (NGOs) and social movements hold and exercise over them through the use of publicity and advocacy, the strength of which comes from an articulated public concern (Lipschutz, 1992; Wapner, 1995; Keck and Sikkink, 1998). That is, by working to shape public opinion transnationally (and thus, public opinion within states as well) on particular issues of international concern, these movements and NGOs utilise the power of public opinion to influence the decision-making of states. In fact, states are accommodating the voice and will of these groups and are including them in various processes, even in decision-making in UN structures, an entitlement reserved in the main for its members, that is, states. For example, NGO representatives constituted a significant proportion of US delegations to conferences like the 1992 UN Conference on the Environment and Development in Rio de Janeiro and the 1994 UN Conference on Population in Cairo (Spiro, 1994: 49). Recently, NGOs played a key role in influencing the drafting of the July 1998 Rome Treaty to establish an International Criminal Court (Benedetti and Washburn, 1999) which, if ratified by sixty states, will effect a significant change in the international system by investing in its prosecutors the authority to override the domestic jurisdiction of states which fail to try criminal cases which concern the international community (see Chapter 7 of this volume). Therefore, states are allowing NGOs access to decision-making which has great importance to how world politics is conducted today. Of course, there are legitimate questions about the 'representativeness' of NGOs and social movements, which must be taken into account when considering their access to decision-making. However, as long as their influence is conducted through the instrument of public opinion, and as long as transnational public opinion is influenced by the reasonableness and workability of the solutions offered, then the access granted to NGOs and social movements can be considered legitimate.

These are examples of bottom-up processes that illuminate the problems that result from the democratic deficits of state-centred world politics. What about more formally institutionalised top-down processes? While the United Nations is not an international organisation of peoples but of states, and while the Security Council upholds the status quo of great power politics that Dewey condemned in the League of Nations, it remains the case that the UN, through the Economic and Social Council, assists at a global level in meeting the needs of individuals in their day-to-day lives with respect to food, water, work, trade, education, culture and development. Embodied in the UN Charter is a conception of international peace and security which resembles that of Dewey and Addams, a conception based on a broad idea of human welfare. Their proposals for people and need-centred international politics conducted through international organisation have been adopted in large measure in the economic and social work that the UN has undertaken.

If there is a case for the empirical relevance of a pragmatist conception of ethical foreign policy, is there also a normative case? There are two main questions here. First, is the aim of wider democratic inclusion in world politics a justifiable one, or is this a typically Western or American imposition? Second, is the guidance offered by the pragmatist notion of growth via democratic inclusion too vague to offer proper prescriptions for how foreign policy should be conducted? What is particularly valuable in pragmatism is that it helps us to navigate between undesirable and problematic alternatives that are often presented as if they were the only available choices: either foreign policy is directed towards absolute, universal moral principles, or it is conducted without regard for ethical concerns altogether. Pragmatism suggests a middle path. It provides a method that allows us to make assessments of how to respond to specific problems within international relations, which work towards growth as a valued end, but without invoking anything more absolute than that as a foundation for prescriptions. While there is an ontological, and possibly Western, basis for its orientation towards democratic inclusion, which may be felt as an external imposition if offered solely on this basis, the pragmatist end in view remains potentially universalisable on the grounds that its methodological arguments for the beneficial character of democratic consultative, deliberative processes are less objectionable than other approaches to addressing problematic situations. A crucial component of this method is the need to leave the determinate content of ethical prescriptions no more precise than growth, so that the solutions tried are not limited by strictures that might narrow their range or creativity. This is the pragmatist hope for the widest possible human welfare, the orientation that should guide the pursuit of ethical foreign policies.

Part II

Instruments and policies

5 Exporting democracy

Margot Light

Introduction

When the question of ethics and foreign policy is raised, the policies that usually come first to mind are the promotion of universal standards of human rights or, more recently, the propriety of military intervention for humanitarian purposes. Respect for human rights is the hallmark of a democratic society and democratic governments rarely implement oppressive policies that require external military intervention for humanitarian purposes. A major objective of a foreign policy that is informed by ethics is, therefore, the institution or renewal of democracy. Promoting human rights is a relatively recent foreign policy goal. Using force for humanitarian purposes is older. Exporting democracy predates both. The United States and some of the former European colonial powers have a long history of fostering democratic development in foreign countries.[1]

Governments have a variety of motives for promoting democracy in other countries. One reason is the belief that democracy is a good system of government, or at least, to quote E. M. Forster, that it is 'less hateful than other contemporary forms of government' (Forster, 1965: 77). But governments also export democracy for self-interested motives: they believe, for example, that it is easier to deal with foreign governments that share the same values. They also associate democracy with peace, and they promote it abroad to increase their own security at home. After the collapse of communism and the victory of capitalism, western governments appeared to think that a market economy would, in itself, generate democracy. More recently, they have realised that democracy is a necessary prior condition for successful economic reform and development. They export democracy, therefore, to make their economic assistance

I would like to thank Margo Picken, Michael Banks and Karen Smith for their constructive advice on this chapter.
[1] It should be noted that the countries that exported democracy were not necessarily fully democratic themselves. In the United States, for example, the franchise was only effectively extended to African-Americans in 1965.

programmes more effective and to promote congenial conditions for investment and trade.

This begs the question of how governments define the democracy they wish to export, and whether it is feasible to export it. It takes various forms in their own states and, when applied to foreign countries, it has been defined differently at different times. Moreover, although there appears to be some general agreement about what it entails in the post-Cold War world, how best to foster it is far less evident. Governments of the advanced industrialised countries also appear to care more about its existence in some countries than in others. It matters more to them that Serbia is democratic, for example, than that Azerbaijan is, although (or perhaps because) their economic interests in Azerbaijan are greater than in Serbia.

Although this chapter concentrates on the period since the end of the Cold War, it begins with a brief overview of the history of exporting democracy as a foreign policy goal. It then explores what democracy means and why governments want to export it. Finally, it examines some of the reasons why exporting democracy has proved far more difficult than it sounds.

History

The United States was the first country to export democracy and it remained an important goal of American foreign policy throughout the twentieth century. Smith traces the promotion of democracy back to the 1898 Spanish–American War, a war that was fought for strategic and economic aims but that ended with Americans 'trying to establish democratic government locally, and then departing' (Smith, 1994: 5). In fact, from the very beginning of its existence as an independent state, the United States hoped that its example would serve to foster democracy abroad. Since 1898 it has simply adopted a more active and, periodically, a more interventionist, method of fulfilling its goal. Well before its entry into the First World War in 1917 'to make the world safe for democracy', it was engaged in exporting democracy to 'its' hemisphere, Latin America, using a variety of political, economic and military instruments. Between 1912 and 1932 alone there were forty episodes during which the United States, while primarily motivated by its own economic and strategic interests, claimed to be promoting democracy in Latin America (Drake, in Lowenthal, 1991: 3–40).

President Woodrow Wilson's Fourteen Points extended America's hemispheric goals to Europe. Wilson hoped that the Paris Peace Conference would result in the establishment of a European order of democratic states. The failure of the League of Nations to defend that order discredited the idea of exporting democracy. The goal re-emerged during the Second World War, however, and the victors were no less ambitious for democracy in 1945 than they had been in 1919. Winston Churchill and Joseph Stalin may have discussed spheres of influence, but the insistence that free elections should take place in the countries liberated from the Nazis also played a large role in the war-time conference negotiations in Yalta, Teheran and Potsdam. The 1947 Truman Doctrine urged the US Congress to vote for the assistance that would enable Greece to become 'a self-supporting and self-respecting democracy'. Every nation, President Truman declared, was faced by a stark choice between totalitarianism, on the one hand, and, on the other, a way of life 'based upon the will of the majority, and . . . distinguished by free institutions, representative government, free elections, guarantees of individual liberty, freedom of speech and religion, and freedom from political oppression' (Truman, March 12, 1947). The Marshall Plan expanded the military and political promises of the Truman Doctrine to the realm of economics, authorising loans for economic recovery 'so as to permit the emergence of political and social conditions in which free institutions can exist' (Marshall, 1976: 24). The Bretton Woods system was intended to ensure an open economic order that would bolster these free institutions.

When the Cold War began, however, anti-communism replaced liberal democratic internationalism as a goal of American foreign policy. The defence of the free world justified supporting authoritarian regimes, it seemed, as long as they declared that they opposed communism. George Kennan advised that in Latin America, for example, 'where the concepts and traditions of popular government are too weak to absorb successfully the intensity of communist attacks . . . we must concede that harsh government measures of repression may be the only answer' (cited in Lowenthal, 1991: 65). This policy had to be made palatable to the American people, and this was done by using the language of democracy. As a result:

The rhetoric of liberal democratic internationalism was to an extent symbolic and manipulative, crafted as much to rally a moralistic but inexperienced American public into an expensive, dangerous, and prolonged involvement in world affairs as to secure the blessings of liberty and justice for other peoples of the world. (Smith, 1994: 140)

Throughout the Cold War, containing communism took precedence in the West over the objective of promoting democracy. Just as the principles of human rights were deformed by the Cold War agenda, as Margo Picken points out in Chapter 8, the definition of democracy was distorted: each of the two superpowers moulded its meaning to suit their stance in the ideological struggle. Few people in the socialist states, and even fewer in Western liberal democracies, took the word *democracy* in the term *socialist democracy* at its face value. Although the constitutions of the socialist states included some of the rights associated with liberal democracy, socialist governments rarely felt themselves bound by their constitutions. On the other hand, what Western governments meant by democracy was equally perplexing given their support for the colonels in Greece and their policy towards South Africa.

American realists like George Kennan and Henry Kissinger opposed the confusion between values and interests, which was implied, they thought, in promoting democracy abroad. British policy-makers, believing in the primacy of national interests and priding themselves on a pragmatic foreign policy, had far more sympathy with realist views than with the idealism underlying attempts to export democracy. In relation to their own colonies, however, they were determined that the establishment of democracy should precede the granting of independence. They had paid scant attention to the democratisation of the colonies in the years of undisputed imperial rule, relying instead on colonial administrators and local chiefs. Once the 'winds of change' of decolonisation began to blow, however, they were intent upon bequeathing Westminster style parliamentary systems to their former colonies, whether or not they were applicable to local cultures and conditions. France, too, assumed that their former colonies 'would grow into worthy pieces of France' (Calvocoressi, 1982: 105). In many cases, what happened instead in both British and French former colonies was a reversion to authoritarianism.

During the Cold War this did not necessarily have a negative effect on relations with the West as long as the authoritarianism was anti-communist. Moreover, there were some democratic successes, for example in India. But even where democracy failed, liberal democratic ideas did not disappear entirely – most military dictators claimed to be temporary and made implicit or explicit promises of future democratic civilian rule. As Mervyn Frost points out in Chapter 3, few political leaders profess themselves to be opposed to democracy. When the collapse of communism internationalised liberal democracy in the 1990s, it was easy for organisations like the Commonwealth to adopt the promotion of democratic values as a core aim (Mayall, 2000: 65).

The Soviet government agreed to discuss human rights and humanitarian principles at the 1972 Conference on Security and Cooperation in Europe as a means of ensuring that the issues that deeply concerned it – for example, international recognition of the inviolability of the post-Second World War borders – were finally resolved. The price of getting

an agreement on borders, security matters and economic relations, however, was the inclusion of Basket Three in the 1975 Helsinki Final Act.
Basket Three pledged the signatories to observe certain human rights
principles. It was a West European initiative; the American administration, dominated by realists at the time, was almost as reluctant as the
Soviet government to include it. It feared that since the Final Act had
no legal force, the Soviet leadership would use the other baskets to le-
gitimise their control of Eastern Europe without making any significant
concessions in the realm of human rights. However, Basket Three proved
a useful instrument when the détente that had made the Conference possible gave way to renewed hostility soon after the Final Act was signed.
By then, President Carter had incorporated the propagation of human
rights into his foreign policy programme. At the first follow up conference in 1977, and at subsequent review conferences in the 1980s, Western
leaders used Basket Three to berate the Soviet government for its poor
human rights record. At the time they seemed to use human rights cyn-
ically to score points in a game that had little to do with democracy. In
retrospect, however, Basket Three helped significantly to empower and
sustain Eastern European and Soviet dissidents in their demands that
their governments should honour the democratic freedoms enshrined in
their constitutions and the obligations they had undertaken in signing the
Final Act (Thomas, in Risse, Ropp and Sikkink, 1999: 205–33).

President Reagan's political views were vastly different from those of
President Carter. He, too, however, included the export of democracy
into his foreign policy programme. In a speech to the British parliament on 8 June 1982, he proclaimed 'a global campaign for democratic
development' (cited in Doyle, 1983a: 205). Within two years Mikhail
Gorbachev had become leader of the Soviet Union. Concerned about
the state of the economies of the socialist states, he launched a set of
reforms which soon expanded from the economic realm to include ideas
about democratising socialist societies.

This brief account makes it clear that exporting democracy is by no
means new. Since the end of the Cold War and the collapse of communism
it has become a far more prominent foreign policy goal, however, and it is
espoused by a greater number of governments and international organisations. How do governments define the democracy they wish to export?

What is democracy?

The frequency with which the term democracy is used in ordinary speech
seems to suggest that everyone agrees what it means. And on one level
they do: they mean that citizens who possess civil and political liberties

can elect their governments and hold them responsible for the policies they adopt. But even this simple definition raises a host of questions: who qualifies for citizenship, what kind of rights do they have, how do they elect their governments, and how do they hold them responsible?

For political theorists, democracy it is a deeply contested term. Indeed, as Robert Dahl, one of the most distinguished theorists of democracy, points out, 'there is no democratic theory – there are only democratic theories' (Dahl, 1956: 1). The contributors to one book, for example, debate the relative advantages of liberal democracy with those offered by other forms, such as direct, deliberative, associational and delegative democracy (Held, 1993). Schumpeter, on the other hand, who saw democratic rule as the exchange of government policies for votes, defined democracy as a system in which a bare majority of citizens have the right to change the ruler (Schumpeter, 1975: 269–83). Dahl himself argued that genuine democracy is an unattainable 'ideal type'; polyarchal democracy is the closest approximation that can be reached in the goal of maximising popular sovereignty and political equality. Polyarchy is a political system in which every citizen has the right to an equal vote and to stand for election, the candidate with the most votes is the winner, everyone has identical information about the candidates and their policies, the orders of elected officials are executed, and decisions taken between elections are subordinate to those arrived at during the election (Dahl, 1956: 84).

It also often seems to be taken for granted that democracy has universal validity, but that, too, is contested, in particular by those who argue that democracy is, essentially, a Western form of government. They point out that it takes various forms in different countries depending on particular histories, traditions, values, social structures and needs. To insist on its universality, therefore, is to 'deny the west's own historical experiences and to betray the liberal principles of mutual respect and love of cultural diversity' (Parekh, in Held, 1993: 167–8). In countries where there is a strong sense of community and the individual is defined in communal terms, governments can be just and accountable to their citizens without adopting the individual freedoms inherent in liberal democracy (Parekh, in Dunne and Wheeler, 1999: 154–8). On the other hand, the pressure from within Asian countries for democratisation suggests that the citizens of those countries demand a greater degree of accountability than their governments have offered in the past. In any case, there are powerful arguments against the idea that universal human rights norms necessarily imply rejection of cultural diversity.[2]

---

[2] See, for example, Donnelly's 'weak cultural relativist' argument that while 'tradition is no excuse for violating internationally agreed human rights . . . that leaves much room

Western governments would not explicitly agree that there are 'Asian values' that differ significantly from Western values. But they did not appear to see the export of liberal democracy to South East Asia as an important foreign policy goal, particularly since the economic performance of the Asian tigers was more impressive than their own, at least until the financial crisis in 1997. In relation to the former socialist countries, however, exporting democracy became a high priority goal as soon as communism collapsed. They proposed representative liberal democracy and, indeed, this was the model that the political elite of the former socialist countries claimed to want. Western governments defined it in terms of a 'procedural definition of democracy derived from Schumpeter and refined by Dahl' (Hughes, 2000: 28).

What does one require in order to establish a representative liberal democracy? It is a system in which control over government policy is constitutionally vested in elected officials. Those officials are chosen and peacefully removed in relatively frequent, fair and free elections in which practically all adults participate, and most adults have the right to run for public office. Citizens should have assured access to alternative sources of information that are not monopolised by the government or by any other single group. Citizens should also be assured of an effectively enforced right to freedom of expression (including the right to criticise officials, government conduct, the prevailing political, economic, and social system, and the dominant ideology), and the right to form and join autonomous associations (including political parties and interest groups).[3]

The criteria that indicate the existence of a liberal democratic regime may be clear, but there is little agreement about the type of institution and constitution that best establish them and ensure their survival. Among established democracies, there is great diversity. Lijphart (1984) divides established democracies into two basic types: majoritarian or Westminster and consensus models. They tend to differ on eight distinct dimensions, six of which concern the types of institutions that are established, the balance of power between them and how they are selected. The remaining two relate to the number of political parties and the range of issues over which they differ. According to Lijphart, the two models are rational (in other words, logically coherent) and empirical (they occur in the real world). But he stresses that they are also prescriptive. In other words,

for historical, cultural and even idiosyncratic variations in implementing these rights' (Donnelly, 1998: 132).

[3] These are the criteria that Dahl (1989: 221) considers mandatory in a polyarchy. They are used by Freedom House to assess the extent of political openness in various countries. See, for example, *Freedom in the World*, 1997–98. Political theorists sometimes add two more criteria when they evaluate the prospects for democratic consolidation in transition states: political accountability and the rule of law. See, for example, Brown, 1999.

'they entail a set of basic choices that have to be made by democratic constitutional engineers in countries that attempt to introduce or strengthen a democratic regime' (Lijphart, 1984: 209).

Dahl's criteria for the establishment of a polyarchy are particularly important in the transition from one-party states, in which elections were held that offered no choice between candidates, and in which citizens did not have the opportunity to exercise elementary civil rights. But constitutional and institutional design are equally significant, since they can contribute to, or undermine, the stability and success of the new democratic system (Di Palma, 1990). Where the transition requires not only political reform but also difficult economic choices which entail high individual costs in terms of uncertainty and poverty, institutions, the balance between them and their legitimacy in the eyes of citizens can be crucial determinants of success or failure. Some scholars (for example, Linz and Valenzuela, 1994) believe that presidentialism (a system in which the executive dominates over the legislature and the chief executive is popularly elected for a prescribed term) jeopardises democratic consolidation. Others (for example, O'Donnell and Schmitter, 1986: 60) argue that there can be no hard-and-fast answer to the question of which particular combination of features will be successful; each national case has to find its own solution. O'Donnell and Schmitter may be right, but trial and error are rarely possible during transition periods, since the consequences of error are likely to be reversion to authoritarianism or descent into chaos.

Governments that aim to export democracy should, therefore, be particularly concerned to advocate the model that best suits the particular conditions of the country to which they wish to export it. They should also ensure that Dahl's procedural criteria are adopted. However, although procedures and institutions are crucial, by themselves they cannot guarantee the successful consolidation of democracy. An active civil society is necessary as is the existence of social capital and social trust. These are far harder to export.

The programmes that Western governments and international organisations have adopted to foster democracy abroad indicate that the characteristics they understand to be essential in a democratic society are, in effect, Dahl's polyarchal criteria. They also aim to support the democratic institutions that have been established in democratising countries. In addition, they pay particular attention to the development of civil society. Two examples will suffice to demonstrate. The four areas of USAID's Democracy Initiative aim to foster competitive political systems; strengthen the rule of law and respect for human rights; strengthen civil society; and promote greater accountability of political institutions and ethical standards in government (USAID, 1997 and see Adams, 1998). The democracy component of the EU's PHARE and TACIS programmes similarly endeavours 'to contribute to the consolidation of pluralist democratic procedures and practices as well as the rule of law' by strengthening the activities of non-governmental bodies, as well as supporting 'the acquisition of and application of knowledge and techniques of parliamentary practice and organisation' and 'transferring expertise and technical skills about democratic practices and the rule of law' (European Commission 1998; Olsen, 1998).

In both cases, conventional security concerns (as opposed to the security deemed to derive from democratic transformation in previously authoritarian states) or simple economic self-interest sometimes take precedence over fostering democracy. And in both cases, far more funding is devoted to supporting the establishment of market economies than to strengthening democracy. Indeed, 'the reorientation of the economies of recipient countries and support for the establishment of market economies' is listed first in the goals of the PHARE and TACIS programmes, before the goal of developing pluralistic political systems. Moreover, funding for the democracy programme was only about 1 per cent of the whole PHARE and TACIS budget in 1992–7 (European Commission, 1998). In 1997 less than half of 1 per cent of the total USAID budget was spent on supporting democracy in the former Soviet Union and Eastern Europe (USAID, 1998). Although the establishment of market systems takes priority, neither the EU's democracy programme nor USAID are concerned with economic democracy, in other words, the provision of equal benefits to the population from the goods and services generated by society.

Nevertheless, the US and the EU, and many other established democracies, take great pride in their democracy programmes. Why do they place such a high value on creating democratic societies abroad?

Why do governments export democracy?

As suggested in the introduction, one reason governments export democracy is that they believe that it is easier to deal with foreign governments that share the same values. Democratic states are believed to share interests as well as values. According to Tony Blair, 'The spread of our values makes us safer' (Blair, 1999). In order to qualify for membership of some international organisations, aspiring states need to demonstrate that they are democratic. Democracy is a requirement for membership of the Council of Europe, for example. Members of the Organisation of American States agreed in 1993 that there was a 'need to consolidate, as part of the cultural identity of each nation in the Hemisphere, democratic structures and systems' (cited in Risse, Ropp and Sikkink, 1999: 9). Before aspiring new members can join the European Union they must demonstrate that they have achieved the Copenhagen criteria, which include 'stability of institutions guaranteeing democracy, the rule of law, human rights and respect for and protection of minorities' (Senior Nello and Smith, 1998: 20).

Shared democratic values are deemed so important because democracies are thought to make better partners. They are accustomed to relations based on the rule of law, and their openness at home makes it easier for potential partners to judge whether they are likely to fulfil commitments. According to Tony Blair, for example, 'it is better to invest in countries where you have openness, independent central banks, properly functioning financial systems and independent courts' (Blair, 1999). President Clinton believed that democracies 'make better trading partners and partners in diplomacy' (*New York Times*, 26 January 1994). Moreover, democracy acts as a constraint against abrupt changes in policy.

The strength of the belief that shared values bind societies in positive ways is vividly illustrated by the reaction of European Union member states in February 2000 to the participation of the extreme right Freedom Party in Austria's governing coalition. Although the Freedom Party achieved 27 per cent of the vote in democratic elections, and is the second largest party in the lower house of parliament, EU member states decided to ostracise Austria by suspending bilateral political contacts while continuing multilateral business within the EU. Gerhard Schröder, chancellor of Germany, explained their stance as 'an expression that we stand for a Europe based on shared values [which] Mr Haider [leader of the Freedom Party] has constantly violated' (*The Guardian*, 4 February 2000). Austrian President Thomas Klestil, while pointing out that the Freedom Party had won its parliamentary seats in a democratic election and 'in a democracy, a parliamentary majority has to be respected', insisted that Mr Haider sign 'a declaration of values of European democracy' before he approved the coalition government (*The Guardian*, 3 February 2000).[4]

Apart from the ease of conducting daily business with like-minded states, governments want to export democracy because they believe that democratic states are more peaceful than non-democratic states. Until the end of the Cold War, it was primarily academics who were interested in the apparent absence of war between liberal democratic states

---

[4] In September 2000 bilateral political contacts were resumed when member states concluded that suspending them had been counter-productive. The EU's difficulty here demonstrates that it is easier for the organisation to insist that aspiring members should be democratic than to regulate the nature of democracy within existing members.

(Doyle, 1983a, 1983b). Policy-makers began to be converted to the democratic peace proposition when the democratisation of the former socialist states seemed to suggest the possibility of a new liberal international order in which democracy within states would be accompanied by peace among them. Since the democratic peace proposition extends only to relations between democratic states and it does not exclude war between democratic and non-democratic countries, converting non-democratic states to democracy would, it was thought, enhance the prospects for international peace. The proposition acquired practical policy significance when promoting democracy in the interests of security was proclaimed a goal of foreign policy. In his State of the Union message in 1994, President Clinton declared that 'Ultimately, the best strategy to ensure our security and to build a durable peace is to support the advance of democracy elsewhere. Democracies don't attack each other...' (*New York Times*, 26 January 1994).

There was opposition to the promotion of democracy abroad in both the academic world and among policy-makers. Realists argued that the potential for war is endemic in the anarchic international system and has little to do with domestic arrangements within states.[5] Some warned that although established democracies might be pacific, democratising states were likely to be bellicose (Mansfield and Snyder, 1995: 79–97). Their reservations had little effect. Anthony Lake, assistant to the president for National Security Affairs, insisted that 'enlarging the community of democracies is in [America's] profound self interest... because the larger the pool of democracies, the greater our own security and prosperity. Democracies, we know, are less likely to make war on us or on other nations' (Lake, 1995). The Charter for European Security adopted by the Organisation for Security and Cooperation in Europe in Istanbul in November 1999, links security to a free, democratic and more integrated OSCE, area (OSCE, 1999).

Governments have a third reason for encouraging democracy abroad: they believe that democratic societies are economically more efficient than undemocratic states. The new British Labour government, for example, launched its White Paper on foreign aid, 'Eliminating Poverty', by announcing that it would pay particular attention in its aid policies to human rights, and transparent and accountable government, building on the government's ethical approach to international relations (Short, 1997). Moreover, democracy is thought not only to improve an individual country's prospects for economic development, but also to lead to greater

---

[5] The best arguments for and against the democratic peace proposition have been collected together in Brown *et al.*, 1996.

prosperity all round. In other words, it is in the economic self-interest of the developed countries to encourage democracy abroad.

The reverse relationship is also deemed to hold; economic prosperity is thought to promote democracy. The rise of fascism after the First World War was attributed in part to the Great Depression and the protectionist policies governments adopted in response. The emphasis on open markets after the Second World War, the Marshall Plan and the establishment of the international financial institutions stemmed from the belief that economic recovery and well-being would make the political climate inhospitable to political movements of both extreme left and extreme right persuasions. A frequently heard justification for 'constructive engagement' with undemocratic regimes (discussed in more detail in Chapter 6) is the argument that democratisation will occur as a spin-off from open markets and increased external trade (Ikenberry, 1999).

In the 1990s Western governments certainly seemed to believe that if the economic systems of the former socialist countries were reformed, democracy would follow naturally. Although they proclaimed that they wished to encourage the development of democracy, their policies were primarily economic. Moreover, the prevailing economic wisdom of the time, now known as 'the Washington consensus', concentrated on swift macroeconomic reform and ignored the fact that neither the institutional structures nor the legal base existed to underpin the economic changes, far less to promote and consolidate democracy.[6] To be fair, the tasks were daunting: everything was important and everything needed to be done at once. But the emphasis on economic reform tended to distract from the even more pressing need to develop democratic institutions and processes. Furthermore, as we shall see later in this chapter, the consequences of the economic reform frequently undermined democracy.

At the same time as the Washington consensus dictated what kind of economic reform should be applied in the former socialist countries, Western countries began to apply political conditions to the economic assistance they were prepared to offer. Karen Smith analyses the conditions the EU attached to its economic assistance from 1990 in Chapter 11. The revised Lomé Convention for 1995–2000 incorporated a clause on 'respect for human rights, democratic principles and the rule of law' (cited in Olsen, 1998). In their bilateral aid policies, individual

---

[6] Joseph Stiglitz, former chief economist at the World Bank, defined the 'Washington Consensus' (also known as 'shock therapy') as 'an ideological, fundamental, and root-and-branch approach to reform as opposed to an incremental, remedial, piecemeal, and adaptive approach' (Stiglitz, 1999). He pointed out that historically the method was associated with Jacobinism in the French Revolution and Bolshevism in the Russian Revolution.

European governments also linked economic development with good governance.[7] The United States Agency for International Development (USAID) launched a Democracy Initiative in 1990, arguing that 'societies which value individual rights, respect the rule of law and have open and accountable governments provide better opportunities for sustained economic development than do closed systems which stifle individual initiative' (USAID, 1990: 2). But democracy, it was thought, would do more than improve the development prospects of aid recipients. It would also assist the donors, since recipient countries would become reliable trading partners and provide attractive opportunities for investment (Adams, 1998: 12).

The governments that are the target of countries that export democracy are, by and large, very willing recipients; they aspire to democracy and in most cases, they want to establish the same kind of liberal democracy that exists in the established democracies. Why then are the programmes not more successful? Why, for example, does democratic consolidation seem so elusive in countries like Russia, Ukraine and Albania?

Why is democracy difficult to export?[8]

Blame for the slow development of democracy in the former socialist states is often placed on endogenous factors, for example, the lack of a democratic history prior to, and the absence of civil society under, communism. People within democratising states, on the other hand, tend to blame exogenous factors. They find fault, for example, with the programmes offered by the advanced democracies and international organisations, particularly with the proportion of funding that goes to outside advisors. The imbalance between the investment in establishing market economies and the support given to democracy programmes suggests that if it is democracy they wish to foster, Western priorities may be wrong. Perhaps progress towards democratic consolidation has been so slow in some countries simply because insufficient effort has been made to foster it. But since democracy appears to have become consolidated in some countries, external factors cannot be the only reason why it has been slow to take in others. Nor can internal factors entirely explain the difficulties some countries have in becoming democratic. In fact, endogenous and exogenous factors feed into one another in complex ways.

[7] Olsen (1998) cites speeches by British Foreign Minister Douglas Hurd and President François Mitterand in 1990 in which they maintained that good governance was a prerequisite for successful economic development.

[8] The arguments advanced in this section are based primarily on the experience of the former socialist states since these are the countries I know best.

The effects of the particular type of economic reform advocated by the West are a good example of the way that external factors exacerbate internal problems, making the establishment and consolidation of democracy more difficult. The Washington consensus concentrated on swift macroeconomic reform and privatisation, and assumed that democracy would develop as a corollary of the market economy. But, as Stiglitz (1999: 8) points out, 'norms, social institutions, social capital, and trust play critical roles' in the success of a market economy. Yet Western-sponsored economic programmes paid little heed to them. Neither the economic reformers themselves, nor their Western advisors seemed aware that political and democratic measures were required to establish the norms, social institutions, social capital and trust that would make a market economy work. Nor did they understand that economic decisions have political consequences; voters, for example, are unlikely to cast their ballots for those who support the macroeconomic programmes that impoverish them.

Moreover, concentrating on establishing a market economy at the expense of other aspects of reform confuses means with ends. The end is not the market economy itself, but 'the improvement of living standards and the establishment of the foundations of sustainable, equitable, and democratic development' that the market economy was intended to produce (Stiglitz, 1999: 3). The living standards of the vast majority of people in the former socialist states fell rapidly and unemployment rose. In Russia, for example, GDP fell 39 per cent in 1991–95. By 1997 63 per cent of the population lived below average income levels (Hughes, 2000). As for equitable development, the second aspect of the Washington consensus – rapid privatisation – simply allowed the accumulation of property and vast wealth in a few hands and opened the door to widespread corruption (Wedel, 1998: 132). The disparities in wealth that resulted from privatisation undermined the support that citizens who were bearing the costs could be expected to give to it. The corruption that accompanied the reform process (and which seemed to be condoned by Western donors) disillusioned them still further.[9] Since the same countries that were exporting democracy inspired the economic reform, confidence in Western models – both economic and democratic – was severely affected. Putnam (1993: 11) points out that 'nothing is more obvious . . . than the fact that effective democracy is closely associated with socioeconomic modernity'. But the consequences for many countries subjected to the Washington consensus was 'pauperisation and de-modernisation' (Hughes, 2000: 23).

---

[9] Wedel (1999) argues that corruption was not simply condoned, but assisted by a small group of Western advisors, some of whom used their advisory role for private gain.

Western tolerance of egregiously undemocratic practices similarly undermined people's belief in democracy.[10] Moreover, Western leaders seem to be victims of the 'electoralist fallacy', that is, the superficial legitimation of elections as relatively free and fair, even when the regimes that come to power are authoritarian (Hughes, 2000: 28). Western governments appear to deem it more important that communists or extreme nationalists do not win elections than that democracy is established. They fear that if communists regain power, they will abolish future elections, overturn the market reforms, and dismantle the democratic institutions that have been established.[11] But by condoning corruption and the use of undemocratic means in the name of establishing democracy, they discredit their own liberal credentials and, more importantly, democracy itself in the eyes of the very people they want to convert.[12]

In considering what endogenous factors make exporting democracy so difficult, it is useful to distinguish between procedure and process. By procedure I mean constitutional and electoral arrangements, voting procedures, laws, institutions and legal instruments to bolster civil liberties and the law. Procedures can be exported, or at least, advice can be offered on which are essential and which work best.[13] Procedures are clearly essential; without them democracy cannot exist. But they are not sufficient to ensure that democracy becomes entrenched. To consolidate democracy, habitual democratic processes are required. Democratic processes are norms, expectations, agreements between citizens and authorities on the limits that those in authority must observe, as well as on the obligations that those over whom they have authority must accept. Some of these processes are established by law, but most arise within society itself.

---

[10] The response of Western leaders to President Yeltsin's suspension and dismissal of the Russian Supreme Soviet in September/October 1993 and the subsequent bombardment of the Russian White House which housed it (and which housed a large number of deputies at the time) is the most dramatic example of this tolerance.

[11] The possibility that religious fundamentalist parties will be elected to power (for example in Algeria) evokes a similar response, and the same disregard for serious infringements of democracy.

[12] The 'two-turnover test' suggests that their efforts to prevent communists from winning elections are misguided. According to Huntington (1991: 267), democratic consolidation is complete 'if the party or group that takes power in the initial election at the time of transition loses a subsequent election and turns over power to those election winners, and if those election winners than peacefully turn over power to the winners of a later election'. In the case of many former socialist states, this means that for democracy to be established, the communists must win one election, lose the following election, and voluntarily hand over power.

[13] Stiglitz's advice (1999: 4) is as pertinent to democracy as to economics: 'Policy advisers put forth policy prescriptions in the context of a particular society – a society with a particular history, with a certain level of social capital, with a particular set of political institutions, and with political processes affected by (if not determined by) the existence of particular political forces.'

They cannot easily be imported from outside. They depend on culture, on habit, on informal networks, on the existence of social capital and social trust.[14]

It is usually argued that the absence of civil society under communism explains why these processes are absent or slow to develop in post-socialist states. It is true that few of the former socialist countries have a democratic past. It is also true that civil society, as conventionally understood in the West, did not exist under communism, and that during Stalinism, society was atomised. Moreover, in Russia and the other post-Soviet states, two world wars and a civil war within a period of forty years contributed to the dislocation of society. But although there were no real non-governmental organisations in the socialist states, after Stalin died there were informal networks, loyalties, interlocking professional groups, and there was social equilibrium. People knew whom they could trust; norms of reciprocity existed, even if they were often used not for civic engagement, but 'to obtain goods and services in short supply and to find a way around formal procedures' (Ledeneva, 1998: 1). And it is the economic reform itself that undermined these links and networks and destroyed existing loyalties.

Rapid change in institutions and procedures, the pauperisation of the majority of the population, huge discrepancies in income between the few winners in the reform and the large majority of losers, produced concomitant changes in society. Established informal networks were disrupted, competition – for jobs, for access to the few remaining services, for access to the 'pickings' of the market – replaced cooperation, and people ceased to know whom they could trust. As a result, existing values and habits were undermined and subverted. The little social capital and social trust that had existed previously were destroyed by the economic reforms. This has had a deleterious effect on the development of the democratic processes that effective democracy requires. Stiglitz (1999: 9) warns that:

If 'reformers' simply destroy the old norms and constraints in order to 'clean the slate' without allowing for the time-consuming processes of reconstructing new norms, the new legislated institutions may well not take hold. The reforms will be discredited and the 'reformers' will blame the victims for not correctly implementing their ill-considered designs.

This is as relevant to democratic procedures and processes as it is to the economic reforms to which he was referring. A critical look at how the new institutions and procedures function is more appropriate than blaming the victims. Unless citizens believe in the integrity of the procedures, laws and institutions that have been set up, democratic processes will

---

[14] Putnam's study of Italian regions (1993) shows how democratic processes develop in strong civic communities and how they contribute to effective democratic government.

not take root. Democratic reform is not predetermined to fail, but the environment in which it takes place requires careful nurturing.[15]

Conclusion

If the results of the programmes implemented by various governments and international organisations in recent years have been disappointing, does this mean that exporting democracy is not a viable objective of an ethical foreign policy? I began this chapter by pointing out that exporting democracy is inseparable from other aspects of an ethical foreign policy such as promoting human rights and humanitarian intervention. Indeed, Frost argues in Chapter 3 that the aim of interveners must always be to facilitate the creation of democracies. Arguing against the export of democracy, therefore, would be tantamount to discounting the possibility of an ethical foreign policy. Moreover, it would be an undeserved vote of no confidence in the people within the democratising states who aspire to live in stable and fully established democratic societies.

The answer, therefore, is not to give up exporting democracy, but to take more care about the manner in which it is done. Those who aim to export democracy should be less ambivalent, for example, about their priorities. Democracy should take precedence over other instruments of policy. If a particular type of economic reform undermines democracy, for example, it should be adjusted and adapted since economic reform is not an end in itself, but the means to ensure a better standard of living and stable democratic development.

On a practical level, there are a number of measures that could improve the manner in which democracy is exported. A degree of coordination (there is very little at present) between individual democracy programmes undertaken by different countries, and between them and those implemented by international organisations, would improve their efficiency and effectiveness. Moreover, better use should be made of the experience gained in past democratic transitions. After all, as we have seen, we have a long history of exporting democracy and this is the 'third wave' of democratisation since the Second World War (Huntington, 1991). Current democracy programmes would benefit from a serious evaluation of earlier successful transitions. Equally importantly, the current

---

[15] The one condition under which democratisation is bound to fail, however, is if political leaders fall victim to the fallacy that they can design their own route to democracy via a period of strong authoritarian rule. Democracy is a habit which can only become established with practice. It cannot be practised under authoritarian rule. The route from authoritarian rule usually leads not to democracy, but to more, or stronger, authoritarian rule.

recipients of, or aspirants for, democratic assistance should play an active role in evaluating and designing programmes.

Above all, those who wish to export democracy should avoid any type of electoralist fallacy. They should be consistent in applying democratic criteria, they should not tolerate infringements, and they should not accept as democratic anything less democratic than they would accept for themselves. They would do well, moreover, to examine their own societies, to ensure that their domestic arrangements are as impeccably democratic as the democracy they wish to export.

6   Ethical foreign policies and human rights: dilemmas for non-governmental organisations

Margo Picken

The problem

The introduction of the 1999 Annual Report on Human Rights of the UK's Foreign and Commonwealth Office (FCO) and the Department for International Development (DFID), which is largely devoted to Kosovo, states:

> Within three months of [the 50th anniversary of the Universal Declaration of Human Rights] this Government sent its armed forces into conflict to defend those same rights . . . Together we stood up for the rights of the people of Kosovo and for the freedoms enshrined in the Declaration. NATO was united in its resolve to defend those rights and the international community was overwhelmingly supportive of our actions . . . This was not a conflict we wanted. But there could not have been a more vivid way of demonstrating our commitment to human rights as enshrined in the Declaration. (FCO and DFID, 1999: 10–11)

Several commentators in Western societies saw their governments' readiness to use military force to defend human rights, together with other events such as the agreement to establish an international criminal court and the arrest of General Pinochet in London, as marking the dawn of a new era for human rights. For others, however, using force in the name of human rights represented a dramatic step backwards in the efforts that had been made since the Second World War to build a just and humane world order based on respect for human rights and the dignity and worth of each person.

Since the end of the Cold War, Western governments have proclaimed with ever greater vigour that human rights are at the centre of their foreign policies. This chapter looks at some of the anomalies that have characterised their policies in the post-Cold War decade, and the dilemmas they present for non-governmental organisations (NGOs) working to defend human rights worldwide or in countries other than their own. Focusing

This chapter builds on Margo Picken, 'Human Rights Policies of the 1990s: Some Hometruths', in Coomans *et al*, 2000.

on the problems risks painting a bleak picture. This would be misleading. The 1990s have seen positive advances in several areas directly and indirectly related to human rights, for example, the emergence of global movements for the rights of women, and campaigns to eradicate the debts owed by the world's poorest countries and to ban the deployment of land mines. Nevertheless, progress in some areas has not been matched by improvement in others, and progress itself often produces new dilemmas.

Hope and disappointment

When governments and peoples of the world commemorated the 50th anniversary of the Universal Declaration of Human Rights in 1998, the Declaration was hailed as a document of major importance, which it has, indeed, proved to be. But it was a disappointment to those who, in the aftermath of world war, had expected something more, and had pressed not for a declaration of moral principles, as favoured by the United States, but for a treaty with the binding force of law. Sir Hersch Lauterpacht, the eminent international lawyer who devoted the war years to drawing up such a treaty, foresaw such a possibility:

Should it be decided to reduce any international bill of human rights to a mere statement of political or moral principle, then, indeed, it would be most likely to secure easy acceptance; for any possible difficulty in agreeing upon its terms will be merged in the innocuous nature of its ineffectual purpose. But if the second World War ought to end, in the words of the British Prime Minister, 'with the enthronement of human rights', then a declaration thus emaciated would come dangerously near to a corruption of language. By creating an unwarranted impression of progress it would, in the minds of many, constitute an event which is essentially retrogressive. For it would purport to solve the crucial problem of law and politics in their widest sense by dint of a grandiloquent incantation whose futility would betray a lack both of faith and of candour. (Lauterpacht, 1945: 9)

If Lauterpacht was disappointed after the Second World War, the following generation experienced a similar disappointment in 1989. Cold War approaches had deformed the ways in which international human rights concepts and principles were interpreted and put into practice, and impeded the development of effective international institutions to oversee the implementation of international agreements to which states had committed themselves.[1] Both East and West had sought equal legitimacy through embracing human rights, but each embraced only those rights

[1] The two principal treaties of general application that translate the provisions of the Universal Declaration into legally binding form are the International Covenant on Civil and Political Rights and the International Covenant on Economic, Social and Cultural Rights. Together with the First Optional Protocol to the Covenant on Civil and Political Rights, which allows individuals international recourse when domestic remedies have

that suited its respective ideology rather than approaching the human rights proclaimed in the Universal Declaration as the coherent whole they were conceived to be. Rather than attempting to reconcile the tensions that inevitably arise, they created false dichotomies between different sets of rights, and between the individual and the collective good. Moreover, in the name of those same ideologies, both East and West also justified or were complicit in repression and persecution in many countries throughout the world.

When the Cold War ended, there was hope that governments and NGOs alike would finally be able to attend to the crucial problems of law and politics about which Lauterpacht had written in 1945. A fundamental rethinking of approaches that had developed during the Cold War would be necessary if credible and effective international and national institutions of oversight were to be put in place. There seemed to be cause for hope. Western governments had emerged as the dominant actors in world affairs, all the more influential in an increasingly interdependent world. The major Western European powers, in particular, had every reason to take human rights seriously given their own recent history and the events in Western Europe that had precipitated the writing of human rights into international law.

Furthermore, other changes held promise of progress towards a more just and humane world. In many African countries, autocratic governments were being replaced by more representative systems. Namibia became independent in 1989, and in South Africa Nelson Mandela was released from prison, the ban on the ANC was lifted, and the apartheid laws began to be dismantled. Some Middle Eastern governments were showing signs of responding to rising domestic pressures for reform. In El Salvador a peace process sought to address the root causes of the repression, civil strife and war that had marked the country throughout the 1980s. Elsewhere in Latin America, the military stepped back from direct rule and, although they remained powerful, civilian governments were elected in their place. In the Philippines, the Marcos regime had ended, and with it the gross human rights violations it had committed. In the USSR and Eastern Europe, more democratic government replaced Soviet rule and basic civil and political rights were being introduced.

Human rights and their advocates had played a part in many of these changes, and the non-partisan strategies they had developed during the

---

failed, they are often referred to as the International Bill of Human Rights. They were agreed in 1966 and came into force in 1976, almost thirty years after the adoption of the Universal Declaration. Committees, working under UN auspices, which are supposed to be composed of independent experts of high moral character, are entrusted with monitoring compliance by states parties to the treaties.

Cold War had been reasonably effective. Although the human rights agenda was undermined by competing ideologies, not all Western governments were caught up in Cold War approaches. Some governments, such as those of Scandinavia, the Netherlands and Canada, pressed by NGOs and by public opinion at home, played a leading role in multilateral forums such as the UN, and the foundations of an international regime to promote and protect human rights were put in place.[2]

The United States became engaged in the mid 1970s after the Vietnam War. While many aspects of President Carter's policies were inconsistent and justly criticised, advances were nonetheless made by his administration which had within its ranks several people who had been active in the civil rights movement. The multilateral and bilateral policies that the United States pursued were generally in keeping with the content and spirit of international human rights law, a commitment that President Carter also signalled when he signed the two core international human rights treaties on civil and political and economic, social and cultural rights in 1977, although he was unable to secure their ratification by the Senate. By the end of the 1970s, with US support rather than opposition, the human rights agencies of intergovernmental organisations such as the UN and the Organisation of American States were on their way to becoming more effective instruments, and US policies were beginning to have an impact, especially in Latin America.

Initially, when the Reagan administration took office in 1981, it tried to jettison human rights issues. Compelled by domestic public opinion to keep human rights on its agenda, however, it rearranged the priorities in ways that suited its own ideology, but which departed significantly from the understanding of human rights set forth in the Universal Declaration and the treaties based on it. It rejected the validity of economic and social rights, underplayed many civil and political rights, and focused primarily on free and fair elections and a narrow understanding of democracy. When, under the Bush administration, the United States eventually ratified the International Covenant on Civil and Political Rights in 1992, it ensured that its own laws would prevail over the provisions of international law. This included reserving the right to put to death young

---

[2] This chapter focuses on the policies of Western governments. However, many newly independent governments of Asia and Africa were active in the first decades of the UN, particularly in response to apartheid South Africa. In 1968, which marked the 30th anniversary of the Universal Declaration of Human Rights, Jeanne Hersch, former Director of UNESCO's philosophy division, wrote: 'Human Rights are not fashionable at the present time, they are in the trough of a wave, not everywhere, but in many countries. This is probably less true in certain developing countries than in developed ones, although one would certainly have thought that the latter would be the main guardians of Human Rights' (Hersch, 1968: 34).

people for crimes committed between sixteen and eighteen years of age, thereby derogating from an 'absolute' and sacrosanct provision of the Covenant which may never be violated under any circumstances. The Human Rights Committee, the body which monitors compliance with the Covenant, regretted the extent of the reservations, expressing particular concern at the reservation in respect to capital punishment, which, it concluded, was incompatible with the object and purpose of the Covenant (Grant, 2000). In many respects the Clinton administration, which took office at the beginning of 1993, continued the policies of the Reagan and Bush administrations. The reservations were not withdrawn, and major international human rights treaties accepted by the large majority of states remained unratified.[3]

Human rights in the 1990s

The opportunity that seemed to exist at the beginning of the decade to strengthen international cooperation to safeguard and advance human rights, and to address the crucial problems of law and politics, soon faded. The policies adopted by the United States, as the dominant world power, became especially influential in setting the agenda for the decade. Western European governments either followed its lead or failed to provide an alternative vision. Much of the decade was marked by 'grandiloquent incantation' with the risk that human rights would fall victim to sloganism. Like most governments, the corporate world also became proficient in the language of human rights and democracy.

During the 1990s, human rights continued to be a source of mistrust in international relations. Intergovernmental agencies responsible for overseeing the implementation of international human rights agreements remained underfunded, weak and unable to discharge effectively a primary purpose for which they were established, namely the prevention of conflict. Western policies were inconsistent, leading many governments and NGOs to ask whether human rights were being misused to advance a particular political and economic agenda.

Several aspects of Western policies raised questions of their good faith, and created dilemmas for NGOs. Although other considerations were paramount, for example, human rights and humanitarian grounds were invoked to justify the Gulf War in 1991. Concerned about linking the use of force with human rights, several governments and NGOs called for international guidelines to govern military interventions on such grounds.

---

[3] These include the International Covenant on Economic, Social and Cultural Rights, and the International Convention on the Rights of the Child which Madeleine Albright signed in 1995. Somalia is the only other member state that has not ratified this treaty.

They met with little success. By the end of the decade, many Western governments and experts argued that an evolving law of humanitarian intervention legitimised NATO's use of military force against Serbia, and that UN Security Council authorisation was not required for interventions on such grounds. While at the beginning of the decade, there had been hopes of a 'peace dividend' which would benefit the poorest and weakest sectors of society, by its end NATO was expanding, the peace dividend was forgotten, and Western militaries were proclaimed as forces for good and symbols of a Western commitment to a just and democratic world order.[4]

The monetarist policies fashionable in the 1990s also created difficulties. Western governments, bilaterally and through multilateral institutions such as the UN and European Union, began to link the promotion and protection of human rights directly with market economic reform although the compatibility of free market economies and human rights, especially economic, social and cultural rights, was by no means evident. Structural adjustment programmes required recipient governments to cut public spending, which undermined their capacity to meet their obligations under human rights law and often created conditions for civil unrest and repression. Debt repayments to Western creditors reduced the capacity of many still further. 'Shotgun' privatisation contributed to corruption and misrule in many countries.

The commercial interests of the defence industry presented the most difficult problem for the human rights policies of the major Western powers, which are also the largest exporters of arms. New guidelines introduced by the British government in 1997, for example, prohibited arms sales to regimes that might use them for internal repression or external aggression. Leaving aside key questions regarding their implementation, the guidelines did not reflect the resolve at the beginning of the decade of the Council of Ministers of the European Community that arms-exporting countries should exercise restraint in selling arms to developing countries, and that these countries should be encouraged to spend their scarce resources on development projects, particularly in the areas of health and education (Council of the European Community, 1991). For its part, the British defence industry argued that arms exports were vital to the British economy, and accounted for one in ten jobs in manufacturing (*The Economist*, 18–24 September 1999: 35–6).

A growing reluctance to recognise and admit refugees also caused NGOs, especially those in Africa and Asia, to question Western sincerity.

[4] In 1998 the State Department budget was $5.4 billion, while the intelligence budget rose to approximately $30 billion following a 10 per cent increase. The administration then proposed an increase for the Defense Department of $112 billion over five years, on top of its $280 billion annual allotment. See White, 1999.

This reluctance often influenced the way Western governments assessed the human rights situation in other countries, causing them to downplay risks. Asylum seekers with good reason to fear persecution at home were deported and/or detained, often for long periods of time, and 'safe havens' and 'protected zones' were created under conditions that were not safe. Policy-makers and the media, faced with the complex world that opened up after the Cold War, also began to oversimplify the causes of political disputes and internal conflicts. Where minorities were involved, these were often labelled as 'ethnic', to the neglect of the many complex causes of conflict, past and present. The effect was to limit the responsibility of the national government and public, and to absolve other governments and outside actors of responsibility.

A foreign policy that seeks to build a stable and just world order based on a reaffirmation of faith in fundamental human rights as laid down in the UN Charter of 1945 is a serious undertaking. Human rights issues cannot be addressed in isolation from other policies. However, throughout the decade human rights were often viewed as a dimension to be added, and genuine dilemmas were glossed over, rather than acknowledged and publicly debated. 'Human rights' were also frequently invoked when a crisis had already occurred and other policies had failed. Rather than being integrated into overall policy, and associated with a long-term agenda of political, economic and social change, they became associated in the public mind with emergencies and a punitive approach – the use of force and the punishment of individuals who, while responsible, were rarely solely answerable for the offence. The energies of intergovernmental agencies such as the UN Office of the High Commissioner for Human Rights, as well as those of human rights NGOs, were also increasingly diverted into internal conflict and war. More resources were expended on crises than on their prevention.

Trade and commerce moved to the centre of the foreign policy agenda of most Western governments. Trade and private investment substituted for aid in many countries, particularly the United States, which gives less aid than any other country as a net percentage of GNP. By the end of the decade, aid budgets were one-third lower than when the decade started, amounting on average to some 0.25 per cent of the GNP of rich countries as against the 0.7 per cent set by the UN.[5] Many development agencies were also charged with incorporating human rights and the promotion of democracy into their programmes, but were often uncertain what this involved. Some began to portray all their development aid as advancing human rights. According to the FCO and DFID 1998 report, for

[5] Britain's contribution was raised to 0.3 per cent in 1999.

example, 'All of the development programme is about promoting rights. It helps to create the right conditions for economic growth or human development which leads to the realisation of rights' (FCO and DFID, 1998: 15).

Assistance and advice

During the 1990s, assisting governments, more recently referred to as 'constructive engagement', became popular, especially in the case of those considered to be 'in transition to democracy'. It was not used in the case of governments considered 'beyond the pale', such as Cuba and Iraq, which were held to require a more robust approach (FCO and DFID, 1999: ch. 3). In effect, this represented a continuation of an approach adopted in the 1980s when governments viewed as allies (often referred to as 'authoritarian') were judged to need help, whereas those who were not allies (often referred to as 'totalitarian') were held to account for their actions. Undoubtedly, governments which come to power following periods of repression and which are genuinely trying to adhere to their human rights obligations can benefit from help. But no government, whatever the legacy it inherits, can be given a blank cheque.

'Constructive engagement' can often mean substituting accountability with assistance. This is an attractive option for governments, diplomats and commerce. It allows for business to continue as usual, while human rights violations are dealt with through quiet diplomacy, friendly advice and technical cooperation. It also has the effect of deflecting criticism before it is made. However, it can leave human rights victims without effective recourse. Moreover, when governments that are violating human rights are assisted and not held to proper account, this can be understood as collusion and collaboration rather than constructive engagement. It also risks legitimising governments that should not be legitimised. The approach within the UN mirrors these policies. 'Protecting' human rights, i.e., holding governments responsible and accountable for their actions and providing recourse to victims when domestic remedies fail, has steadily given way to the 'promotion' of human rights and helping governments to do better or to mend their ways. The United Nations' technical cooperation programme in the field of human rights, implemented under the leadership of the High Commissioner for Human Rights, has grown dramatically in recent years, and now has projects with over sixty governments (United Nations Secretary-General, 1998).[6] The

---

[6] Stark examples of where assistance replaces holding to account include China and Angola.

programme, and the assumptions behind it, are in urgent need of thorough and independent evaluation as to their effectiveness in advancing respect for human rights in practice.

Meanwhile, the treaty bodies that are responsible for ensuring that States parties comply with the provisions of the treaties that they have accepted – considered by many to be the backbone of longer-term institution building in the field of human rights – remain depleted of resources, and unable to function as envisaged. Few governments, including Western governments, have been willing to support effective and independent multilateral oversight of their policies and practices.

Towards the end of the decade, there were some signs that more attention was beginning to be given to the longer-term agenda. The analysis in the 1999 UK Annual Report on Human Rights, for example, was more informed with regard to many issues, including the roots of conflict and the need to prevent conflict, even if it was less convincing about how the problems were being dealt with, and the range of solutions on offer. Poverty, education, housing and health began to be addressed in terms of human rights, due not least to the efforts of NGOs such as Oxfam. In his 1999 report on the work of the Organisation, the UN Secretary General stressed the need to shift from a culture of reaction to one of prevention, and for governments to place the welfare of all citizens over narrow sectional interests (United Nations Secretary-General, 1999a; 1999b). He has also called for the 'mainstreaming of human rights' although it is not clear what this will amount to in practice. However, the decade was perhaps best summed up by Martin Woollacott, in November 1999, as having been one of constant compromise with injustice and exploitation and of having the worst of both worlds – of diluted moral standards combined with unconditional economic demands (*The Guardian*, 19 November 1999).

Non-governmental organisations and Western publics

In 1995, Goenawan Mohamad, the well-known Indonesian writer and journalist, argued that 'there is a risk of letting the issue of human rights become prominently a problem of international relations, to be negotiated in meetings of government officials and diplomats. The issue is increasingly perceived as a matter of international precepts and principles. In other words, a kind of foreign assignment to countries which have no means to refuse.' In Indonesia, he noted, people had forgotten their own past; to many 'human rights is just an international protocol that the West wants the "Third World" to comply with. It has nothing to do with a genuinely internalised need.' He concluded that:

No nation has a common past, and common guilt and common indifference. A nation consists of victims, murderers, bystanders, fellow-travellers . . . Viewed this way, you cannot expect that an Australian businessman or an Australian spook will raise the issues of human rights when he or she meets with his or her Indonesian counterpart. They have their own things to worry about. This applies also to government officials. A meaningful international support for the cause of human rights will eventually depend on how people with the same concern help each other internationally. Ultimately, of course, it is the people who are directly affected by human rights abuses who will decide what their survival will have to rely upon. (Mohamad, 1995)

Human rights are about good government and the responsible exercise of power for the common good. All societies need vigilant citizens and independent institutions to ensure that power is not misused, that governments are kept decent and honest, that states honour their international agreements and assume their responsibilities and duties towards their own citizens and to each other with regard to human rights. Governments are unlikely to develop the commitment that is necessary of their own volition.

Had it not been for an active citizenry in the West after the Second World War, and had the task been left to diplomats and statesmen alone, human rights would not have been given the central place they were accorded in the UN Charter. The Universal Declaration of Human Rights might well have met the fate of most UN declarations and remained a dormant document. Few governments at the time could have anticipated the emergence of movements of concerned citizens determined to hold them to their word. Gathering force in the 1960s and 1970s, organisations of active citizens became vocal advocates for human rights, insisting that states honour the commitments they had made.[7] Trade unions, religious organisations, peace movements and the Red Cross were among those that played a vital role. Founded in 1961, Amnesty International based its mandate on the Universal Declaration of Human Rights and helped to set basic standards for non-governmental advocacy. It drew to its membership committed individuals initially from Western Europe, and eventually from all regions of the world, who worked on behalf of individuals in countries other than their own, and helped to popularise the values and universality of human rights.

The non-governmental landscape has changed considerably in recent decades, in both positive and negative ways. In one of the positive developments, people in all regions and most countries of the world from

---

[7] For a history of the human rights movement see Zalaquett, 1981/83.

different cultures and backgrounds now lay claim in organised fashion to the universal validity of the provisions of the Universal Declaration of Human Rights, and the subsequent treaties to which it gave birth, to support principles of democracy, justice and equality within their own societies. Often fragile and beleaguered, they nonetheless have become effective forces. However, their task is not easy. Not only have they to contend with their own frequently hostile governments and publics, they have also to deal with the contradictions that mark Western policies and practices. The greater these inconsistencies are, the less recourse they have to principle, and the more the principles themselves are confused and undermined.

Under the 'constructive engagement' approach, those laying claim to human rights and exposing their violation can also be viewed as troublemakers. This was often the case, for example, in Latin America, when the majority of countries were declared to be 'in transition to democracy'. For many people the term 'human rights' was narrowly associated with brutal dictatorship, and portrayed as being 'against' government. When the dictatorships gave way to elected governments, a view emerged that human rights were no longer at issue, and that organisations which monitored and reported on the conduct of their governments were too negative, should stop pointing out the problems, and instead should work constructively with their governments. Some donor agencies stopped funding human rights organisations in the region in the belief that the problems they had been addressing had been resolved.

Within Western societies the dynamic has been different. Organisations advocating for human rights in other countries and worldwide have come to inhabit a separate universe from organisations working for human rights at home. There are complex historical and political reasons for this divide, but the human rights endeavour would be strengthened if the divide were bridged, particularly as the world becomes more and more interdependent, as domestic and foreign policies are increasingly interconnected, and as those working for human rights at home in Western and non-Western societies face common problems. Indeed, one of the most effective contributions Western governments could make to advancing respect for human rights worldwide would be to bring their domestic policies and practices into compliance with the letter and spirit of their international obligations, and to fully support effective independent multilateral institutions to oversee their own conduct and that of other governments.

In the United States, in particular, the term 'human rights' has been more commonly associated with foreign policy and with practices in other countries rather than at home. Organisations working within the

United States to end police brutality, cruel, inhuman or degrading treatment, and racial discrimination, for example, have not generally viewed these problems as human rights issues, although there are signs that this is beginning to change. However, misconceptions about basic principles and concepts of human rights, many of which were formed during the Cold War period, are widespread in most Western societies. Often ignorant of the past, as well as of the values that underlie non-Western religions and philosophies, human rights tend to be seen as values that Western societies have and generally respect, and that others lack. Events that helped Western societies to 'internalise' the values of human rights in this century – a legacy of slavery, colonialism, the Depression, the Spanish Civil War, two world wars, the Holocaust, decolonisation, and the civil rights and anti-Vietnam War movements in the United States, for example – are also now passing into history for younger generations. A keener sense of history and a greater degree of scepticism are needed.

The movement for human rights in Western societies in some respects is not as strong today, or it is more dispersed. For historical reasons, almost all organisations working to safeguard and advance adherence to human rights worldwide have been headquartered or based in the West. Most do not have worldwide memberships that inform their policies and programmes and that can also support them financially. The majority in fact are not membership organisations, and many are essentially national organisations working internationally. Trade unions and established religions with their worldwide memberships and constituencies are not as directly engaged as they used to be, in part, perhaps, because their own memberships and influence are diminishing, because they feel excluded by the 'professionalisation' of human rights that has taken place, or because they are committing their energies to related fields. Church organisations play an active role in Jubilee 2000's campaign for the cancellation of debts, for example, and in campaigns against the arms trade. The very successes referred to above – the dismantling of apartheid, the fall of Soviet communism, the retreat of dictatorship in Latin America – have also meant that many who previously advocated for human rights have moved to other issues.

Western public opinion is more confused. At one level, everyone is in favour of 'human rights' as they were during the Cold War. At another level, there is greater tolerance of practices that should not be tolerated, or a feeling of confusion and helplessness to affect events. The issues are made to seem more complicated, and power is made to seem more dispersed. The media, which could be counted upon for incisive analysis and sound investigative reporting to bring out the facts, has also changed. Its attention span is shorter, and there is less in-depth, continuous coverage of events. The media also has to contend with an increasingly sophisticated government and corporate 'spin' when it comes to human rights matters. Public concern continues to be aroused, however, when the issues become clear and intelligible, as in the case of Rwanda, East Timor, or China and Tibet. Jiang Zemin's visit to the United Kingdom in October 1999 visibly demonstrated the contradictions that had characterised UK policies towards China during the preceding years, and the public reaction to them.

A related but different trend has been that for lack of ideological alternatives, ever-increasing claims are made on human rights to remedy all injustice and wrongdoing, although this was not their intent, nor can they carry such a burden. A pitfall here is that human rights may become so elastic and diluted that they lose what should be special to them, which is that they 'should identify those elementary claims that need to be met if a properly human life is to be lived' (Vincent, 1990). Human rights cannot replace or be a substitute for politics, ideology or religion.

Changing perceptions and new actors

In the years since the Cold War, a profound transformation has taken place in the perceptions, as well as the political and economic contexts and patterns of violations of human rights, requiring deeper analysis of their causes and the underlying economic, political and social factors. This is a controversial terrain, and it is much more difficult for human rights organisations whose expertise lay traditionally in international law, fact finding and objective reporting of violations of human rights.

In the 1990s many new actors entered the human rights field. As attention turned to conflicts within societies, for example, different sets of actors, new to working within politically charged and fragile societies, became involved, each bringing its own particular professional culture and analysis. They included those from the peace and security fields, who had previously worked on East–West issues, refugee organisations whose focus shifted to the 'internally displaced', and humanitarian relief organisations which were required to work in altered, and far more complex, circumstances. As conflict resolution became the vogue, conflict resolution experts also moved in, often with little or no understanding of the nature of the specific conflicts they were seeking to resolve which came to be commonly described as 'complex emergencies'.[8] Other actors, such as

---

[8] The situation was further complicated by weak international legal regimes governing situations of internal armed conflict (weak because of the long-standing anxiety of all governments regarding outside intervention in their internal affairs), and a genuine confusion as to which legal regimes to apply, and in what circumstances. Some governments

the World Bank, government and non-governmental development agencies, and the UN Development Programme also became engaged.

The new actors invoked human rights or were dealing with human rights issues without invoking them. But many were ignorant of the history, as well as the actual content and purpose of international human rights agreements, and they were further influenced by the prevailing misconceptions. New terms that came to dominate the international discourse and agenda of the 1990s compounded the confusion. The Universal Declaration of Human Rights had been an attempt to define in clear language a set of basic values that were indispensable to a peaceful world. The new terms, while they all relate to the human rights agenda, tended to distract from it. Many have no universally agreed-upon definition, are unclear in their meaning, and do not readily translate into other languages.[9] In many respects the terminology of the 1990s seemed to represent a step backward from the clarity of thought that was needed.

Human rights are about controversial matters. However, current policies tend to blur over, or do not acknowledge, competing interests. The UK 1999 Annual Report on Human Rights, for example, admits that 'We are still often faced with difficult decisions in uncertain circumstances, and sometimes unwelcome options. And we have other aims and aspirations – for national security, economic prosperity, quality of life and poverty elimination – that our policy must also reflect' (FCO and DFID, 1999: 23). But the report does not explain the difficult decisions, uncertain circumstances and unwelcome options, nor does it explore how apparent contradictions might be resolved for the common good.

The report calls for partnerships between government and NGOs, between government and business, between business and civil society, as if the ambitions and roles of human rights advocates and of NATO, Rio Tinto Zinc and Jubilee 2000, of the poor and of the rich, of the arms trader and of the campaigner against the arms trade are similar and can be reconciled under the banner of human rights. One of the troubling consequences of this assumption is that it gives rise to a confusion of

and NGOs began to claim a 'right' to humanitarian intervention, which fuelled these apprehensions. Human rights were often invoked to override considerations of national sovereignty in ways that did not always help the efforts of human rights organisations which are also concerned with questions of sovereignty and self-determination as provided for in Article 1 of both the International Covenant on Civil and Political Rights and the Covenant on Economic, Social and Cultural Rights.

[9] They include democracy, transitions to democracy, civil society, rule of law, governance, 'humanitarian' intervention, human development, human security. The meaning and content of the term democracy, for example, which had been passionately debated in the interwar period, was the subject of similar debate in the 1990s. H. G. Wells and George Orwell are worth reading in this respect. See, for example, Orwell, 1968 and Chapter 5 of this volume.

roles. For example, organisations such as Amnesty International and UK Save the Children, perhaps from a desire to influence government policy, now have staff working in the Foreign and Commonwealth Office which in turn plans to second staff to human rights NGOs. The dilemma for human rights organisations is whether such a relationship compromises their independence, if not in reality, then in terms of perception.

Corporations have also begun to understand the importance of human rights, as well as the need to respond to public concern. However, they resist formal regulation or mechanisms to oversee their conduct, opting for voluntary codes of conduct instead. NGOs are grappling with the difficult question of how they should relate to the business sector. What are the responsibilities of the corporate sector towards society? What is the role of governments, especially in those countries where they are headquartered, in ensuring that they exercise their considerable power in ways that respect and uphold human rights? How can their policies and practices be brought within the law?

Paradoxically, as human rights have become more fashionable and all embracing, the task for organisations advocating for human rights has become far more exacting, if not overwhelming. They are required to monitor the policies of those who act 'for' human rights as much as the practices of governments that are in breach of their obligations. They must also develop strategies that are well conceived, feasible and precise in the measures they are calling for. Unrealistic or vague requests for action and responses that are inadequate (in the case of 'friends'), or excessive (in the case of 'enemies') can seriously undermine their efforts to secure human rights and build a universal culture of human rights.

They must also give far greater priority now to educating themselves, the new actors, and Western publics and polities about the basic concepts, philosophy and principles underlying the international human rights documents, and to making the human rights discourse intelligible and accessible. As Neelan Tiruchelvam, the prominent advocate for human rights from Sri Lanka, pointed out, too much of the discourse on human rights has taken place 'in an esoteric language and idiom, which is unintelligible to vast sections of the polity'. He felt that the human rights movement had failed to expand the base of support for the 'secular, democratic and pluralistic values of human rights' (Tiruchelvam, 1993: 89). He had Asian organisations in mind in the context of the 'Asian values' debate as to whether the provisions of the Universal Declaration of Human Rights applied to Asian societies. It applies as much to Western societies, however, which suffer from their own 'cultural relativism'. But this task cannot be shouldered by human rights organisations alone. It is one that we all share as concerned citizens. Human rights, in Lauterpacht's words are 'conceived as a means to enable man to do his duty, in freedom, to man and society' (Lauterpacht, 1950: 327). The duty of individuals, in accordance with the Universal Declaration of Human Rights, lies in striving 'by teaching and education to promote respect for these rights and freedoms . . . and to secure their universal and effective recognition and observance'.

Resources and funding

Jealous of the independence which is essential to their effectiveness, many human rights NGOs either do not accept, or are cautious about accepting, direct government or corporate funding, especially in relation to their monitoring and reporting activities. Instead they rely on support from the public, philanthropic foundations, church organisations, development agencies which have some degree of independence[10] and intergovernmental bodies such as the European Commission. The United States has an array of philanthropic foundations and wealthy individuals, but acceptable sources of financial support are far more limited in Europe. Those organisations that strive for independence are consequently often short of funds.

At the beginning of the decade, only a relatively small number of donor agencies supported activities to advance respect for human rights. This has changed as more governments, governmental development agencies, the European Commission and corporations have become engaged. They have become influential actors in setting the agenda even though many, as relative newcomers, do not fully understand the field, and some have their own particular agenda. Yet their policies and practices are rarely subject to critical independent review, in part because no-one wishes to bite the hand that feeds, and also because donor agencies rarely invite independent outside evaluations of their programmes.

Donor agencies decide what to fund, and who should and should not receive financial support. With few exceptions, most restrict their funding to specific projects, rather than contributing to an organisation's overall activities and overheads. This not only affects the ability of NGOs to plan their activities in accordance with their own priorities, it also undermines

---

[10] Scandinavian development agencies, such as the Swedish International Development Authority (SIDA), have more independence than their UK or US counterparts which makes it easier to accept funding from them. SIDA's Director and board are formally appointed by the government, which is guided by nominations put forward by political parties and 'civil society structures'. SIDA is also protected by a law stating that all 'agencies' are independent and should be allowed to run their programmes without government interference, although they must stay within budget and broader annual instructions.

their long-term stability and allows donor agencies undue influence in setting their agendas as well as the overall priorities of the field. Many donor agencies are also risk averse, and it is often difficult to obtain support for controversial projects. Concerned to promote their own public image, some also seek public credit for their support, as if they owned the projects they fund. For example, the European Commission often makes its support conditional on the prominent display of its logo. Corporations make similar demands, and affluent individuals also like to see their names associated with good causes.

Many NGOs working to protect human rights find it difficult to accept these conditions. Corporations and governments that are in good faith should encourage the establishment of, and channel their support through, independent funds. This would also allow them to support potentially controversial projects without being associated with them. There are models for this, for example the Swedish NGO Fund for Human Rights which was established in 1990, and the European Foundation for Human Rights which was supported by the European Commission for several years. Sadly, the Commission recently terminated this support, and the Foundation is winding up its affairs.

The United Nations

Human rights NGOs have invested a great deal of energy and hope in the UN. Yet the UN is a much-reduced organisation in chronic financial difficulties, for which the United States, which has been heavily in debt to the organisation, is largely responsible. The United States has used this leverage to lead a move to 'reform' the UN, which, as one commentator has put it, has been tantamount to its 'privatisation'. Other Western governments have either supported these reforms or have been mute in their criticism. The regular budget of the UN has been reduced in real terms, and voluntary contributions provided by the rich member states, and latterly from wealthy individuals, have increased.[11] Voluntary contributions are earmarked to support activities of the contributors' choice, thereby adding to their already considerable power. The reforms have also affected staff recruitment. Posts financed from the regular budget have been reduced, and the recruitment of persons seconded by their

---

[11] Currently, on a yearly basis and in rounded terms, the United Nations is financed at a level of $1.2 billion from assessed contributions to the regular budget, $1.8 billion from voluntary contributions to the same regular budget, and $1.4 billion from assessed contributions to the budgets for peacekeeping operations. This relates to the UN proper, and not to its programmes, notably the UNDP and the WFP. See documents of the 5th Committee of the General Assembly of the United Nations, UN New York, 1999, in particular A/Res/54/250A-C, A/54/6/ Rev. 1, and A/C.5/54/48.

governments, from private firms, or taken on as short-term consultants has risen (Baudot, forthcoming). In some cases, governments 'pay for' posts which are occupied by nationals from the contributing country.

All areas of UN activity have been affected by these reforms. Several staff in the Office of the UN High Commissioner for Human Rights, for example, are on short-term contracts, and almost half of the office's annual budget is now met from voluntary contributions. Thus the statement in the UK Annual Report on Human Rights for 1999 that the UK provided $11million in voluntary contributions to the High Commissioner's Office, and that this was its highest ever level of support, should be seen within this overall picture, about which the report is silent (FCO and DFID, 1999: 69). Peacekeeping operations are budgeted for through a separate procedure and on a case by case basis. Funding from the United States is always involved, and each peacekeeping operation must now be presented as a matter of course to the United States Congress. While undoubtedly the UN needed to change, these reforms have damaged multilateral response capacities and reduced the moral standing and credibility of the organisation which is essential to its role in all fields, but especially so in the field of human rights.

Conclusion

The UN Charter remains a landmark document. Its human rights provisions 'were adopted, with deliberation and after prolonged discussion . . . as part of the philosophy of the new international system and as a most compelling lesson of the experiences and lessons of the old' (Lauterpacht, 1950: 147).

Although the treaties they have accepted legally bind Western governments, they have yet to assume their obligations at home and abroad fully. The role of governments is to respect and protect human rights, and to further their enjoyment, but not to monopolise them. Nobody expects the ways forward to be easy or straightforward, but at least an honest attempt should be made to look for them.

NGOs advocating for human rights have been influential and have had moral force precisely because they have stood apart. The ethical policies and the new actors of the 1990s have produced a confusing landscape and blurring of lines. Human rights organisations are now increasingly invited to work with Western governments in a common effort to uphold human rights and to assist in building democratic institutions around the world, but in accordance with an overall agenda and conditionalities that are largely set, and often manipulated, by these governments. While such invitations can be seen as a step forward, they create new dilemmas, the greatest of which is how human rights organisations should position themselves so as to maintain their independence and traditional vigilance, particularly since the policies of the 1990s have yet to show convincing results.[12]

In developing an alternative agenda, NGOs might heed Rene Cassin, the French jurist who played a prominent part in drafting the Universal Declaration of Human Rights. In accepting the Nobel Peace Prize in 1968, he said that organisations of civic society should not be distracted from the immediate tasks at hand, that they should concentrate their main effort for as long a time as necessary on the work already done to bring about tangible results. 'Not to implement the measures already worked out, even if they are insufficient, would be playing into the hands of those who wish to block any progress'.[13]

They might also heed Goenawan Mohamad's view that meaningful international support for the cause of human rights will eventually depend on how people with the same concern help each other internationally (Mohamad, 1995). Now that national and local organisations work in most countries of the world to secure respect for human rights at home, and now that Western nations have become the dominant powers in world affairs, perhaps organisations working from within Western societies to secure respect for human rights worldwide could best express their solidarity with peoples elsewhere by challenging their own societies to confront the anomalies that characterise Western domestic and foreign policies today.

---

[12] For a fascinating case study of democracy building initiatives in Kazakhstan, see Luong and Weinthal, 1999.

[13] He had principally in mind the two covenants on civil, political, economic, social and cultural rights adopted two years previously which require as a first priority the organisation of a system of guarantees within each state for the benefit of all individuals without discrimination. Most states, including Western states, have yet to put such a system in place. See Cassin, 1995: 383–4.

7 The international criminal court

Spyros Economides

Introduction

There are many examples after 1989 of the international community's interventionist tendencies on the international stage. Kuwait, Cambodia, Somalia, former Yugoslavia and East Timor have all been the objects of a newly found, albeit selective, interventionist policy. While geopolitical and economic interests – and more traditional rules of public international law – have often shaped the rationale of the powerful state actors instigating and enacting these interventions, the prime catalyst in securing wider state support in both word and deed has been ethical and humanitarian concerns. Humanitarian intervention is the catchphrase that came to embody this concern in the 1990s, especially in the foreign policy declarations of Western states and the proclamations of the major international organisations such as the European Union (EU) and the United Nations (UN).

In the West, the state that most vociferously proclaims the newly acquired moralism in its post-Cold War foreign policy is the United Kingdom (UK). Only ten days into the tenure of the New Labour government, Foreign Secretary Robin Cook explained that the UK's foreign policy would be bound by an 'ethical dimension' and that 'the Labour Government does not accept that political values can be left behind when we check in our passports to travel on diplomatic business' (FCO, 1997b). This was headlined as the most important departure in British foreign policy under a new government. The Clinton administration also took up the mantra, but it was less direct in its declarations about the role of an 'ethical dimension' in foreign policy. Nevertheless, the administration held up the interventions in Bosnia and Kosovo as indications that it would not tolerate what it saw as massive abuses of human rights and crimes against humanity, and that it would take action against the perpetrators of such gross violations of international law.

Concern with the inadequacies of public international law in dealing with those suspected of committing 'war crimes, genocide and crimes against humanity', together with the new-found concern with ethics and foreign policy has driven forward the founding of an International Criminal Court (ICC).[1] The initial impetus towards holding individuals criminally responsible for crimes committed against humanity in the contemporary era was provided by the *ad hoc* war crimes tribunals created in relation to the conflicts in Rwanda and former Yugoslavia. These tribunals were established under the aegis of the UN Security Council and were based on the precedent of the International Military Tribunal at Nuremberg and its sister body in Tokyo. They also have the 'legal' backing of the Universal Declaration of Human Rights and the Convention on the Prevention and Punishment of the Crime of Genocide, which the vast majority of states proclaimed the benchmark of international standards of human rights and the prevention of crimes against humanity.

Historical precedents

The most important precedent set by the International Military Tribunals at Nuremberg and Tokyo were that they 'extended the traditional scope of international humanitarian law, in adding international criminal law and justice to the laws of Geneva and the Hague' (Beigbeder, 1999: 27). Both Tribunals were primarily US initiatives and they were tainted by the accusation of meting out 'victors' justice'. They were generally seen to be highly politicised in that they were not convened as the result of an international treaty, and hence were of dubious standing in customary international law. The Nuremberg Tribunal was the product of an agreement concluded during the Second World War between Winston Churchill and Franklin D. Roosevelt, which made clear that German 'war criminals' would be punished.[2] Their bilateral agreement was extended to nineteen signatory states in August 1945 and it started operating on 14 November 1945. During its 11-month lifespan, the Tribunal tried twenty-four defendants and seven organisations indicted of violating any or all of the three jurisdictional elements upon which the Tribunal was based. These three elements were crimes against peace, war crimes and crimes against humanity.

---

[1] The International Court of Justice (ICJ), the primary judicial body of the UN and the 'international community', has no jurisdiction over individual criminal responsibility. Its function is to act and decide over disputes brought to it by consenting states.

[2] Churchill and Roosevelt could not initially agree on the method of punishment. It was feared that a lengthy trial would give those being prosecuted the opportunity to use the proceedings for propaganda purposes or that the trial could become a focus for groups that still supported the Nazis. Churchill and Roosevelt even aired the possibility that those suspected of the crimes might be shot on sight.

Despite certain differences in the technicalities of the personnel and legal procedure, the International Military Tribunal of the Far East – the Tokyo Tribunal's official designation – had the same jurisdiction as its sister body in Nuremberg. Again primarily an American project, the Tokyo Tribunal was constituted via the Potsdam Declaration of August 1945 which was initially signed by the United Kingdom, the United States and China and to which the USSR later acceded.

Although they were highly politicised, both Tribunals injected the notion of morality and introduced the legal concept of crimes against humanity into customary public international law, and 'substitut[ed] legal process for the victims' urge for revenge' (Beigbeder, 1999: 27). They also made novel contributions to international criminal law by indicting and prosecuting individuals (rather than states or peoples) for crimes committed against peace, humanity and the laws of war. Ultimately, the Nuremberg and Tokyo Tribunals provided the historical, legal and judicial basis for the Tribunals relating to former Yugoslavia and Rwanda.[3]

In May 1993, the UN Security Council confirmed a decision made earlier that year to establish an International Criminal Tribunal for former Yugoslavia (ICTY), to prosecute violations of international humanitarian law under Chapter Seven of the UN Charter. Arguably, the ICTY, which was established while fighting still continued on the territory of former Yugoslavia, was meant to substitute for the lack of effective international intervention. Nonetheless, it was the first time in the history of the UN that the Security Council created a judicial body to 'maintain and restore international peace and security' under Chapter Seven of the Charter (Beigbeder, 1999: 150). Using the Nuremberg precedent, the ICTY was to have the same jurisdiction over individuals suspected and indicted of violations of international humanitarian law, but its mandate excluded crimes against peace and the prosecution of organisations. In attending to some of the perceived deficiencies of the Nuremberg process, the architects of the ICTY ensured that the Court's composition would be international, thus refuting possible charges of 'victors' justice' (this was not immediately applicable as fighting continued in former Yugoslavia). Furthermore, those convicted would have a right to appeal, and the ICTY would not have a right to try an individual *in absentia*, as had occurred at Nuremberg.

In November 1994, the Security Council created a similar judicial organ to deal with crimes committed during the conflict in Rwanda. Called the International Criminal Tribunal for Rwanda (ICTR), it shared the

[3] Useful sources on the Nuremberg and Tokyo Tribunals include Best, 1984; Ginsburgs and Kudriavtsev, 1990; Marrus, 1997; Minear, 1971; Röling and Cassese, 1993; Smith, 1981; and Taylor, 1992.

ICTY's legal basis and jurisdictional powers with slight variations to take the differences between the conflicts into account. The major difference between the two Tribunals was that because the Rwandan conflict was classified as an internal conflict, the ICTR had no mandate to prosecute war crimes, but was tasked with prosecuting those indicted of genocide and crimes against humanity inflicted in a widespread and systematic manner on civilian populations.

Both Tribunals were severely constrained by temporal and territorial limitations: set up to deal with specific crimes in specific areas at specific times, they had no remit to act outside the prescribed territorial limits or in preventing future violations.[4] Similarly, neither had an enforcement mechanism for executing warrants and both relied on the voluntary co-operation of member states and the political and military will of the West to enforce indictments and bring those accused before the Tribunal for prosecution.[5]

The need for a permanent court

In this context, the wheels were set in motion for the creation of a permanent international institution to punish individuals indicted of gross violations of human rights, crimes against humanity and genocide. Trinidad and Tobago led the campaign for an ICC. Plagued by criminal problems related to international drug trafficking, they requested that the UN reconvene the International Law Commission. The proposed institution would not only have a deterrent effect on potential violators of the humanitarian code of conduct but would also have such broad-ranging, and permanent, jurisdictional powers that it could prosecute and punish criminals without the consent of states.

An optimistic argument would suggest that the proposal for an ICC represents a significant shift in the politics of international justice and indicates a growing, broad-based desire to individualise responsibility for crimes committed against some basic laws and principles of the international system. The rules and laws forbidding genocide, war crimes and crimes against humanity have long been agreed. The most important and relevant are the 1948 Universal Declaration of Human Rights; the 1907 Fourth Hague Convention, pertaining to the law of warfare; the 1948 Convention on the Prevention and Punishment of the Crime of Genocide; the 1949 Geneva Conventions and the two supplementary Protocols

---

[4] The legal terms for these restrictions on territory, individuals and time are 'ratione loci, rationae personae and ratione temporis'.
[5] The most useful material on the ICTY and the ICTR is Goldstone, 1996; Hampson, 1993; ICTY, 1996; Klinghoffer, 1998; Meron, 1997; Meron, 1998.

of 1977 pertaining to protection of any person affected by armed conflict; and the 1984 Convention against Torture and other Cruel, Inhuman or degrading Treatment or Punishment. What has been lacking up to now is a mechanism of enforcement and prosecution.

The major lacuna in international law has been well illustrated by the case of General Pinochet, the former Chilean president who was arrested in London in October 1998 based on a warrant issued by a Spanish court alleging that Pinochet was responsible for the murder of Spanish citizens while serving as president of his country. A second Spanish warrant after his arrest broadened the accusation to include systematic acts of illegal detention, murder, torture and disappearance of people. The initial decision of the British High Court stipulated that on the first charge neither the United Kingdom nor Spain had jurisdiction over crimes committed in Chile and hence extradition was not warranted in this instance. The second charge, which was simply put as a charge of 'crimes against humanity', fell under the aegis of customary international law and thus complicated matters for the English Court. The High Court further decided, however, that as a former head of state, Pinochet was protected by traditional sovereign immunity and that meant that he could not be prosecuted for criminal or civilian legal violations in foreign courts. The House of Lords later overturned the second decision, making General Pinochet liable either to stand trial in the United Kingdom, or be extradited to stand trial in Spain, on the basis of violations of international humanitarian law. This was a significant shift in the direction of endorsing the concept of holding individuals of all rank and status responsible for their criminal actions and violations of agreed conventions and treaties in international law.

It was hoped that the creation of the ICC would render the complicated and highly politicised Pinochet example redundant by transferring authority for the prosecution of such cases to an international tribunal; the ICC could confront suspected individual criminals head on. In the words of the UN Secretary-General, '[The ICC] promises at last, to supply what for so long been the missing link in the international legal system, a permanent court to judge the crimes of gravest concern to the international community as a whole – genocide, crimes against humanity, and war crimes' (cited in The Coalition for an International Criminal Court, Press Overview, 1998).

On 15 June 1998, 160 states convened to negotiate a statute and 'Final Act' for the proposed ICC. The UN had conducted the preparatory work for this set of negotiations between 1995 and 1998, using as a starting point the work carried out by the International Law Commission (ILC), in the late 1940s. The UN had tasked the ILC soon after the end of the Second World War to codify the principles and procedures of Nuremberg and Tokyo, as a precursor to creating an ICC, in the form of a 'Criminal Chamber of the International Court of Justice'. Between 1951 and 1957, the ILC and an adjunct Special Committee convened by the UN General Assembly to draft a statute for an ICC, drew up and tabled a number of draft texts which the Assembly rejected. While justifications were found for rejecting the drafts (for example, the lack of a clear definition of the crime of aggression), the work of the ILC and the Special Committee was stymied by the onset of the Cold War and their findings remained moribund until after 1989 (Beigbeder, 1999: 187–8).

The Rome negotiations

After almost five weeks of sometimes rancorous negotiation in Rome, the vast majority of the participating states voted to accept the statute and Final Act.[6] During the five-week period, the delegates raised 1,400 points of disagreement over the text, many of them trivial but some reflecting the reluctance of many parties to take the vast leap over the state-centred custom of public international law.

The statute consists of 128 articles in 13 parts, commencing with the establishment of the Court, its seat and relationship with other international bodies such as the UN, through to the jurisdiction of the court, the penalties it can impose and the process of enforcement.[7] As we will see, the question of jurisdiction was the most contentious part of the statute, since it brings into question the traditional power of the state, as against the principle of individual criminal responsibility.

The first contentious issue concerned definitions of the crimes over which the Court would have jurisdiction. Of the frequently mentioned troika of crimes, genocide, war crimes and crimes against humanity, there was a great deal of disagreement about the third. The first two were dealt with more easily as they had been previously specified and defined in the Geneva Conventions. Nevertheless, the negotiators went to great lengths to ensure that there was no ambiguity or possibility of multiple interpretations of genocide and war crimes. Genocide, under Article Six of the statute, is defined as a series of acts, 'with intent to destroy, in whole or in part, a national, ethnical, racial or religious group'. The acts include

---

[6] The vote was 120 in favour, 7 against and 21 abstentions. As the vote remains unrecorded, there is no public evidence of which states voted against the statute. They have been variously reported to include the USA, China, Israel, India, Bahrain, Qatar, Vietnam, Iraq, Libya, Yemen, Sri Lanka, Turkey and the Philippines. The USA, China, India and Israel appear most consistently as states that voted against it.

[7] For the most concise and precise account of the 13 Parts of the statute, see the summary produced by the Coalition for an International Criminal Court, 1998.

not only injury and death but also, 'mental harm', 'measures intended to prevent births within the group; and forcibly transferring children of the group to another group' (United Nations Diplomatic Conference of Plenipotentiaries on the Establishment of an International Criminal Court, Article 6). The definition of War Crimes, under Article Eight, refers to the relevant provisions of the Geneva Conventions dealing with illegal acts against 'persons and property', which have been generally accepted as the ethical code of conduct in time of war.

The definition of crimes against humanity was more problematic in that the negotiating parties found it difficult to delimit the range of crimes that could fall under this category. Following heated debate, a lengthy list of crimes was compiled to cover a series of prohibited acts 'as part of a widespread or systematic attack' on a civilian population. In one characteristic example which set the tone for the discussion, the Arab League states, led by Syria, argued that these crimes should only apply at times of inter-state conflict and should not include conflicts internal to states. This brought them into direct opposition with the negotiators from more 'liberally minded' states such as Germany and Canada, who wished to cast the net of this clause as widely as possible. The list of prohibited acts included traditionally forbidden acts such as torture, murder, extermination and forced enslavement. But Article Seven also incorporated a series of crimes that reflected concerns with specific acts that had occurred since 1945. They include apartheid (with the South African experience in mind); 'forcible transfer of population' or ethnic cleansing; rape and forced pregnancy (a reference to actions in the Yugoslav wars and Bosnia in particular); enforced disappearance of persons (reflecting the experience in certain Latin American states); and clauses relating to gender persecution (which caused discomfort among many Islamic states), and enforced sterilisation (which China did not like).

The objections raised during the debate about definitions reflected the controversy surrounding the attempt to proceed to the creation of an all-powerful ICC. Several particular examples illustrate the inherent complications involved in attempting to define and universalise crimes in the face of objections from specific states on specific issues. One example stems from including in the definition of a war crime 'the transfer, directly or indirectly, by the Occupying Power of parts of its own civilian population into the territory it occupies' (Article 8). This led to heated opposition from the Israeli delegates, who saw it as a direct attack on Israel's policy of settling the West Bank. The Israelis accused the Egyptians, among other Arab states, of having wilfully forced the acceptance of this provision knowing that Israel could not accept it. Despite many attempts to mediate a formulation of this clause acceptable to all parties, no compromise agreement could be reached. Although the voting record was not made public, it is generally agreed that Israel was one of the seven states that voted against the final draft of the Treaty. It is paradoxical that Israel had been a long-term supporter of the creation of an ICC in principle, yet in practice had to reject it due to one unpalatable clause.

Another example is the Indian proposal to define the use of nuclear weapons as a war crime. India presented this as an ethical and humanitarian attempt to rid the international system of a category of weapons that has always been the subject of moral debate. Nevertheless, the enduring tension between India and Pakistan over disputed territories, which has led to a spiralling conventional and nuclear arms race, was always understood to be the prime motivation behind the Indian proposal. Not surprisingly, it met with opposition from nuclear powers such as the United States, and its NATO allies. While for the United States this was simply another of the many US objections to the treaty, for NATO, and especially for the nuclear states, France and the United Kingdom, it presented a dilemma. Either they supported the United States in fighting the clause, thus safeguarding their own nuclear arsenals – a vital element in their military strategies – and the coherence of the NATO alliance, or they supported its inclusion in the hope of pacifying a wide variety of other states whose assistance they needed to create a strong ICC.

After much wrangling, and in the matchless fashion of international diplomacy, a compromise was agreed that resulted in blurring the issue. Under the definition of war crimes, a clause was inserted which forbids the use of 'weapons, projectiles and material and methods of warfare which are of a nature to cause superfluous injury or unnecessary suffering or which are inherently indiscriminate'. While this definition includes nuclear weapons, the draft included the proviso that the clause would only come into effect once the use of nuclear weapons had already been comprehensively banned by international treaty. Such a treaty does not yet exist. While this pays lip-service to the view that the use of nuclear weapons should be classified as a war crime along with other weapons of mass destruction such as chemical and biological weapons, and it leaves the door open for future amendment of the statute to include nuclear weapons, the nuclear powers were more than satisfied with the fudge. India's more direct proposal was thus eliminated from the draft treaty and the final statute.

In the negotiations over the definitions of war crimes and crimes against humanity, a significant area of discussion related to the threshold at which the jurisdiction of the ICC would become operational. In principle, the ICC would be able to indict and try individuals irrespective of their rank in their particular military or paramilitary formation or unit. The lowliest of footsoldiers or the grandest of generals could be held responsible for committing crimes defined under the statute. In practice, many states found it problematic that the envisaged vast machinery of the ICC would kick in even if one soldier, acting alone, committed something defined as a war crime or a crime against humanity. These states, led by the US and including all those with a large military presence on foreign soil primarily in a peacekeeping capacity, feared that the Court would become a forum for the politically motivated prosecution of soldiers involved in duties beyond their borders. Individuals would become targets not only because they might have committed crimes but also, and, perhaps especially, because they happened to be nationals of a particular state. To overcome this objection, the negotiating parties had to search for a suitable level of condemnable activity at which individuals or small groups would no longer fall under the jurisdiction of their own legal machinery, whether national or military, but would instead be answerable to the ICC.

In the case of war crimes, it was agreed that the ICC would have jurisdiction only if the crimes committed by an individual or group formed 'part of a plan or policy', 'or as part of a large-scale commission of such crimes'. Indeed, the crimes would have to be defined at a level of 'seriousness' to warrant ICC intervention. This implied that the superiors of the offending individuals or groups would also be held accountable for having ordered these condemnable acts. An opt-out clause was negotiated with great difficulty, after much prompting from the French delegation. It partly covered the concerns of those states that maintain large military units abroad, whether as peacekeepers or in more traditional defensive roles such as US troops stationed in Germany. It allowed a moratorium on the war crime provision of the treaty if the acceding party so wished.[8]

Alleged 'crimes against humanity' would have to be deemed 'widespread or systematic'. This formulation was reached after lengthy deliberation as to whether the wording should be 'widespread *or* systematic' or 'widespread *and* systematic'. The former was finally deemed sufficient in that 'systematic' made clear that there existed a pattern to the crime and 'widespread' covered the level of criminal activity, each constituting enough of a threshold to invite the ICC's attention. This also covered the case of mass murders which many states felt could be challenged by the Court as falling under its authority, thus limiting sovereignty by bypassing domestic legal and criminal systems.

With respect to the general application of the trio of 'core crimes', two further controversies arose. It was agreed that in the cases of genocide and

---

[8] Although this concession sufficed for France to put its signature to the statute, it did not persuade the United States of the merits of the text on this particular point.

crimes against humanity, the provisions of the statute would be applicable in times of both war and peace. Accepted as a norm prior to the negotiations, this caused much consternation as it challenged the principles of the right of domestic jurisdiction and non-intervention in the internal affairs of sovereign independent states. While it showed a desire to establish a judicial body with widespread powers beyond those already existing in the international domain, it provoked misgivings as to the rights the negotiating parties were handing over to an institution over which they would have little control and could not effectively block. Their trepidation was reinforced by another controversy involving the applicability of the provisions on the core crimes to internal conflicts as well as to international conflicts, which have constituted the more traditional domain of international law and, more importantly, the UN Security Council.

An unresolved controversy revolved around the desire of a number of states – and of the non-governmental organisations (NGOs) which were represented at the Rome Conference – to include a fourth category of crime, that of aggression. It proved impossible to reach agreement on a definition of the crime of aggression. Many states, with the US at the forefront, complained that if the proposed Court were to have sole right in determining what constitutes an act of aggression, this would contravene the authority of the UN Security Council. Under Chapter Seven of the UN Charter, the Security Council has singular rights and competence in determining acts of aggression. Furthermore, General Assembly Resolution 3314 clearly stipulates and defines aggression as an act of state(s), and all UN members are bound both by the decisions of the Security Council and this Resolution. Nevertheless, many UN members insisted that this particular interpretation was too narrow and would inevitably and preemptively disarm an effective and independent ICC. Those arguing against the exclusive rights of the UN in this area cited the precedent set by the Nuremberg and Tokyo Tribunals in the area of individual responsibility. If the international community wished to create a viable court with powers to indict, prosecute and ultimately enforce penalties on those accused of the defined crimes, then it should be an institution devoid of the usual balances of power struck by states in existing international organisations. It should be an independent organ removed as far as possible from the state-bound limitations of existing treaties and agreements. Nevertheless, lurking beneath the surface of this seemingly well-intentioned position was a traditional piece of power politics. India, for example, argued vociferously against the predominance of the United Nations, and especially the Security Council, in determining what constituted a crime of aggression. There can be no doubt that India, like many other negotiating parties, perceived the independence and strong jurisdictional powers of the Court as a *sine qua non* of its effective functioning. Yet paradoxically, like the US, India was in fact championing its own state rights – and grievances – by attacking the pre-eminent position of the UN Security Council. Snubbed by the 'Great Powers' for many years, India has had well-vented and documented ambitions to join the fraternity of the Permanent Five. Always rebuffed, India used the proposals regarding the ICC's jurisdiction to challenge the power of the Security Council and its permanent members.

The major paradox in this instance is that states such as the United States and India took diametrically opposed positions to protect and further their own national interests from possible erosion by a more independent 'global institution'. This was a traditional clash of state interests. What was supposed to be a major departure from the traditional conduct of international relations was coloured by that very same method of conducting international affairs. The definition of what constitutes aggression remains the sole prerogative of the Security Council.

Sovereignty and international law

Beneath the issue of complementarity with the United Nations – and especially the Security Council – is possibly the most important principle of international relations at stake in the negotiations over the foundation of the ICC. Implicit in the debates on ensuring complementarity with the UN, which, after all, is an international organisation comprising member *states*, is the contentious problem of the relationship between international law, whether customary or criminal, and national jurisdiction. That is, the major question underpinning all the debates was whether the negotiating parties were willing to cede sovereign rights and allow powers to the new Court which would go beyond the existing provisions of public international law. As indicated in the debate over including the crime of aggression within the ICC's remit, complementarity was the key problem in considering the relationship between the ICC and national courts.

The US was at the vanguard of a group of states which insisted that the conference would have to concede the preeminence of domestic or national courts, and hence the precedence of domestic jurisdiction over that of international law and ICC jurisdiction. In other words, domestic judicial systems will have the first responsibility for prosecuting those suspected of war crimes within their jurisdiction; the ICC 'will act only when national courts are unable or unwilling to exercise jurisdiction'. The US argued strongly that if the primacy of national courts was not maintained, it would be unrealistic to expect states to sign the treaty, because they would be loathe to cede so many sovereign rights to the ICC. The treaty would ultimately raise serious constitutional issues that would have a detrimental effect on the process of ratification by national legislatures even if governments signed it. Complementarity between the ICC and national criminal jurisdiction would, therefore, have to be maintained. This is what ultimately emerged from the negotiations in Rome. The ICC can only take unilateral action in investigating or prosecuting crimes when the domestic judicial system of a state has failed to do so, or when it is requested to do so by the UN Security Council. If domestic courts are investigating or prosecuting a suspected crime, the ICC has no authority unless the Security Council steps in and, under Chapter Seven of the Charter, authorises the ICC to pursue the case. In this case no state can prevent the ICC from proceeding, whether or not they have ratified the statute, as Chapter Seven decisions by the Security Council are binding and legally enforceable in all states. As the ICC is acting under the authority of the Security Council in the maintenance of international peace and security, neither the nationality of the accused nor the territory of the state upon which the crime was said to have been committed is relevant.

Thus the principle of complementarity between the ICC, domestic legal – and hence state sovereign – jurisdiction and the UN, ran through the draft statute in a triangulated fashion. In name, the ICC is to have jurisdiction over a whole raft of defined crimes, 'when either the State in whose territory the crime was committed, or the State of the nationality of the accused is party to the Statute'. In practice, however, through the tireless opposition of the US and other states – primarily the Permanent Five of the Security Council, India and some Arab countries – the inclusion of provisions which asserted the sovereign rights of states and the preeminent authority of the UN Security Council severely undermined the powers of the ICC. Thus what is proposed is a much-circumscribed Court that will only be able to act if invited to do so by states or the Security Council.

Another major sticking point in the negotiations was the role and powers of the independent prosecutor. It was clear that if the Court was to have autonomous powers beyond the control of traditional state interests or the interests of international organisations, the Prosecutor should have the right to instigate investigations irrespective of whether invited to do so by a state(s) or the Security Council. These powers, as we have seen, were severely limited by the triangular notion of complementarity outlined above. Yet a large group of about sixty states argued in favour of a prosecutor with wide-ranging powers. Having lost the argument on the basic principles, a rearguard action was fought to ensure that the prosecutor still retained residual rights to trigger the investigative procedure independently. At stake here was not only the real and symbolic right of the Court to act independently of state interests, but also the Court's ability to take action based on information provided by victims of crimes and/or by NGOs.

The independent rights of the prosecutor were set out in Article 15, and they started from the premise that s/he would always defer to States conducting their own domestic investigations. In a placatory gesture, the prosecutor was given the power to initiate investigations without referral from either the Security Council or a particular state. Nonetheless, this independent power was bound by a series of restrictive conditions including, at the outset, the submission of all evidence pertaining to the case to a three-person 'Pre-Trial Chamber' consisting of independent judges. They would have the right to decide whether or not the case merited prosecution, and would have to take into account the testimony of the states/suspects who could challenge the jurisdiction of the Court at this stage. The impartiality of the case and the 'seriousness' of the suspected crimes would be examined according to the criteria set out in the definitions of the 'core crimes' and the jurisdiction of the Court. While these safeguards seem logical and fair in the context of allowing the prosecutor leeway to conduct investigations without being bound by state or Security Council consent, when taken in conjunction with the principle of complementarity, it is clear that the ability of the prosecutor to act alone is extremely narrow.

Even if the Court was to proceed with an investigation instigated independently by the prosecutor, and which had been cleared as admissible by the 'Pre-Trial Chamber', the Security Council would still have the right to terminate the investigation. Initially, the draft text stipulated that the Court could not undertake any investigation that was being considered by the Security Council unless the Council explicitly allowed it to do so. In the final text this was amended to place the burden on the Council by making it clear that the Court could take action unless explicitly forbidden to do so by the Council. This compromise was intended to forestall the possibility of the Court interfering with the Security Council's attempts to maintain international peace and security. The case of the Dayton Accords on Bosnia springs to mind here. The Serb leader, Slobodan Milosević, was a vital participant in the Dayton negotiations and only he could deliver a deal. If an independent Court had indicted him during or prior to the talks, the negotiations would not have taken place and the work of the Security Council would have been derailed by the activity of the prosecutor and the Court. However, the compromise leaves the Security Council, and especially the Permanent Five, with an effective veto, which allows them to have a case deferred for a renewable 12-month period.

In other words, the outcome was yet another set of elaborate checks and balances between the independence of the prosecutor, the Security Council and the rights of party States. The compromise guarantees the right of the prosecutor to conduct investigations as long as they do not interfere with the Security Council's agenda, and it gives the Security Council and party States the right both to question and to stall the activity of the prosecutor and the Court. If the intention was to make the Court an innovative departure in international law and international relations by giving it powers beyond the traditional state-bound rules of the international system and the ICJ, then this compromise put paid to yet another element of that intention.

The dissent and dispute that characterised the debate about jurisdiction affected all areas of negotiation. Discussion about the penalties that the Court can impose was stalled as it was impossible to deal with different types and levels of sentencing until the question of the death penalty had been addressed. While a decision on the death penalty was deferred until the end of the negotiating period, it clouded all other exchanges, since a majority of states specified that they would be unable to sign the statute if the final text gave the Court the right to impose the death penalty. Opposing them, a number of Islamic states insisted that the death penalty should be an option since it is an intrinsic part of their domestic legal systems and of their cultural heritage. They were joined in their opposition by diverse countries such as the US and Trinidad and Tobago. The final compromise reflected the principle of complementarity underpinning the entire negotiations. The clause on the death penalty was struck from the statute, but the text makes it clear that the penalties that the Court can impose are not prejudicial to the types of national penalties that can be imposed under the domestic judicial systems of State parties (United Nations Diplomatic Conference of Plenipotentiaries on the Establishment of an International Criminal Court, Article 80). This ensured that even though the Court cannot pass the death sentence as this would contravene the will of the majority of member states, this does not mean that there is a widespread international consensus in favour of the general abolition of the death penalty. Nor can any state's domestic arrangements be judged or hampered by the provisions of the statute. The protection of national sovereign rights left its mark yet again on proceedings.

In any event, the Court can impose penalties that range from fines, a specific length of imprisonment, to life sentence. An attempt was made to limit the maximum sentence to 30 years' imprisonment, as many states were opposed to the principle of handing down life sentences. In the end, a compromise was reached which gives the Court the right to hand down a life sentence if the crime is deemed grave enough, but includes a clause stipulating a regular review procedure and the right to claim parole irrespective of where the sentence is served. In terms of enforcing the punishment, the statute indicates that sentences will be served in 'a State designated by the Court from a list of States which have indicated their willingness to accept sentenced persons' (Article 103). Alternatively, the sentence will be served at the designated seat of the Court in The Hague.

The issue of financing the Court proved no less contentious than other matters. Moreover, it was debated in the context of the financial crisis in which the UN finds itself after many years in which major contributors such as the United States have withheld their contributions. Here the clash was between those advocating mandatory state contributions, those arguing in favour of voluntary state contributions, those promoting the United Nations as the main source of funding, or a combination of all these options. The last position prevailed, since it was a compromise in the spirit of complementarity. Sources of funding will include the 'assessed' contributions of party States, the United Nations and voluntary contributions from other sources including individuals, corporations and NGOs. In the case of the UN funds, there was a debate about whether the Security Council would be responsible for ensuring payment to the Court on the basis of each case referral or a fixed recurrent sum. Ultimately the statute left it up to the UN General Assembly to decide what form UN contributions will take based on the agreement that the UN will be a major contributor.

Conclusion

The issue of jurisdiction underlies all the legal and political compromises forged in the attempt to launch the ICC. The outcome of the Rome conference was a statute that still contained many loose ends so that follow-up sessions were planned to deal with them. The principle of complementarity, which informed much of the debate in Rome and became the cornerstone of the final agreement, sacrificed the power and independence of action of the ICC at the altar of preserving state sovereignty. The statute of the Court can be characterised as emblematic of a habitual clash in international relations between state-centrism and universalism, with internationalism stuck in the middle. State-centrism was reflected in the intransigent positions held by a number of countries with respect to the handing over of sovereign rights to the proposed Court. Universalism was expressed by those states that saw in the Court the prospect of creating a new institution with powers beyond those usually found in international organisations, which could both act as a deterrent and punish those indicted of crimes against humanity without having to consider state interests. Internationalist positions were taken by those who certainly wished to see progress in the process of the universal protection of human rights and, more generally, the protection of an agreed humanitarian code of conduct, but who realised that it would not be possible or even practical to circumvent the long-standing rights and activities of either states or international organisations, such as the UN and its affiliates.

State consent, and where relevant, the consent of international organisations, has always been the hallmark of customary international law, especially as manifested in the principles and workings of the ICJ. Proposals for an ICC which could function effectively without the imprimatur of state consent were constantly rejected by those who were unwilling to cede state sovereignty to a body beyond their control. Once a state has ratified or acceded to the statute of the ICC, it has accepted the Court's jurisdiction. No further state consent is required by the independent prosecutor in bringing an indictment before the Court (irrespective of how circumscribed those powers are). This proved to be the simplest and most persistent sticking point, as it highlighted the fundamental tension between state sovereignty and the independence of the ICC. Despite the many concessions made to dissenting parties and the compromises built into the Treaty, the basic principle of state sovereignty and state consent proved sufficient for states not to sign, or not to ratify, the statute, thus temporarily consigning the ICC to the waiting list of international initiatives.[9]

The ICC certainly represents a trend towards holding individuals responsible for crimes committed against the international humanitarian code of conduct. The main question which remains unanswered, however, is whether it will prove a strong enough judicial organ, with enough backing from the international system of states, to allow it to name, indict and prosecute those suspected of humanitarian crimes on a systematic and comprehensive basis. Inevitably, as individual cases are brought in front of Tribunals such as the ICTY and ICTR, and high-ranking individuals such as Pinochet are subject to indictment under international humanitarian law, there will be an increase in the body and codification of an international criminal law, which will enhance the workings of the ICC.

[9] A further attempted compromise suggested giving states that disagreed with the scope of the Court's jurisdiction a 10-year period of grace during which they would be exempt from this jurisdiction. Even this was insufficient to satisfy dissenters like the United States, France, China and Russia. Here a bit of politics was played in that one of the reasons why this initiative failed was because of a break in the coherence of the five permanent members of the Security Council (P5); the United Kingdom, the remaining P5 member opposed the proposed amendment, breaking ranks and hence solidarity, and giving enough impetus to other states to push through a majority view rejecting the amendment.

But to ensure that the ICC can function as a strong, quasi-independent court, states would have to accept its authority in all instances, rather than accept it on an *ad hoc* basis which simply serves to undermine the principle of universality of international humanitarian law. A court in name but not in practice is a very apt characterisation of the current status of the ICC.

Thus, at a time when the ethical dimension of foreign policy is supposedly gaining in strength, and when humanitarian and moral concerns occupy a higher slot on the international agenda, the inability to gain consensus on the remit and powers of the ICC shows the inherent problems of dealing with state sovereignty and divesting states of their traditional rights. While those in power may preach universalism with respect to the protection of certain core values internationally, in reality the application of their beliefs remains rather selective, if not discriminatory. The assertion made by the British Secretary of State for Foreign Affairs that political values cannot be left at home, but must be exported, is laudable. Nonetheless, the discussions on the creation of the ICC and a series of other events in the 1990s demonstrate that, while in principle there may be a desire to 'export' human rights and humanitarian concerns, in practice an ethical foreign policy may be intended primarily for domestic political consumption. Thus, rather than domestic political values being 'exported' in the form of an ethical foreign policy, instead the symbolism of an ethical foreign policy is being imported to bolster the popularity of governments within specific – and especially Western – states.

Foreign policy agendas will continue to be affected by ethical and moral dilemmas, especially when a vocal public opinion demands action against those acting unethically and/or immorally. What is in question is the willingness and ability of states to be consistent in pursuing an 'ethical dimension' to their foreign policies and formulating a position where the 'national interest' is always best served through pursuing an ethical policy. If consistency and universality are not at the root of an 'ethical dimension' to foreign policy, the policy will remain selective and discriminatory in its attempts to serve a narrower interpretation of the national interest.

Ultimately, the creation of the ICC hangs in the balance, and its fate will be decided by states. By May 2001, almost 34 months after the adoption of the statute by majority vote, 140 had signed it, while only 30 countries had ratified the treaty. The statute will only come into force 60 days after the sixtieth ratification, and even then many states will reject its jurisdiction and authority.

Constructing an ethical foreign policy:
      analysis and practice from below

K. M. Fierke

Critical theorists, among others, have argued that theorists and scholars of
international relations do not write in a vacuum, rather they are embedded
in a historical context which shapes their reflection and analysis of the
world (Cox, 1986). The historical canon of international relations, from
Thucydides to Machiavelli to Hobbes – most often drawn on in sound-
bite form to support realist themes – emerged from thinkers who had in
some way participated in, and later reflected on, the dramatic changes
occurring around them. This chapter is a much more modest effort to
reflect self-consciously on the relationship between theory and practice,
and how this gives rise to certain conclusions about an ethical foreign
policy. It grew out of an invitation to discuss an ethical foreign policy from
the perspective of my pre-academic experience in the peace movement
and my subsequent research. The chapter begins with a brief biographical
sketch of my experience. This is followed by elaboration on four points
that link this experience to the question of an ethical foreign policy.

Background

In the 1980s, I worked at four different levels of political organisation
relating to nuclear disarmament: as organiser of a city-wide campaign, as
strategist for a campaign in the state of Minnesota, as one of the first three
staff in the national office of the US Nuclear Weapons Freeze Campaign,
and then as editor of an international networking publication based in
the Netherlands. After six years of travel and work, I returned to grad-
uate school to gain a deeper understanding of what I had witnessed.
The Intermediate-range Nuclear Forces agreement had been concluded

Karen Smith invited me to participate in the LSE Cumberland Lodge conference on Ethical
Foreign Policy in November 1998. The offer was intriguing – I had never before been asked
to reflect on my practical involvement; but it was also challenging since it required blending
personal with theoretical experience in a way that I have rarely done and is uncommon
in academic fora. There is, however, an unquestionable link between my pre-academic
experience and my approach to scholarly analysis.

(in late 1987) and, as I was preparing for my Ph.D. preliminary exams, the Berlin Wall was crumbling. The changes were in full swing as the dissertation prospectus was being written. The outcome is a book, titled *Changing Games, Changing Strategies: Critical Investigations in Security* (Fierke, 1998), which provides a framework for thinking about changing East–West security relations over the last twenty years, from the Helsinki Final Act to the NATO–Russia Founding Act. Although the term 'ethical foreign policy' is never used, the role of moral discourse in international relations is one theme of the book.

The following analysis is organised around four points relating to critique, language, dialogue, and analysis. They represent reflections, based on my earlier experience as an activist, as well as my later work as a scholar, on the possibilities for an ethical foreign policy.

A critical mirror

The first point is that an ethical foreign policy requires the existence of individuals and groups who will hold up a critical mirror to the government regarding its own practice. The claim that such a mirror is necessary relies in part on an acceptance of the realist argument that the moral discourse of states potentially disguises other interests. However, rather than offering an excuse to discount the role of moral discourse, as realists tend to do, the argument provides a point of departure for examining the relationship between moral justification and action. The critical recognition of this relationship opens up the possibility of pressuring leaders to act in accordance with their moral claims.

Nicholas Wheeler and Tim Dunne (1998) have argued that Labour's ethical foreign policy represents a significant departure from the foreign policy of past governments; that is, no government over the last fifty years had presented an ethical framework for judging policy. Having read hundreds of foreign policy texts from the last twenty years, however, I would make the contrary argument: leaders often claim to have an ethical foreign policy; that is, they justify their policy in moral terms. In this respect, the Labour government's policy is only a departure from the past in so far as it explicitly asked to be judged in terms of an ethical framework.[1] In other words, what was implicit in the justifications of state leaders in the past, has been made explicit.

One obvious example in the context of the Cold War was the justification of nuclear deterrence. Particularly in debates with the peace

---

[1] According to Wheeler and Dunne (1998: 847) 'In the preceding fifty years, there had been no public articulation of a conceptual framework for understanding the means and ends of foreign policy.'

movements, government officials relied heavily on moral arguments about deterrence: deterrence was just because it had blessed Europe with an unprecedented period of peace (see, for example, Hofmann, 1984). Human rights were also an important point of departure, if inconsistently, for conservative governments in particular.[2] In discussions of the interpretation of the Helsinki Final Act, Western governments repeatedly focused on the implementation of the human rights accord (NATO 1975–80), in contrast to the Soviet emphasis on disarmament. Lord Carrington (1983), for instance, referred to the moral obligation and responsibility of Western governments towards those activists in the Eastern bloc who were pressuring Eastern governments to uphold the human rights promise of Helsinki.

The claim made by Wheeler and Dunne raises a question about the difference between Labour's ethical foreign policy and the moral discourse of states which is an everyday feature of foreign policy. By placing Labour's ethical foreign policy in a longer tradition of moral justification, I do not intend to question the sincerity of the Labour government, or ask whether this policy is qualitatively different from past policies. Many people, including the authors, have pointed out the inconsistencies between this commitment and actual practice. Instead, my purpose is to turn the realist argument about moral discourse on its head. Realists have argued that the moral discourse of states is a disguise for other interests. E. H. Carr (1964) pointed to the role of the British Harmony of Interests in convincing others, including the victims of British imperialism, that their interests were the same as the Pax Britannica. Some realists, not least Kissinger (1977), have recognised that moral discourse plays an instrumental role in constituting the power of the state to act.

What is implied, but less often directly asked – John Vincent (1991: 121–2) is a notable exception – is why do states bother to justify their policy if it is based on pure interests? They bother because their power to act is dependent on the support of their citizens, who provide the resources and soldiers to project power and who must be convinced of the legitimacy of doing so. As Hannah Arendt (1986) has pointed out, power should not be equated with the capacity to use violence. Power necessarily depends on numbers and on legitimacy. Power and violence are actually opposites, and the use of the latter without popular support is a sign of the absence of power.

---

[2] Accusations regarding human rights were, of course, selective and focused primarily on those states with political ties or sympathies with the Soviet Union. As Donnelly (1994: 241) points out, the Cold War also provided a framework for justifying support for regimes which abused human rights, as evidenced in US support for Haiti, South Korea, the Shah in Iran, Pinochet in Chile and Mobutu in Zaire.

If one assumes that the power to act is fundamentally dependent on providing ethical justifications, then exposing a discrepancy between promise or justification and practice can provide an important incentive for states to align their practices with their words. In this respect, whatever the motives of the Labour government, its explicit articulation of an ethical foreign policy provides an opportunity for critics to hold it accountable for its promises.

Changing Games, Changing Strategies analyses the relationship between challenges to state policy in both East and West relating to human rights and disarmament, and changes in practice. My conclusion was more nuanced than the idea that states, confronted with a discrepancy between language and practice, realign the latter with the former. Instead, I found – counterintuitively perhaps – that changes in practice by states corresponded with changes in language, as they selectively adopted the language games of their challengers to their own purposes. For instance, the shift made by President Reagan and President Gorbachev towards arguments that undermined the logic of nuclear deterrence corresponded with moves toward disarmament by both, and with President Reagan's decision to develop the Strategic Defence Initiative (SDI). In so far as one of the outcomes of the cruise missile debates was the politicisation of foreign policy (Villas-Boas, 1984), one might understand the emergence of an explicit ethical foreign policy by Labour against this background. The relationship between changing discourse and practice brings me to my second point.

Language and context

The claim that language and context are important is less controversial than it was ten years ago. After Gorbachev's New Thinking and the victory of liberal ideals, more scholars are ready to concede the role of meaning, norms and interpretation (Onuf, 1989; Kratochwil, 1989; Wendt, 1992; Katzenstein, 1996; Adler, 1997), if not language itself, which is reflected in the movement of constructivism from the margins to the centre of debates within the discipline.[3]

Building on the work of the later Wittgenstein (1958), I approach language as explicitly intersubjective, and language use as a form of action that is constitutive of the political world. Wittgenstein draws on the game metaphor to illustrate that language use is necessarily based on shared

---

[3] Conventional constructivists such as Wendt have been criticised for failing to take language seriously (Zehfuss, 2001). The introduction by Katzenstein, Keohane and Krasner to the 50th Anniversary issue of *International Organization*, 1998, claims that the debate between rationalists and constructivists has moved to centre stage, replacing earlier debates between realists and liberals.

rules, much as two players must share the rules of chess to engage in play. *Changing Games, Changing Strategies* elaborates on his concept of a language game, demonstrating how speech acts and other types of practice within the context of the Cold War were given meaning within a context of shared rules. The point is that there is a tendency to become caught up in the language games of one's context and, once caught up, the range of conceivable possibilities is constrained by the boundaries of a dominant game. My concern is less about truth or falsehood, than about how the boundaries of truth and falsehood come to be defined within particular contexts, and how this shapes the parameters of thinkable and justifiable action. Adam Michnik (1981: 70–1) made the point in relation to the context of Eastern European communism:

What do I mean when I say that the Poles allowed themselves to have a language imposed upon them after 1945? One example is the attitude toward the German question. The role of Stalin in the annexation of territories and in the victory over the Germans was only mentioned positively. To do so was to accept a language that was compromised. One was free to say many things of Stalin – whether it was true or false was irrelevant – as long as the rhetoric was positive. To be sure, those who played this game (journalists, for example) understood full well that it was a game with rules. Their readers, however, were not always so well informed. Due to the long habit of covering Stalin's real face with a mask, the mask seemed more real than reality.

Michnik's point is that these language games did not necessarily involve lies, although they might; rather, playing the game involved knowing the rules and what could and could not be said in relation to any particular subject.

While Stalin is the extreme example, the same was arguably true in a general sense within the Cold War, both East and West, as it is in any intractable conflict. In the context of the Cold War, within the United States – and Western Europe as well, I suspect – one knew what could and could not be said if one wanted to avoid being labelled a communist sympathiser. In most cases, this was probably less conscious than part of operating within the language and assumptions available to actors embedded in that historical context. During the Cold War, everything – from internal dissidence to wars in the Third World – was given meaning in terms of the conflict between East and West, and this defined the boundaries of our thinking. The result was a set of implicit rules, a language game, on the basis of which one could manoeuvre in all kinds of ways, but within clearly defined constraints.

The common tendency in politics is to make a distinction between language and action. When I began as an activist, I shared this assumption, and was always thinking about finding the most effective political action that would turn the situation around. Randall Kehler, who was the director of the Nuclear Weapons Freeze Campaign, once commented to me that speaking was an important form of action in itself. In a situation where everyone knows the boundaries of what can and cannot be said, crossing those boundaries, to speak the unspeakable, can be a very powerful act. Post-structuralists have argued that dominant discourses reproduce a particular worldview by silencing alternatives (Campbell, 1993, 1998). In this respect, speaking can be an important act that breaks the silence. This resembles Michnik's point that the imposed language of communism began to lose its force once workers made their voice heard.

Contra the post-structuralists, I would argue that the phenomenon of being constrained by our language is not simply due to efforts of the establishment to impose and reproduce a realist game. It is, first of all, a feature of language itself. To speak meaningfully, we necessarily speak in a language that will resonate in the experiences of those around us, and thus in a shared language. The dependence of language on shared rules is perhaps even more the case in a political environment where one is trying to communicate a message with meaning to a larger public.

In order to a make a critique, peace movements had to find a way to speak meaningfully in their context, just as state actors did. This became clear when I went to Germany in 1982 on a speaking tour as a representative of the American Nuclear Weapons Freeze Campaign; it was most apparent because I was confronted with a different peace movement culture, which approached the problem of nuclear weapons, the political analysis and the possible solution in a dramatically different way than in the United States. I remember sitting in a meeting with a group of representatives from the German peace movement, and feeling like an actor following a script. I knew how to respond in a whole range of different ways but there were clear boundaries of what I could say as a representative of the Freeze Campaign, boundaries that were not as evident when operating within the American context. In the United States, the discussion emphasised bilateral solutions and nuclear deterrence was assumed rather than challenged, as it was in the European context. The American discussion was also primarily focused on the military aspects of the nuclear arms race, and it largely ignored the political relationship between East and West. The first two points give rise to two conclusions about the requirements of an ethical foreign policy.

Dialogue

Given the tendency to become imprisoned in the assumptions of our context, it is imperative that an ethical foreign policy creates the space and conditions for real dialogue, which, as Andrew Linklater (1996: 286) said, involves a situation where we 'accept that there is no a priori certainty about who will learn from whom and a willingness to engage in a process of reciprocal critique'. By contrast, Labour's ethical foreign policy has often relied on a monologue reminiscent of the Cold War.

A particular language game has been used repeatedly in a range of different situations of intractable conflict, and has been heard with a disturbing frequency more recently from President Clinton, Prime Minister Blair and Foreign Minister Cook. In the Cold War, it was argued that the Soviet Union only understands the language of force. In the Middle East, South Africa and Northern Ireland, it was argued that terrorists only understand the language of force. In Iraq it was argued that Saddam Hussein only understands the language of force. And in Kosovo, it was argued that Slobodan Milosević only understands the language of force.

The assumption underpinning these statements is that one should avoid talking to terrorists, criminals, etc., either because one cannot believe anything they say, or because they do not deserve to be heard. In most cases, both sides to a conflict make similar claims about the necessity of a forceful response. While the dynamics of these various conflicts differ, I would argue that this mutual argumentation becomes a common game into which the participants become locked, and by which conflict is reproduced. This gives rise to two different questions: first, in a situation where the only common language is one of force, how does dialogue become possible; and second, why would mere talk be effective? The first question is important given the range of conflicts that have, if only temporarily, moved towards some kind of resolution since the end of the Cold War. But I want to start with a personal reflection regarding the question of effectiveness.

While working for the Freeze Campaign I was asked to head a task force to analyse the feasibility and desirability of a strategy of non-violent direct action or civil disobedience. The campaign had followed an explicitly political strategy of trying to influence elections and lobby representatives, but some were arguing the need for more. During the process, I analysed some of the more prominent examples of this type of movement, such as the US civil rights movement or Gandhi's Indian campaign, and asked what had made these examples of non-violent direct action particularly effective.

I concluded that it was not the civil disobedience *per se*, but rather the choice of actions that cut through the logic of the conflict by 'acting as if' the desired state of affairs already existed. If, in both cases, the victims lived in a context structured by a hierarchy of rules defining the place and possibilities of African-Americans or Indians, respectively, then they, the members of the movements, would act as if they lived in a world where they had the rights they desired. In the American south, African-Americans sat in the front of the bus, even though by law they had to sit in the back; they sat at lunch counters for whites only and entered schools for whites only. In India, the campaigners began to spin their own cloth instead of buying British, and they collected salt from the sea. In Poland, Solidarity used a similar strategy, which one commentator called 'being what you want to become' – if you want to have a trade union, organise a trade union, if you want to speak freely, speak freely (Weschler, 1982: 56).

The logic of the strategy is twofold.[4] First, by acting 'as if', you begin to construct a different world and, at the same time, defy the power of the old over you. Second, the authorities usually respond by overreacting, often using force in response to normal everyday acts like taking a seat in a bus or speaking freely. Their overreaction brings the implicit violence of the structure into the open, making it impossible to maintain the veneer of moral justification. According to Martin Luther King, the goal of non-violent direct action is to dramatise a situation in order to make a real dialogue possible (Washington, 1986).

The Cold War was a different kind of conflict in so far as it involved two relatively equal powers. Nonetheless, at the time, I asked myself what acting 'as if' would mean in this situation. People were climbing over fences to beat missiles into ploughshares, or chaining themselves to the fence at the Pentagon, but these actions did not seem to have quite the same power; they did not cut into the logic of the conflict, or expose the violence underlying the Cold War. In both cases the activists were likely to be accused of being pawns of the other side. What kind of action would disrupt a pattern of mutual recrimination and self-justification, and where would it come from if the participants were themselves unable to step out of their mutual game?

In Europe in 1984, I found that part of the peace movement had discovered such an action. European Nuclear Disarmament (END), from the early 1980s on, had set the goal of acting as if the Cold War was over, as if they were citizens of a United Europe, no longer divided into East and West. It is interesting, in light of the failure to predict the end of the Cold War, that in 1982 E. P. Thompson (1983) told a small group in Hungary that the new peace movements in East and West had set themselves the astonishing objective of breaking down the Cold War itself in the next ten years. They planned to do this by engaging in a dialogue with their independent counterparts in the East. This dialogue resembled Habermas' notion of discourse ethics. The idea is that when you confront someone in a different position from yourself, when you step

---

[4] For a deeper analysis of the logic behind this type of strategy, see Fierke, 1999.

outside of the language games of your own context, you are forced to redefine yourself and your own moral position *vis-à-vis* the other.

The act of dialogue, in this case, cut into the logic of the Cold War, in so far as the conflict was sustained by a division between self and Other which made it thinkable to destroy the enemy. The threat to use force, and the possibility of exterminating the Other, requires their dehumanisation (Thompson, 1980: 26).[5] Moving beyond the logic of deterrence or the logic of force required an act of renaming, of giving an identity to the people of Eastern Europe. Since the superpowers were trapped in the rules of the Cold War game, the impetus for an alternative had to come from outside. As the Russian, Yuri Medvedkov (1983), stated in 1982:

Today the top leaders of the two camps are not on speaking terms; they are not ready even to 'tango' as one of them put it. It means it is up to us to provide alternative forms of constructive East–West dialogue in order to shorten the time needed for the business-like attitude of the politicians to the settlement of their disagreements.

Against the background of states either refusing to talk, or bargaining from two fixed positions, of the disarmament debates in the West, and the repression of human rights activists in the East, a background in which independent initiatives on both sides were believed to be part of a psychological war instigated by the other (see, for example, Hofmann, 1984; LFEE, 1980), the two groups began a dialogue across the division of Europe. One of the first acts was to rename the Other as someone who, like the self, was human, and with whom one could engage in speech. It required making the Cold War, rather than other human beings, the enemy.

This effort has been largely invisible or forgotten. But at the time, it was visible to Eastern authorities, and – as evidenced by some of Reagan's language changes – probably to Western ones as well. It was clearly seen as a threat by the Eastern European authorities, since Western activists were often expelled from Eastern bloc countries for attempting to talk with their independent counterparts (see, for example, Voute, 1987; Jones, 1987). Members of official peace councils in the East, who had assumed the Western peace movement to be their ally, began to accuse participants in this dialogue of being accomplices of NATO, which was only reinforced by Reagan's adoption of a language – very similar to that of the peace movements – of breaking down the wall between East and West (Soviet Peace Committee, 1984).

---

[5] Social psychologists, such as Kelman and Hamilton, 1989, who analysed the American involvement in Mylai, also make an argument about the role of dehumanising language in preparing soldiers for warfare.

The process of dialogue was destabilising to the maintenance of a conflict that required clear lines of self and Other who did not communicate except by means of threatening to use force. And it was destabilising to the identities of the movements themselves. When the Western peace movements originally proposed the idea, the hope was to recruit the Eastern human rights activists to their cause, so that they would no longer be accused of seeking unilateral disarmament (see, for example, Reagan, 1983; Thompson, 1983). But through the process of dialogue, they had to revise their understanding of peace, and its relationship to human rights, as the Eastern Europeans made it clear that this concept had a very different, and less than positive, meaning for them.

Changing Games, Changes Strategies traces the eventual adoption of this game by Reagan and Gorbachev, and their transition from a game within which they were politicians involved in self-interested negotiations to one in which they were human beings engaged in a dialogue about the stakes of their relationship to one another. The message is also clear in William Wohlforth's book, *Witnesses to the End of the Cold War* (1996), which is based on discussions with policy-makers in both East and West (see also Oberdorfer, [1991] 1992). Negotiators on both sides emphasised how important the human element was; that they began to see the other as a human being like themselves. In this respect, the Cold War was not just about barbed wire running through the middle of Europe, it was about barbed wire running through people's hearts and through societies.[6]

I have recently begun analysing a range of post-Cold War contexts to look at the continuing conflict between a logic of dialogue and a logic of force, from NATO expansion, to Iraq, to Northern Ireland and the Middle East. My preliminary observation is that in all of the cases where there has been some movement toward transforming a seemingly intractable conflict, it has begun when actors – thought only to understand the language of force – began to talk face to face. In Northern Ireland, the British government held secret negotiations with the IRA, and Gerry Adams, John Hume, and Albert Reynolds were involved in continuing dialogue. The United States played an important role in encouraging a non-violent resolution of the conflict. In the Middle East, non-governmental organisations (NGOs) had been attempting to construct a dialogue between Palestinian and Israeli organisations for years (see Rothman, 1992), and the state-level peace process was given impetus by secret talks in Oslo.

This argument can be made even in relation to Iraq. When Kofi Annan went to Baghdad during the UNSCOM crisis, Tariq 'Aziz's response was

---

[6] This particular wording comes from Beresford, 1983 in a letter to the Soviet Peace Committee.

that this was the first time that the UN had bothered to listen to the Iraqi position, to their legitimate grievances in this situation ('Aziz, 1997, 1998; Iraqi Leadership, 1998). Prior to the Agreement on Mutual Understanding, Iraq had won the sympathy, or at least the self-interest, of Russia, China and several Arab states. While these actors wanted Iraq to comply with UN resolutions, they emphasised the importance of resolving the conflict on the basis of a logic of dialogue rather than force (see, for example, China, 1998; Safronchuk, 1998; Iran, 1998; Isma'il, 1998). It is not that the threat of force played no role in reaching an agreement; I have doubts about this, but will concede that it may have. The key issue is the effect of the face-to-face meeting. This is a very controversial statement in Britain and the United States, where only two scenarios have been presented in the press about how to deal with Iraq: either Saddam Hussein is a criminal like Hitler who has to be eliminated, or he is a bad boy playing cat and mouse who has to be hit hard (see Fierke, 2000). Both language games provide a framework for reasoning that justifies the use of force.

Kosovo seemed a more difficult case since people were being slaughtered and force seemed the only short-term option. At the beginning of Michaelmas term 1998 I was organising a special tutorial at Oxford with a student from Bosnia.[7] At his first session he described his experience working with Carl Westerdorp in the Office of the High Representative in Bosnia. Then he reported the views about US negotiator Richard Holbrooke, which he had picked up from people working on the ground in Bosnia. They tended, he said, to think about the situation quite differently than the people in Brussels. They thought that the most important thing about Holbrooke was not that he is tough and can deliver on a threat, but that he had developed a relationship of respect with Milosević after several years of interactions. They had a face-to-face relationship, and Milosević responded to being treated like a legitimate leader. This contrasted with Milosević's refusal – at that time – to deal with Cook because Cook treated him as a pariah who only understands the use of force.

His second point was that on the ground in Bosnia, dialogue, although frustrating, was preferred and understood to be more effective in the long term. You can hurt people or leaders materially by pounding them with weapons, but you do not win their hearts and are more likely to increase support for the existing government, a lesson which became conventional wisdom during the NATO campaign against Kosovo. You can use force, but in the process, all the work that has gone into negotiations and into building trust is destroyed. As untenable as this may seem, it is

---

[7] The student, Elvir Camdzic, was originally from Tuzla.

important to emphasise that this was a Bosniac,[8] who had lived through the worst of the atrocities, speaking about a Serb leader.

There are cases where using force is the only option, and it is not my point that we should all become pacifists. The NATO bombing campaign in Bosnia, for instance, created the conditions for a stabilisation of the situation and an end to the fighting on the ground. My main concern is to raise a question about whether we do not often assume too much about force, or assume that it is a solution when it may, in fact, prolong and reproduce conflicts that have some potential for resolution if the legitimate concerns of both sides are taken into account.

Martin Luther King ([1967]1972) said that a riot is at bottom the language of the unheard. One could say the same of terrorism. Groups such as the IRA or the PLO have legitimate historical and present grievances.[9] In so far as the use of violence by the weak makes it easier to marginalise them, these groups have probably contributed to their own silencing, and might succeed in achieving their own demands more effectively by choosing other tactics. But the point is that the weak often resort to violence out of frustration at being ignored, silenced or brutalised. The key question is how do you break through the dynamics of tit-for-tat violence, or negotiations involving a dialogue of the deaf, in order to create space for the consideration of other options? Each context has to be analysed in terms of its own dynamics, but outside intervention by a third party, whether NGOs, the UN or other states, seems to be a crucial ingredient.

My other concern is to reinforce the idea that 'mere talk' is not irrelevant. One important contribution of the moral and the ethical, as well as the critical, traditions is their emphasis on a common humanity, and of morality consisting in having to look the Other in the eyes and give an account of the reasons for our actions. Philosophers in the Wittgensteinian tradition, such as Stanley Cavell and Hannah Pitkin (1972: 150–2), have argued that the moral emphasis on the 'I–Thou' relationship occurs in the realm of individual human relationships, not in the realm of politics. It represents one form of life, which emphasises healing tears in the fabric of human relationships, and is distinct from others, such as the use of force, which only deepen the wounds, and create enemies for life. Dialogue and reconciliation occur in face-to-face relationships between human beings. The examples, however small, and however limited, suggest that in

---

[8] Bosniac is the preferred term for referring to Bosnian Muslims.
[9] The use of the term terrorist is a positional language, applied by those in power to groups outside or marginalised from the political process. The meaning of acts of violence changes with position. Today's terrorist may be tomorrow's freedom fighter or government leader.

assuming too much about the success of force, we have not looked closely enough at the human, psychological and spiritual dynamics of intractable conflict.

Since the end of the Cold War there has been a tendency for the United States and Britain to elevate the use of force in relation to selective Others, without a clear idea of how or why it would be effective. The justification for doing this is cast in terms of the moral superiority of the West. The word dialogue is used to mean we expect you to adopt our position, rather than we expect to listen and also grow from this process. This is highly problematic from two of the wealthiest countries in the world, which are also the two top arms exporters, and have a more extensive history of imperial exploitation, in one form or another, than any other country in the world. At present the military strength of the United States is more than that of the ten other major countries in the world combined (MacGinty, 1997: 242).

As the numerous missile gaps during the Cold War, or the US bombing of the pharmaceutical company in Sudan demonstrate, inaccurate information about threats has often been used to justify a forceful response. As post-structuralists have argued, claims of moral goodness are often used by those in power to marginalise and silence those who are culturally different and less fortunate. Labour's ethical foreign policy is a sign of hope, and the possibility of good citizenship on the part of states, but it should first and foremost be an expression of that dialogue of states which is so central to the international society tradition (see Watson, 1982).

Dialogical analysis

My final point is that if all of us, academics and political actors alike, have a tendency to become locked into the assumptions of our context, it is useful to think about more dialogical forms of analysis, particularly when asking questions about processes of change.

The standard approach of the social sciences is hypothesis testing. We begin with a theory that is used to generate assumptions, from which we formulate a hypothesis to test against the world to see whether they correspond. There is an objective world out there and we can compare our words with it to see whether our words are correct. Realists, for instance, begin with assumptions that states are the most relevant actors and we should therefore focus analysis on states, which are only interested in maximising their power. Moral discourse is only a disguise so we need not bother with language. This point of departure provides a justification for selectively choosing from the detail and, not surprisingly, one is likely to see what one is looking for.

A more dialogical approach makes it possible to examine the relationship between the moves of political actors occupying different positions and to do a conceptual mapping of change. While engaged in the research for *Changing Games, Changing Strategies*, several layers of patterns began to emerge from both a shared and a contested language. Actors in any one position consistently made arguments that relied on a specific language game.

Take the concept of deterrence. NATO argued that deterrence was a prison that could not be escaped. After Reagan introduced SDI, he argued that defensive technologies would make it possible for us to escape the prison of nuclear deterrence. The peace movements argued that we needed to be liberated from the prison; and Gorbachev argued that the guillotine needed to be destroyed to make way for more civilised form of politics based on shared norms.

What one notices in this example is that each of the parties was articulating a distinct moral argument about nuclear deterrence, but they relied on a shared language in doing so. The key object was deterrence as a prison. The question was the form of action to be taken in relation to that prison: staying inside, escaping, being liberated or destroying the structure. These each related to a moral argument:

> NATO: The prison cannot be escaped: we should maintain deterrence because it is a blessing that has prevented war in Europe for the last forty years (Hofmann, 1984).
>
> REAGAN: The prison can be escaped: we should develop technologies that will allow us to find security in ways other than threatening mutual destruction (Reagan, 1985).
>
> PEACE MOVEMENTS: We need to be liberated from the prison: we are trapped in a way of thinking that is imprisoning us and keeping us from thinking about alternative solutions (Kaldor, 1984).
>
> GORBACHEV: The guillotine should be destroyed: we can develop a form of international politics based on civilised norms, but need to destroy our reliance on deterrence and balance of power thinking (Gorbachev, 1987).

Once the shared components of a political language are identified it becomes possible to trace a transition, from one language game to another. By language game I mean the language and practices woven together (Wittgenstein, 1958: para. 7). The structure of the change and the patterns are to be found in the context itself, not in an *a priori* theory.

The problems with hypothesis testing became evident against the backdrop of the ending of the Cold War. From the mid-eighties on there was a series of surprises that were neither predicted nor explainable on the basis of realist assumptions. Yet five years later the conventional wisdom about the end of the Cold War was that the West had won it, a zero-sum realist argument about winners and losers, one that reinforces the idea that this was solely about states in competition with one another.

If one goes back and engages in a dialogical analysis in which a wider range of voices are allowed to speak, including states and social movements in both East and West, and traces the change over time, we come to a very different conclusion about the meaning and significance of the end of the Cold War.[10] We then see that the victory argument was imposed at a particular point, and that it has influenced how we are constructing the present and future. But the transformation itself was constructed out of the conflict between a logic of force and a logic of dialogue. This tension continues to be constitutive of post-Cold War international politics.

A more dialogical analysis is not primarily critical in the sense that it includes a range of actors or practices that would be ignored in more traditional approaches. Some might argue that there is nothing critical about the mere description of a change, even if it includes more critical voices. It is critical because it makes us look again, in a fresh way, at our assumptions about the world because they have become too familiar. In this way, new spaces are opened up for thinking about the meaning of the past and the present and, therefore, how we construct the future.

Conclusion

The explicit articulation of an ethical foreign policy is a positive development, so long as it increases the potential for holding the government accountable for its promises. However, as a policy of one of the top two arms contractors in the world, there is some danger that the moral dimension of the policy may be used to build support for actions that might otherwise be questioned. There was a glaring inconsistency between the sale of British weapons to the Indonesian government – which was repressing the independence movement of East Timor – and the claim to an ethical foreign policy, an inconsistency that did not go unnoticed. By contrast, in Kosovo, few questions have been asked about the relationship between the explicitly humanitarian mission, led by Britain and the United States, and who profits from this situation, either in terms of arms sales, contracts for reconstruction, or an expansion of power in the region. There are enough historical examples of moral principle being put

---

[10] It is important to emphasise that this is not a subjective phenomena but intersubjective. The focus is not on public opinion but rather how practices are given meaning.

to work for national interest or power to recommend vigilance in this case.

A foreign policy that is ethical in practice requires that individuals and groups be ready to hold up a critical mirror to government action. In fact, since the British Labour government introduced its ethical foreign policy, it has been confronted time and time again with accusations that its actions do not correspond to its words. In this respect, the explicit articulation of an ethical foreign policy has provided a framework for others to make a comparison between policy and implementation.

The flip side of this vigilance is a willingness to engage directly in dialogue with those most affected by this policy. The mantra of moral goodness, articulated by the powerful, often silences the voices of the less powerful behind maxims that they 'only understand the language of force'. The Balkans is a case in point. In the context of the Dayton negotiations, the Serb leader Milosević was seen as a pivotal player in reaching an agreement (Holbrooke, 1998); by the time of Kosovo, it was claimed that he understood no language except that of force, as if this was an essential quality of the leader that transcended time and space. Similarly, Iraq was once a patron of Western arms sales; it fell into disfavour with the invasion of Kuwait; since that time every interaction with Iraq has been presented as if the Gulf War were still underway, and as if the use of force is the only conceivable response. As a result, the United States and Britain failed to take adequate advantage of the negotiated solution to the UNSCOM crisis that was reached between Iraq and Kofi Annan, and arguably contributed to the breakdown of that agreement. In both cases, the context of action came to be dominated by maxims regarding the moral superiority of Britain and the United States *vis-à-vis* an evil Other. The point is less one about the use of force, which is in some cases justified; it is rather about the tendency to become caught up in the dominant assumptions and language games of a context. In a situation of conflict, these assumptions are likely to presume the moral superiority of the self and the need to silence the Other. When both sides engage in this behaviour, the conflict will be reproduced.

A dialogical form of analysis can be brought to the service of both efforts. It provides a means to look beyond the arguments of one's own context, both narrowly and broadly conceived, to more thickly describe how outcomes are constructed through the interactions of different players. Through such an analysis the role of the less powerful – such as social movements or weak states – in constructing outcomes, can be brought to the surface. This role is usually either assumed away or ignored.

Part III

Case studies

9   The United States and the ethics of post-modern war

Christopher Coker

In general the period since 1989 can be said to have been a period of progress for US foreign policy. It began with the collapse of communism and the fall of the Berlin Wall, and continued into the Gulf War and the conflict in Kosovo. It was not without setbacks, of course: the ill-fated UN intervention in Somalia, and the years it took to reach the Dayton Accord during which 250,000 people lost their lives. A New World Order was not born. The world may be safer for democracy than at any time in the twentieth century, but many democratic regimes, including Russia, have not fared well and at the very beginning of the period – in Tiananmen Square – the democratic movement in China was brutally suppressed.

Still, the United States has been at the centre of the management of the international order since the Cold War ended. It led the coalition that evicted Iraq from Kuwait. The war against Serbia was largely American led and conducted. And it has played the dominant role in trying to prevent nuclear proliferation.

The collapse of communism made possible a brief moment of euphoria between 1991 and 1994 when it seemed possible for the United States to restructure the world on new foundations. The idea of a world order based not on power but on international law flourished. In truth, it had less to do with building a new world order than with a new public order based on an operational linkage between principles and means. The means were the *ad hoc* coalitions put together by the United States in the Gulf and Somalia – coalitions of the willing. The principles were enshrined in the famous UN Resolution 688, which was deemed to have given the international community the right for the first time to intervene in the internal affairs of other countries.

The United States has remained interventionist ever since. For all the talk of neo-isolationism and self-containment, it seems to have returned to that period of self-confidence which Senator Fulbright wrote about in the mid-1960s in *The Arrogance of Power* (Fulbright, 1967). America is now more omniscient in the world system than it has been at any time in the past thirty years.

How can we explain this astonishing reversal? It is not enough to say that the new context (the post-Cold War environment) favours the exercise of American power. For even if opportunities have arisen, the question remains: why has the United States seized them? While the United States remains confident in its economic power, it is clearly not as great as it was thirty years ago. 'If God wills America will have another chance to show the world she was born to serve humanity', proclaimed Woodrow Wilson. 'We are Americans: our sole responsibility is to work for freedom', proclaimed George Bush (cited in Smith, 1994: 179). The ideological link between the two assertions is easy to see, but the rhetoric has worn thin since 1991. The United States is no longer the ideological power it was. It certainly has no stomach for sustained military campaigns.

Something else seems to have been at work, and it is not ideology. A number of explanations come to mind. Some see the exercise of power in terms of the post-Cold War phenomenon: unipolarity in a unipolar world. Others think that it results from a power vacuum that will eventually be filled by America's partners or enemies in Asia. Still others see it as a vindication of crude market economics. When American politicians explain their actions, however, one must look at the ethical foundations, for they talk the language of ethics more and more.

The Americans began this period holding the ethical high ground of the international order. Ethics were deeply involved in the resurgence of American power. The removal of the Soviet Union from the international system left the United States in possession of the intellectual high ground. Capitalism had never enjoyed such a good press. The American Way appeared to be vindicated. The Soviet Union may have lost the Cold War rather than the United States winning it, but as the leading power in the coalition that faced down Soviet communism, America played the largest role in its eventual demise. It emerged from the Cold War with a restored sense of the moral certainty that it had lost in Vietnam. Despite the widespread criticism on ethical grounds of actions such as the bombing of Belgrade and the continued use of sanctions against Iraq (and the human suffering they produce), the Americans themselves harbour few such doubts. The main reason for this is that they have discovered something new: humanitarian interventionism.

Historically, the United States was the first country to make human rights a centrepiece of foreign policy. But the human rights issue was only an item in a much broader agenda during the Cold War. It was useful in outmanoeuvring the Soviet Union after the 1975 Helsinki Final Act and embarrassing a variety of lesser actors from China to dictators in the Middle East. The agenda has now been expanded. The United States, President Clinton proclaimed after the Kosovo conflict, will now only fight humanitarian wars (cited in Krauthammer, 1999: 8). Kosovo is not the first such campaign. Arguably, the United States was prepared to use force for moral ends much earlier, from the declaration of no-fly zones for the Kurds at the end of the war against Iraq, to the transformation of NATO, largely under its own prompting, from a self-defence organisation into an international police force. The force of US humanitarianism, rather than geopolitical interest, can be detected in a series of actions which ended in the bombing of Belgrade, from the first shot the alliance ever fired in anger against the Serbian air force in 1994 to the airlift to Sarajevo (which was more extensive than the 1948 Berlin airlift which many historians consider to be the first 'shot' of the Cold War).

Humanitarian war

It would be easy to multiply such instances – the general pattern is clear. But the fact that each of these actions was defended on humanitarian grounds does not necessarily make them 'ethical'. New lines of inquiry present themselves. Instead of looking at the ethics of US policy, we might look at the nature of the United States as a society, as well as at the nature of what has been called 'post-modern' war. For if we look at humanitarianism as a purely contingent factor, the ethics of American power can be seen in a different light.

When President Clinton told the American people that the United States would only fight humanitarian wars in the future, he meant that it would only fight for people oppressed or repressed by ethnic cleansing, genocide or political oppression in its many forms. Humanitarianism means intervening on behalf of other people and taking the human rights agenda much further than in the past when breaches were occasionally punished by sanctions. It means a pro-active policy on behalf of others, including, if necessary, recourse to war.

I would argue, however, that American policy was a great deal more ethical in inspiration when it was ideological; it is a good deal less ethical in a post-ideological age. We must start with the Vietnam War and what appeared to be the end of the American Century. And we must consider the type of society the United States was becoming in the early 1960s, long before the Cold War ended.

The American Century and the will to power

They are of the day before yesterday and the day after tomorrow – they have as yet no today. (Nietzsche, 1966: 71)

All the wars the United States fought from its entry into world history in 1917 were ideological: they were fought to make the world 'safe for democracy'. In trying to systematise peace as a condition of a liberal international order, the Americans were prepared to resort to war to construct that order, and to police it once it was in place. In that regard its wars were also ethical. The American Century and war were, in part, synonymous, a point that comes out particularly vividly in the speeches of General Cummings, a character in Norman Mailer's novel *The Naked and the Dead* (Mailer, 1948).

In retrospect, the novel is not quite as anti-war as it is often made out to be. Mailer's concept of heroic individualism – the theme of much of his writing, the hero who goes out to battle and discovers his creative power by the tasks he sets himself – is in the same tradition as Leo Strauss' contention that a nation measures its power not by weighing its capabilities and choosing its tasks, but by setting itself roles and finding whether or not it has the power to perform them.

Mailer's novel was a text for the times. Indeed, if we seek a definition of the American Century it is Cummings' concept of history or historical energy: 'There are countries which have latent powers, latent resources, they are full of potential energy so to speak. And there are great concepts which can unlock that, express it. As kinetic energy a country is organisation, co-ordinated effort: your epithet, fascism' (Mailer, 1948: 321). The last remark is a reference to Cummings' interlocutor Robert Hearne, who had suggested that there is a process of osmosis in war: that the victors always tend to look like the vanquished. Let us deconstruct the text. The American Century was founded on

1. The latent powers and resources of America. The United States was quite simply the most powerful country in history – certainly the most powerful in the twentieth century, a fact grasped early on by writers such as Joseph Conrad. In *Nostromo*, written in 1904, a character remarks:

   We shall be giving the word for everything: industry, trade, law, journalism, art, politics and religion, from Cape Horn clear over to Smith's Sound and beyond too, if anything worth taking hold of turns up at the North Pole. And then we shall take in hand the outlying continents and islands of the earth. We shall run the world's business whether the world likes it or not. The world can't help it – and neither can we. (Conrad, 1990: 94–5)

2. Great concepts were needed to unlock and express that power. The twentieth century was an intensely ideological age and liberalism was the strongest ideology. Its forms, if not its message, were aped by all the other ideologies that paid lip service to parliaments, elections and

even references to the Rights of Man (differently defined, of course, in the fascist case: not the brotherhood of man but the brotherhood of one's fellow countrymen).
3. A country is kinetic energy. That is the point. The resources of the nation-state harnessed to the ideas of the twentieth century created a formidable force. America, claimed Gary Wills, became an 'ism' in the course of the twentieth century (Wills, 1992: 422–6). This combination of forces was made possible by nationalism, the real force of the twentieth century which all the major ideologies, liberalism, communism and fascism, harnessed for their own ends.

America's principal rivals in the twentieth century were Nazi Germany and the USSR. As a nation-state the Third Reich was formidable, as was the Soviet state at the height of the Great Patriotic War. But the United States was the most formidable of the three, and it needed war as a medium to express its energy. As Cummings adds, 'historically the purpose of war is to translate America's potential into kinetic energy'. His was an authentic modern voice and it was not entirely coincidental that the Cold War should have followed almost immediately upon the end of the Second World War.

Mailer's novel is intriguing because it captures some of the themes of this debate, albeit unconsciously. 'We are out of the backwaters of history', remarks Cummings, to which Hearne remarks somewhat ironically, 'We have become destiny, eh?' (Mailer, 1948: 61). What was the American Century if not the wish to make the world safe for democracy (and, later in the 1970s, diversity, before democracy once again kicked in)? What was the American Century but the belief that America was the destiny of everyone else? Most Western intellectuals, however critical of America they might have been in these years, stopped going to Moscow after the purges in the 1930s.

Cummings also adds: 'We are in the middle ages of a new era, waiting for the renaissance of real power'. The middle ages was not 1948 when Mailer published his novel. It was 1942, the year in which the novel is set, the year that the publicist, Henry Luce, declared the coming of the American Century, and Henry Wallace 'the age of the Common Man'.

What made the United States formidable in the Cold War was its wish to impose its will on the rest of the world. The will to power was very 'American'. Hearne may have referred to a process of osmosis, claiming that having defeated fascism, the United States would itself become a fascist state. And indeed Cummings' philosophy is couched in fascist terms, although he is not a fascist, but a Nietzschean who respects Germany's challenge to the United States but concludes that it is not powerful enough to succeed. What makes Cummings an authentic figure is that his vision of the world can be found in other contemporary American writings, and particularly in the philosophy of the three great twentieth-century American philosophers: Charles Peirce, John Dewey and William James, most notably in the latter's writings on 'the will to believe'.[1]

James' voice, speech, and even his turn of phrase, were authentically American. His philosophy was both ideological and ethical. It was ideological in its liberalism; it was ethical in that it required the United States to exert itself for others, including the common man. James deliberately employed such characteristic expressions as 'cash value', 'results' and 'profits' in order to bring his ideas within reach of the 'man in the street'. He spoke with a force and directness that made his philosophy of pragmatism second nature to his fellow citizens. He elaborated a philosophy of action.

Its first principle was 'purpose'. If our experience discloses an unfinished world, he argued, a world with a future, with aspects that are still in the making, we must ask what part we have in shaping that process. We cannot decide what is morally good or bad until we have a moral order. If we do not want such an order, we cannot be made to believe in what is good or bad by rational argument. That we make moral distinctions and take them seriously, James argued, is decided by our will, not our intellect.

When Woodrow Wilson declared war on Germany in 1917, he confidently asserted that 'our object is to vindicate the principles of peace... we are glad to fight for the ultimate peace of the world' (cited in Iriye, 1985: 36). The idea that war was being fought for peace was the ultimate conclusion of America's historic mission to rid the world of tyrants, whether they took the form of eighteenth-century kings or twentieth-century German emperors. It was inevitable that Soviet commissars would be added to the list later. In that sense the Cold War was indeed a war, rather than an armed peace, for it could only end in the unconditional victory of one side, and the unconditional surrender of the other.

James' second principle was 'effort'. Effort tells us that we are free, that our will (or free thinking) is capable of bringing about change. We are not passive spectators but actors in our own history. It is not enough, however, to await evidence that will confirm us in this opinion. If we resolutely refuse, for example, to consider the possibility of God's existence until we have proof of it, we will fail to put ourselves in a place where we may find proof, or where we may experience the reality. The 'cash value' of abstract ideas, James once declared, is such that they can only be known

---

[1] For the place of the 'will to believe' in James' overall thinking see Ruth and Putnam, 1989: 27–46.

when lived through. Only by wishing to believe in the possibility of their existence from the outset will we be willing to act in ways that will put us in the presence of them (if they are there to be found). And that may require that at some point we fight our way into history.

Effort, of course, was endless in the twentieth century. Dean Acheson told the American people in 1946, after the Wilsonian order had collapsed and another war had been fought to punish those held for responsible for its failure, 'the need for effort will always be with us' (cited in Smith, 1995: 90). There appeared to be no end to America's labours, only a constant striving.

The final element in James' work was 'will' itself. For effort would be of little avail if it were no more than a blind will to power. Our efforts must be governed by our purposes, and our purposes, in turn, must be framed by our beliefs. A belief that has nothing to do with conduct is not a proper belief. Our conduct, however, must be informed by ideas. In the end, we hold our beliefs through our will to believe (Bird and Smith, 1963).

If German thinkers (and General Cummings) can be said to have subscribed to the will to power, American liberal thinkers like James believed with equal force in the will to believe. Few liberal writers of importance ever doubted the veracity of their convictions even in the darkest moments of their history. The need to believe was all the greater, of course, in the conflict with twentieth-century totalitarianism.

In short, the ethics of the period placed great emphasis on instrumentality. To be legitimate, power had to be exercised for a purpose, preferably a grand design. It had to be seen to be used in pursuit of a goal. This readily translated into the language of the new order that Wilson introduced into public discourse in 1917. It also readily translated into the ideological categories that the United States, like others, began to use. Ethics become ideological and future-oriented.

Early in 1916 Colonel House, President Wilson's personal representative, told the French that if the United States did enter the war, it would want to see the end of German 'feudalism' which it held responsible for the conflict (cited in Gardner, 1986: 11). Twenty-five years later Mary Lindberg wrote *The Wave of the Future* in which she argued that a global contest between the forces of the future and those of the past was at stake in the Second World War (cited in Lukacs, 1976: 514). And it was as a power of the future that America saw its role in an ethical (that is, historically sanctioned) light.

The Vietnam War and the end of Americanism

The 'will to believe', and with it America's commitment to an ideological foreign policy, foundered in the Vietnam War. The war was fought in the name of a great theme: the war against totalitarianism, and it was packaged in grand historical terms. But during the war the soldiers exited history by living in a permanent present, in a world in which they were determined to put the injunctions of history behind them. It was also the last exercise of America's collective will to power, the last test of national 'virtue'. On both counts – its belief in History (in the upper case) and the willingness of its citizens to fight their way into it – the country was found wanting.

The young no longer heeded the siren call of History. They were not quite so willing to march to the sound of history's metanarratives. At the height of the Vietnam War a contemporary writer entitled the chapter of a book, 'The Revolt Against Obligation'. The extent of that revolt was marked. Of the 2 million young men who were called up, an unprecedented 139,000 refused to be drafted. In *Libra*, Don DeLillo calls Kennedy's assassination 'the seven seconds that broke the back of the American Century' (DeLillo, 1988: 181), but the Vietnam War was the main event which discredited America's collective will to power.

In 1969, J. H. Plumb predicted that historical metaphors such as manifest destiny, which had mobilised the nation in the past, would soon lose their hold over the American imagination. They were already less powerful than they had been. 'The past has served the few', he wrote, 'perhaps history may serve the multitude' (Plumb, 1969: 67). He meant by the multitude the individuals who comprised it. For the war saw the emergence of what Ulrich Beck calls 'reflexive modernisation'. What he means is that the post-modern era dissolves the traditional parameters of an industrial society, such as class culture, or family ties. Beck calls it 'a social surge of individualisation' (Beck, 1997: 87). There is a tendency, in other words, for the emergence of individualised forms of existence which compel people to put themselves, not History, at the centre of life.

But the Vietnam War not only challenged America's understanding of History. It also brought into question its collective will, or rather its willingness to assert it. For towards the end of the war it came to be situated in an ethical discourse which was distinctly 'post-modern', and which challenged one of the central premises of the will to power. Post-modern communities do not embrace an ontology that is concerned only with the language of self; they tend to derive their identity from the conditions that make social life possible. In other words, 'we' are always ethically situated, for our sense of self is derived from a prior ethical relationship with others. We have a duty to think of others as well as of ourselves when we act. What is important is not that states should act in the world but that they should engage in the world and, in the process, forge a world in which it is possible to live in peace with others.

What is this if not a 'negative ironic' tradition. Negative irony requires one to have no metaphysical position either for or against war, only to see it for what it is: brutal. If metaphysics was a precondition of modern warfare, the abandonment of metaphysics is a precondition of post-modern war. Put more simply, what we see is what Isaiah Berlin called 'negative liberty' – the extent to which the individual is permitted to exercise his ironic conscience without interference by the state (Berlin, 1969: 160). Or as Richard Rorty, America's most distinguished post-modern philosopher writes:

> Metaphysics hoped to bring together our private and our public lives by showing that self-discovery and political unity could be united . . . The ironist [by contrast] should reconcile himself to a private public split within his final vocabulary to the point that resolution of doubts about one's final vocabulary has nothing in particular to do with attempts to save other people from pain and humiliation. (Rorty, 1989: 120)

It is only, to use Berlin's terminology, by abandoning 'the conviction that all positive values in which men have believed must in the end be compatible, and perhaps, even entail each other', that a post-modern society is able to act, and use war as an instrument of policy. For it challenges the belief that the state is an end in itself, and allows civil society to assume its dominant ethical stance: a contempt for cruelty.

In that sense the Vietnam War can lay claim to being the last modern war because it was the last war in which the United States sought – and failed – to impose its will on another power for a metaphysical end. Fifteen years later it may still have talked of creating a 'New World Order' but by then such metaphysical language was seen as trumpery. As an American Secretary of State admitted a few years later, given that it disliked fighting wars, the most powerful nation in history was going through a 'period of recalibrating [its] expectations' (Albright, 1994: 8). The United States, to quote Whitman, is no longer so ready to 'sound its barbaric yawp over the rooftops of the world'.

No less important after Vietnam, the United States also had to design a new technology to fight wars, one that would minimise enemy casualties. It had to find a new formula for what can be called 'humane warfare'. Like most other industrial powers, it found that it could no longer fight war by modern means. When it fought its next major war in the Gulf in 1990–91, it did so by post-modern methods.

Let me invoke Nietzsche here because more than any other modern philosopher, he wrote about the will to power; he dominated the modern imagination (implicit in the dialogue between Hearne and Cummings). What makes him still such an attractive thinker – even in the post-modern era – is that he abominated metaphysics and absolute truths. He was an ironist who once notoriously defined truth as 'a mobile army of metaphors' and was among the first philosophers to suggest that the world should abandon the quest to 'know' the truth.

But Nietzsche was also rooted to the nineteenth century in his claim that not only should we abandon the search for the truth, but in seeking what is true for *us* we should also 'reconsider cruelty and open our eyes, [as] almost everything we call "higher culture" is based on the spiritualisation of cruelty, on it becoming more profound' (cited in Lyotard, 1984: 158). As a thoroughly modern man, Nietzsche hoped to see a society in which citizens would once again be soldiers, and their rulers commanders. He disliked liberal societies because he claimed that they were unwilling to fight for their freedom. His statement that 'war educates for freedom' is consistent with this reasoning, for true freedom, he insisted, lay not in granting constitutional rights, but the freedom to commit oneself to a goal and hold oneself accountable for the consequences of one's own actions (Nietzsche, 1990: 72). And that was Clausewitz's definition of war too: 'the sum of available means and the strength of the will' (Clausewitz, 1993: 86). This was the true expression of the will to power as well as the only reality of the idea for them, freedom. War provides the experience of being an effective agent in the world, one who is able to transform what 'is' into what 'will be'.

Clearly, such a view cannot be squared with the post-modern sensibility which is averse to cruelty, and even the stereotyping of enemies, and has little stomach for war. Nietzsche's view is based on his own ontological construction of a man 'who seeks above all to discharge [his] strength – life itself is the will to power'. With this ontology he tried to connect the private and public spheres – private self-realisation with the public – a more aristocratic political society – a nobler one, a community as the will to power.

For Heidegger this was a case of replacing one metaphysics with another. Nietzsche's claim to distrust philosophy and philosophers and see the former as a sickness of the soul could not be trusted: 'a regard to metaphysics still prevails even in the intention to overcome metaphysics'. Our task, therefore, 'is to cease all overcoming and leave metaphysics to itself' (Heidegger, 1972: 24). And indeed, the defining characteristic of the American way of warfare since Vietnam – with its non-committal lip service to universalism, its half-hearted dislike of cruelty, its ironic stance on life – is that it has taken Heidegger's prescription very much to heart.

The United States went into the Vietnam War expecting that the 'will to believe' was enough. It left it recognising that times change. The ethics of the will to power rested on a contract with history. The ethics of the post-modern world involved a contract with others. The will to power, like many other nineteenth-century ideas – progress, history and, in the American case, manifest destiny – barely took into account other people or nations or individuals, or when it did it subsumed the latter into larger categories to be redeemed or rescued, or even punished, as the power that was 'willing' saw fit. The ontology of the will to power was ethical, but it was intensely self-referential. It referred everything back to the source of that will. In that sense it was self-absorbed and self-regarding and in the end – in Vietnam – self-reproaching as well.

Project *versus* projection

America is no longer engaged in great projects. It no longer finds legitimacy in a vision of the future; instead, it has been reduced to managing the present. The 'crisis of meaning' – the subject of a book by Zaki Laidi – is expressed in a disquieting gap between expectations of change (the need to act, to project oneself into the future before one is caught out), and an ideological discrediting of grand schemes and grand narratives. The United States may project its power into the future but not in tune with a particular project.

A project implies an effort to move into the future to realise one's destiny, to move from the present, not to deny it but to transcend it. By projection Laidi means the need to tie the present even more strongly into a future brought nearer by the compression of time. Crisis management has become the central political objective. The United States claims that management prevents it from reflecting on a project, but, in fact, the absence of historical perspective makes it a slave of contingency or the state of emergency. And emergency does not constitute the first stage of a project of meaning: it represents its active negation (Laidi, 1998: 11).

This is a great contrast with the past. When Secretary of State Dean Rusk first appeared before the Senate Foreign Relations Committee, he assured its members that what distinguished the United States from other countries was the fact that it had no interests, only responsibilities. This was the language of the project: to make the world safe for democracy. Today the United States is unwilling to discharge any responsibility because it evaluates actions largely in terms of cost (both economic and human). In the absence of any major project or design whatever measurement is there? That is the reality of the post-Cold War era.

It is interesting that Laidi specifically takes humanitarian intervention as an example of the gap between projection and project. The United States has instruments of power but lacks a policy. Humanitarianism by default has become an instrument of power, not a source of meaning. Somalia and Kosovo are two cases in point.

In Somalia, the United States committed 25,000 troops for a humanitarian project after years of neglect, and just as quickly pulled them out when they ran into trouble. In Kosovo, it found itself drawn into a crisis that arose from the collapse of the Rambouillet talks which precipitated a 79-day air war with Serbia. Kosovo was part of a larger crisis of state dissolution sparked off by America's lack of interest in Yugoslavia after the end of the Cold War, and particularly, its willingness to countenance its break-up in recognising Croatia as an independent state in 1991. Humanitarian intervention only took the form it did because the US lacked a political strategy. As months went by, the humanitarian policy became an end in itself. Humanitarian policies cannot prevent conflicts and nor can they contain them; they are no substitute for a policy (Laidi, 1998: 109–10).

In the end the absurdity was reached in Somalia that humanitarian organisations had to deal with the casualties of the US 'humanitarian' war. Another absurdity occurred in Kosovo where humanitarian intervention precipitated the mass expulsion of 1.2 million Kosovars. When NATO ground forces finally arrived, they were unable to stop the ethnic cleansing of Serbs: in six weeks the number of Serbs in Pristina fell from 40,000 to 2,000.

Kosovo was heralded as the first 'humanitarian war' in history but it was a strange case of humanitarianism when NATO forces in the US-led and directed conflict were not prepared to risk their lives for the people in whose name they were bombing Belgrade. The armed forces of the world's nineteen most powerful military powers waited for the air war to establish a 'permissive environment' in Kosovo: a theatre in which Serb forces would have been so bloodied that they would have been incapable of offering further resistance if a land invasion had been attempted. Just as most late-nineteenth-century commanders kept their cavalry back rather than commit them to a frontal assault against entrenched infantry, today's generals seem reluctant to commit their infantry until the bombers have broken the back of enemy forces on the ground.

In the aftermath of the war, the Americans issued what came to be known as the Clinton Doctrine: a ringing affirmation of their willingness to go to war for humanitarian aims. But it was hedged with so many qualifications that it is clear that the United States will be reluctant ever again to risk the lives of its ground forces except where there is an overwhelming national interest (such as oil), or a strategic principle at stake. Like charity, humanitarianism begins at home in the unstated agreement between public and politicians that there are no humanitarian interests for which an American soldier can legitimately be asked to lay down his life.

Post-modern war

The problem, however, goes much deeper. Without a grand project, projecting military power has no particular rationale. This is why when American forces intervened in Somalia, Haiti and Yugoslavia, we saw a pattern of rapid force projection, hesitation, uncertainty and retreat. There has been no consistency or follow through, not only because there is no master plan or grand design: the means used have not only been disproportionately military; the military means themselves have been suspect ethically. The way America now projects force is itself unethical, or open to the criticism of being unethical.

One example was the bombing raid on Baghdad called 'Desert Fox' in late December 1998, a seventy-two-hour burst of bombs and missiles which was intended to disarm Saddam Hussein from the air. The mission involved some 650 strike and strike-support missions by land and carrier-based aircraft. More than 400 cruise missiles were launched, which exceeded the number used not only in the Gulf War, but also during the Kosovo air campaign. Within weeks the operation resumed against more than 70 air defence targets. In January and February more bombs were dropped than during 'Desert Fox'. So commonplace were the air strikes that they did not even make the evening news.

The operation was an excellent illustration, in fact, of the demands of Ulrich Beck's 'reflexive modernity'. In his most recent book, he argues that new and all-powerful sensibilities to new dangers are a reflection of a fundamental shift in the nature of modernity. He believes that it is the distribution of risk rather than of wealth that characterises the second phase of modernity. Indeed, there has been such a shift in focus that power can be measured through the ability of a government, or alliance, to contain, minimise or transfer risks (Beck, 1998: 136).

This helps to explain the shift from deterrence to dissuasion that has become the chief characteristic of American post-Cold War strategy. Detecting and controlling a potential risk, by pre-empting weapons accumulation, or degrading the weapon stocks of potential enemies, reflects America's power as a military 'manager'. In Kosovo the Western alliance was not 'at war' so much as engaged in a policing operation to preserve human and democratic rights and to minimise the risk posed by Serbia to the stability of the Balkans. Instead of a war, it was restyled 'a risk management strategy with missiles'.

Risk societies seem to need new enemy stereotypes. Beck lists three categories: the interchangeable enemy (for example, Islamic fundamentalism and/or Iraq); the abstract enemy (which can include asylum-seeking foreigners, or migrants); and mobile enemies (such as criminal cartels, the arms trade and nuclear proliferation). Again, this seems particularly apt in the light of Kosovo, where at times it was difficult to know whether the threat identified by NATO was the Serbian leader, Slobodan Milosevič, or the principle of ethno-nationalism, or the Kosovar refugees gathering on the edge of Western Europe prepared to demand school places, decent housing and reduced hospital waiting lists. All three were, at one time or another, invoked by Western leaders to justify the air campaign.

What is especially troubling about the phenomenon is that, in the absence of a concrete enemy, there is no end to the risks that the postmodern world faces. Iraq may be chastised but the threat of nuclear proliferation will remain. Serbia may enter the democratic fold but until the world is entirely democratic, the democracies will face the prospect of war indefinitely. The more intractable and deep rooted the threats, the more there will be a market for 'security managers'.

That means that post-modern societies face the prospect of endless war – in part, because, in Beck's words, 'it is possible to have enemy stereotypes without enemies' (Beck, 1998: 110). In other words, a problem may be insuperable whatever the outcome of a specific military campaign or diplomatic initiative. Both with respect to Iraq, with which the United States has been effectively at war since 1990, and to Serbia, with which it has been at war since 1993, the phenomenon we are discussing is very similar to what Virilio has called 'pure war', a term he takes from Clausewitz's *On War*. For 'pure war', he claims, is the realisation of the Clausewitzian concept of a war without respite:

Under Bonaparte war was waged *without respite* until the enemy succumbed and the counter-blows were struck with almost equal energy. Surely it is both natural and inescapable that this phenomenon should cause us to turn again to the pure concept of war with all its rigorous implications. (Virilio, 1997: 27)

Napoleonic warfare did, indeed, seem to be endless as one allied coalition followed another until Napoleon was finally defeated twenty-five years later. Napoleon was interested in the military, not political dimension; everything else was peripheral. In pursuit of his aims, he was prepared to turn the private into the public, life into war, the individual into the collective will. He was even prepared to 'requisition' the nation, to turn it into a supremely effective instrument of war. Today's technologies permit the post-modern world to carry out war without respite, but this time without undue cost to itself socially or economically. Clausewitz's model of pure war has now been 'realised', albeit in a form which Clausewitz himself might have difficulty recognising.

And, like Napoleon's campaigns, America's military operations are founded on insecurity. Chateaubriand said of Napoleon that he was haunted by insecurity, by 'an existence which because there was nowhere to stop was put to the hazard each morning' (cited in McManners, 1966: 88). Military historians have seen the fact that there was nowhere for him to stop – that he was drawn ever onwards even into the steppes of Russia – less as a psychological necessity of Napoleon's nature than a necessity of the post-revolutionary situation. Napoleon could never be at peace with his neighbours because the *ancien régime*, led principally by Russia and England, could never be at peace with a post-revolutionary order.

In the post-Cold War world, the United States finds itself equally insecure about the future. Just as Napoleon had to combat the old order, it has to combat countries that wish to challenge its position, or terrorist movements that are trying to subvert the old order it is trying to prop up. The problem is that maintaining the status quo calls for more effort than maintaining the bipolar Cold War regime. The old deterrent structure of the Cold War 'don't do that' has been replaced by a more active dissuasive policy of 'if you don't do that...' And the dissuasion is now carried out regularly by stealth bombers and cruise missiles.

This deterrent strategy has three features worth discussing. First, every surface of the planet is in contact with every other. 'Only connect...', are the opening words of E. M. Forster's *Howards End*, in which he described how unconnected were the lives of his contemporary Londoners. Today there is not a single point on the globe that cannot be seen. Satellites render everything transparent; they provide a 'vision-less gaze'. Everything can be detected. Almost nothing can be concealed. The radiant arc of a communications satellite 22,300 miles above earth synchronises time and transforms the globe into a single homogeneous space. The conquest of time and space, the dream of the nineteenth-century romantics, has now been realised.

This, writes James Der Derian, represents a new regime of power in international relations. Human intelligence lacked ubiquity and high resolution. The technical intelligence system does not rely on a human filter at all. The computer identifies and assesses information and relays it to military analysts. A new dialectic has arisen between the observer and observed. What you see you strike, whether it is a missile system about to be activated, or a nuclear programme about to go on line (Der Derian, 1992: 31).

Every point of the globe is also on camera. Military missions have been known to be governed by television schedules, especially in Libya in 1986, the first bombing in history that was scheduled for Prime Time TV. It was staged for the precise moment when the networks opened their national news programmes. This convenient arrangement allowed the network anchormen to switch at once to Tripoli so that their viewers could watch events live on television.

The second feature of the new deterrent strategy is that the United States can strike from anywhere in the world. According to *The Economist* (30 September 1995), distance has been abolished. In the age before firearms, the speed of a weapon was limited. You could see the trajectory of an opponent's javelin and parry it with a shield. You could not see a bullet's trajectory, of course, but you could move out of range. Today, however, everyone and everything is within range, and the United States has the capability to strike wherever it wants to. It no longer even needs fixed bases.

'The revolution in military affairs' (the application of new information technologies) is making it possible to give serious consideration to 'disengaged conflict': the chance to fight a war from a distance without the network of bases and overflight facilities that proved so important to America as recently as the Gulf War. To quote an article from *Scientific American* (272, 12 (December 1995): 74): 'In the long term scenario aircraft carriers, tanks, fighters and bombers may cease to have a primary role in the post-modern theatre of war. Most US forces may be stationed at home.'

Third, Umberto Eco argues that we have changed the rules of politics. Where others talk about the end of history, Eco talks about the end of politics as we have traditionally understood the term. The United States does not fight wars to change regimes or impose new world orders. It fights to deter things from happening. What we have is a 'warlike politics', a 'war without respite', a Clausewitzian formulation even if it challenges Clausewitz's concept in suggesting that war is no longer a continuation of politics but politics a continuation of war (Eco, 1997: 16).

Pre-emptive air strikes have become the means by which the post-modern world tries to disarm the rogue states of the modern, to decelerate history, to buy time to stop the modern world from using weapons of mass destruction, to assist it to make history on its own terms.

Deterrence, writes Jean Baudrillard, did not end with the Cold War. The nuclear stand-off kept the two superpowers at peace with each other for forty years. The difference today is that deterrence is taking the form of *dissuasion*, the relentless application of force 365 days a year.

Deterrence is a very peculiar form of action: *it is what causes something not to take place*. It dominates the whole of our contemporary period, and it tends not to produce events but to cause something not to occur, while looking as though it is a historical event. Or else events do take place instead of some other events which did not. War, history, reality, and passion – deterrence plays its part in all these (Baudrillard, 1998: 17).

In this world there is no prescription for victory. 'The wars of ideology call for total victory; the wars of interest for victory; in the pre-modern world victory is not a relevant objective', according to Robert Cooper, a British diplomat. We need, he adds, to get used to the idea of double standards. Post-modern societies may operate by one set of rules when dealing with each other, but when dealing with others they may need 'to revert to the rougher methods of an earlier era: force, pre-emptive attack, decapitation, whatever is necessary for those who live in the nineteenth century world . . .' (Cooper, 1996). Victory is no longer an objective. Post-modern societies do not fight wars to secure a final peace; they use war to manage insecurity. Unable to aim for a decisive victory, governments try to manage conflicts and claim victory when a risk is reduced to manageable proportions. Wars are no longer wars, they are police actions. For there is no 'peace', no world order, no imperial mission, only the endless prospect, to quote President Clinton, of 'a world in which the future will be threatened'.[2]

Deterrence is not only the preferred option, it is the only option, even if this may mean allowing regimes like Saddam Hussein's to remain in power indefinitely. Over forty years ago Kenneth Walz claimed that 'in war there is no victory, but only varying degrees of defeat'. It was a proposition, he added, that 'had gained increasing acceptance in the twentieth century' (Walz, 1959: 1). It may have even greater currency in the twenty-first.

In sum, post-modern societies are principally interested not in victory but in safety; they are primarily interested not in attaining the good but preventing the worst. And they are plagued by risks and threats. What is the difference between the two? Risks involve controllable consequences; threats uncontrollable consequences. The United States can devise a regulatory regime for risks: a form of accident insurance. It can impose sanctions on countries trying to upgrade their nuclear weapons programmes like India and Pakistan; it can enforce intrusive verification regimes like UNSCOM in Iraq. But there is no insurance against threats. The US must act before a risk becomes a threat. It has even evolved a new terminology to describe its actions: 'degrading', or 'attriting' the enemy's capabilities before they can be put to use.

If Clausewitz called violence the 'essence' of war, in an age of pure war, violence has taken a particular form: that of terror. As Baudrillard

---

[2] 'Remarks to the Veterans of Foreign Wars on Kosovo', The White House, Office of Press Secretary, Eisenhower Hall, Ft MacNair, 13 May 1999: 89.

contends, the problem of security so haunts our societies that it has long ago replaced liberty as the most important factor of life. In the Cold War the West fought to protect its liberty at the risk of nuclear destruction. Today our risk-averse societies crave security, and are ready to devise appropriate strategies to obtain it. Gone is the constellation of social alienation and class war; in place of it we have a constellation of terror. And the response? In order not to be taken hostage ourselves we have to take others hostage, or at least we must be willing to threaten to (Baudrillard, 1990: 39).

For if we move from the humanitarian agenda to that of national security, the Americans find themselves living in a world in which the major threat comes not from states but from non-state actors (often, of course, sponsored by governments). The most recent is the wealthy Saudi exile, Osama bin Laden, whose terrorist base in Afghanistan was targeted by 75 Tomahawk cruise missiles in October 1998. This was the first time that an individual had been targeted by a state using cruise missiles.

There is no doubt that the balance of power between the state and the individual has shifted markedly, if not yet decisively, in the information age, in favour of the individual. Capital accumulation, the ability to form networks of electronic communications, the ending of the national monopolies of effective weapons, the way in which the new communications have freed organisations and individuals from the constraints of specific locations, all these things, in the case of bin Laden, made him the first sovereign terrorist. It was especially significant in this context that his terrorist network was described by *The Washington Post* (21 August 1998) as 'a stateless confederation of terrorist groups without strict hierarchy, government or territory', but one that was all the more dangerous for that. In the same article, a high-ranking official called bin Laden 'a transnational actor in and of himself'. In the modern era legitimate authority was subsumed by the concept of state sovereignty; in the post-modern era state sovereignty has been subsumed by acts of individuals. Acts of terrorism are increasingly classified not in the category of social crimes but of war.

Such a conclusion, however, begs many questions: is the war against terrorism really a 'war'; and is it a high-intensity or low-intensity affair? Unfortunately, the potential for it to become warlike and to pose a high-intensity challenge is great. Instead of a state of siege, politics has become a state of emergency in which traditional diplomacy has been replaced by 'anti-diplomacy' (Der Derian, 1992: 89). In a state of 'pure war' the United States has dispensed with declarations of war. It no longer distinguishes between war and peace, only between war and an armistice.

The problem is that the post-modern notion of deterrence raises an embarrassing question. Every side has anti-terrorist special forces: Delta Force (the United States); the SAS (UK); the GSG-9 (Germany), but does the prefix, 'anti', before terrorism support the distinction? Were not the cruise missile strikes on Khartoum and Kabul in 1998 terrorist acts, in the absence of a declaration of war? Terrorist or not, they seem to represent the future face of warfare.

A risk or threat may be dealt with in the person of a dictator or a regime, but even if the person is removed or corralled, the problem (nuclear proliferation, for example) will persist. It will merely metastasise or reappear in a different region or form (from ethnic cleansing in the Balkans to ethnic cleansing in East Timor).

Limited war has taken the form of peacekeeping at the beginning of the twenty-first century by default, not design. The ethics of world order have been superseded by those of crisis management. We now have the ethics of triage: we bandage up some societies, hospitalise others, and let others suffer on their own. Triage is a perfectly ethical activity, of course, but it is what is demanded at the time. It is also necessarily selective. The United States acts in the name of humanity – that is the language of humanitarian wars – but it now finds itself quarantining off parts of the world and thus diminishing its former inclusive view of humanity. Perhaps this is one of the unforeseen consequences of its humanitarian agenda.

Conclusion

Nobody schooled in twentieth-century history can regard the use of American power as undesirable or sinister in itself. It remains the world's ultimate guarantor of law and order, tested and found reliable whenever international law blatantly breaks down as in Kuwait. More baffling is what the purpose is of the exercise of American power in a post-ideological age.

Vietnam showed 'the arrogance of power'; and the need to find a new ethical basis for it. It required a new ideology of power. Instead, America has no grand purpose in mind. Its power is largely reactive. It is risk-aversive, and therefore unmindful of the risks others have to run. It is still struggling to target the evils of the world with the blunt weapons of the Cold War. Air power and cruise missiles do not always allow ethical choices when it comes to targeting. Our weapons are not precise enough yet to select targets without risk of collateral damage. The threat of massive retaliatory force contained totalitarianism in the second half of the twentieth century, but it cannot police the internal conflict of states. For all its bluster, no one in America really minds enough about Saddam or Milosevìc to fight them to the death or demand their unconditional surrender, an ethical requirement in the past. The game is not worth the candle. The United States talks the language of humanitarianism, but it does not have the will to adopt a policy that would enforce it. Until it does, its ethical pretensions will be open to challenge.

10 Blair's Britain: a force for good in the world?

Tim Dunne and Nicholas J. Wheeler

On 12 May 1997, the new Labour government's foreign secretary, Robin Cook, informed an expectant audience of the course he intended to plot for British foreign policy. He announced 'a global foreign policy' which was to be guided by the goals of security for all nations, prosperity, protection for the environment and 'an ethical dimension' (FCO, 1997b). This part of the mission statement dominated the media coverage the following day, but there were other hints of a radical departure from the pragmatic conservatism that had dominated British foreign policy for fifty years. New Labour's view of British identity seemed quite different from the jingoism that dominated the Thatcher governments. Sovereignty talk, so loud under the previous government, was nowhere to be heard. There was no mention of 'threats' to national security, no elevation of the principle of non-intervention in Britain's domestic affairs. In their place, we heard 'internationalism', 'promoting democracy', 'promotion of our values and confidence in our identity', 'a people's diplomacy' and so on.

The most significant discursive departure concerned the priority to be accorded to the promotion of human rights: 'Our foreign policy must have an ethical dimension and must support the demands of other peoples for the democratic rights on which we insist for ourselves. The Labour Government will put human rights at the heart of our foreign policy...' (FCO, 1997b). Whilst Cook's predecessors would have concurred with the priority accorded to the goals of security, prosperity and protection for the environment – even if they would not have been so open in announcing them – they would definitely not have been comfortable with his missionary call to 'make Britain once again a force for good in the world' (FCO, 1997b).

How does this claim stand up four years later? Has New Labour delivered on its promise to place human rights at the heart of foreign policy, or has Cook's policy been so buffeted by events that it looks little different

We would like to thank Chris Brown and the editors for their helpful comments on an earlier version of this chapter. Some of the ideas build on our contribution to Little and Wickham-Jones, 2000.

from that which preceded it? Cook's predecessor, Lord Hurd, has argued that Labour's foreign policy is not the radical departure it professes to be. They have merely adjusted the compass 'by two or three points', not 180 degrees (Hurd, 1997: 25). The journalist John Pilger believes that New Labour has returned to the realism that has always framed British foreign policy. In his words: 'The announcement [i.e. the Mission Statement] was, of course, at odds with the historical record, which shows that since 1945 Tory and Labour governments have had almost identical foreign policies, none of which have upheld human rights' (Pilger, *The Guardian*, 25 January 1999).

This chapter does not agree with the 'business as usual' position of the critics, but it supports the growing ranks of those who point to the increasing discrepancy between the moral rhetoric of the Blair government and its subsequent practices. To explore just how far the Labour government has failed to live up to the human rights standards it articulated in May 1997, we set up a benchmark by which to judge the government's ethical foreign policy. Despite reiterating the need to place human rights at the centre of foreign policy, the government has not elucidated a conceptual framework for deciding the priority to be accorded the various principles in the mission statement. Building on our earlier study, this chapter furnishes such a framework which is predicated on the proposition that the state should act as a 'good international citizen' (Wheeler and Dunne, 1998: 847–70). Does Britain qualify for admission to the select group of 'ethical states' (Lawler, 1994)?

In the first section, the concept of good international citizenship is developed as a litmus test by which to assess the government's commitment to human rights in foreign policy decision-making. The next section examines the historical record to see whether the priority Britain has accorded to the human rights dimension meets the standard demanded of ethical states. We focus on three cases that illustrate the dilemmas and trade-offs that regularly confront foreign ministers who wish to pursue a foreign policy committed to the promotion and defence of human rights. The foreign secretary has placed considerable faith in the dialogical approach to human rights diplomacy, and the centrepiece of this, as we discuss below, has been the government's attempt to initiate a dialogue with the Chinese government on human rights. We draw attention to the constraints that inhibit the government from making human rights the defining basis of its relationship with China. The second case we focus on is Indonesia and we argue that the government had more room for manoeuvre in censuring and sanctioning the Suharto regime. Its decision to subordinate human rights to commercial considerations in selling arms to the Indonesian government manifestly fails the test of good international citizenship.

A commitment to dialogue in the diplomacy of human rights assumes that the participants are open to the possibility of changing their position. Recent cases of ethnically motivated violence in Kosovo and East Timor raise the question of what the good international citizen should do when a government rejects the minimum standards of common humanity that have been legitimated by the society of states. Does NATO's 'humanitarian war' against the Federal Republic of Yugoslavia (FRY) demonstrate that using force in defence of global humanitarian norms is, in exceptional cases, a necessary component of good international citizenship? Or is one of the lessons of the war in the Balkans, as some argue, that evil means rarely bring about good ends? (Booth, 1999: 11). A highly controversial aspect of the intervention in Kosovo concerns the legal authority with which 'Operation Allied Force' was launched. This raises the question of how the good international citizen should balance the conflicting claims of legality and morality in such cases.

Good international citizenship revisited

The debate about how those charged with the responsibility of high office ought to act is as old as politics itself. Realists have long claimed that the responsibility of leaders is to promote the security and welfare of their own citizens over utopian ideals of common humanity. States cannot afford the luxury of propagating their own values in an uncertain and dangerous world. Instead, they should be guided by hard-headed security interests and commercial considerations. The implication is clear: governments that bring human rights into the diplomatic dialogue risk weakening the security of the national community which they are entrusted to protect. Realists point to the fate of those like Jimmy Carter whose human rights policies could not stand the collapse of superpower détente, degenerating into the inconsistencies which Stanley Hoffmann labelled 'the hell of good intentions' (Hoffmann, 1981). There is an inescapable tension between national security and human rights in foreign policy-making, and governments pursuing a realist course will always steer clear of any temptation to take the moral high ground.

Set against this, liberals have long argued that there is a mutual interdependence between the provision of national security, the strengthening of international order and the promotion of human rights. The idea of good international citizenship should be seen as one version of this older liberal belief that order and justice can be reconciled. A decade before Cook enunciated an ethical dimension to British foreign policy, the Australian Labor Party sought to pursue a form of ethical statecraft that it called 'good international citizenship'. The idea has become intimately associated with Gareth Evans, the minister for foreign affairs from 1988 to 1996, although its origins go back to Canada's commitment in the 1960s to an internationalist foreign policy (Lawler, 1999). Evans argued that Australia had to promote an internationalist agenda on global challenges such as peacekeeping, peace enforcement, arms control, the environment, drugs and refugees. These issues, he maintained, could only be addressed through international cooperation (Evans, 1989; Hanson, 1999).

Foreign policy thus springs from the principles of democracy, human rights and good governance. Evans recognised that Australia would not be credible in arguing for human rights internationally 'if in our national policies on Aboriginal affairs, immigration or the like we are seen to be indulging in double standards' (Evans, 1989: 16). States that speak the language of good international citizenship will be mistrusted if they do not uphold principles of democratic governance at home. Evans emphasised that 'in the longer term, the evolution of just and tolerant societies brings its own international returns – in higher standards of international behaviour, and in the contribution that internal stability makes to international stability and peace' (Evans, 1989: 12).

The British foreign secretary and prime minister have not drawn directly from their Australian counterparts' insights and experiences. But like the Labor governments in Australia, New Labour is committed to developing institutions and rules for collective action by the international community. In a phrase that could have been lifted from Bull's *The Anarchical Society*, Cook argued that membership of the 'international community' brings with it an obligation 'to abide by the rules' (FCO, 1997c). The implication is that states that abuse human rights forfeit the right to be treated as legitimate members of the international community, and should become the subject of international scrutiny and censure.

How, then, does good international citizenship help governments in setting the compass of an ethical foreign policy? There was a certain 'Goldilocks' quality about Evans' formulation: he wanted to reject a policy based purely on self-interest ('too cold'), while steering clear of a cosmopolitanism that sought to replace the states-system with a universal community ('too hot'). What, then, is 'just right'? Chris Brown correctly argues that, at its core, the Blair government's ethical foreign policy is an attempt to 'reconcile the national interest with the norms of international society' (see Chapter 2). But the devil is in deciding what to do when the national interest and the norms of international society are in tension, and in agreeing on which norms of the society of states should be privileged in particular cases where they are in conflict. Without explicit criteria, the debate becomes a somewhat sterile argument between politicians defending Britain's 'interests', and the press believing that an ethical foreign policy means the consistent application of principles irrespective of widely divergent contexts.

Andrew Linklater has suggested a conceptual way of steering a course between the protection of vital national interests and respect for the norms of international society. Ethical states are not required to sacrifice their vital security interests out of fidelity to the rules of international society, but they are required 'to put the welfare of international society ahead of the relentless pursuit of [their] own national interests' (Linklater, 1992: 8–9). Given that respect for human rights is central to the 'welfare of international society', states that are good citizens not only have to place order before the pursuit of narrow commercial and political advantage, they are also required to forsake these advantages when they conflict with human rights. This is the litmus test by which we propose to evaluate the success of Cook's diplomacy of human rights in enmeshing Asian states into a dialogue about justice.

Dialogical statecraft

In his most significant contribution to defining the character of the government's ethical foreign policy, the foreign secretary claims that a dialogue on human rights can avoid the twin perils of a 'row' or 'kow-tow' (*The Daily Telegraph*, 14 November 1997). This suggests that he sees the most significant challenge for the diplomacy of human rights as lying in Asia. Cook rejects the low priority the previous government accorded to human rights, but argues that more will be achieved through 'dialogue' than public confrontation. A genuine 'dialogue' is not an occasion for lecturing or hectoring as realist critics have contended; rather it is an opportunity for an 'open exchange of views' (FCO and DFID, 1998).

China and the human rights dialogue

China is a hard case for applying the test of good international citizenship because security interests are paramount in Britain's bilateral relationship with China. In his first year in government, Cook did not shy away from putting human rights more firmly on the agenda than his Conservative predecessor had; quite the opposite, he made the bold claim that the government's dialogue with China on human rights had achieved more in one year than the Conservative government had achieved in the previous ten (BBC Radio Four interview, 4 April 1998).

Is Cook's claim that there is a middle way between 'row' and 'kow-tow' just a slogan which covers up the reality that, after a few high profile exchanges on human rights, Britain gets on with the traditional business of diplomacy? The difficulty in evaluating Cook's strategy is that we cannot know how much more might be achieved by adopting a tougher stance.

The dilemma is illustrated by the foreign secretary's trip to China in January 1998. Cook requested the release of twelve dissidents but only raised these cases at a junior level within the government (*Electronic Telegraph*, 20 January 1998). During a four-hour meeting with Chinese foreign minister, Qian Qichen, he decided not to mention any of the individual cases on his list, instead discussing human rights in general terms. Moreover, having said that he would provide a platform for the victims of human rights abuses, the foreign secretary declined to meet Wei Jingsheng during his visit. Cook later claimed that China's release of its most famous dissident in November 1997 was a vindication of the policy of dialogue. However, the human rights campaigner, who spent eighteen years in prison, refuted Cook's claims. Not only did Wei Jingsheng criticise the foreign secretary for not meeting him, he later castigated the part Britain played in refusing to table a resolution censuring China at the 1998 UN Human Rights Commission. British policy, he argued, was a 'disgrace' which lifted 'pressure from the Chinese Government' (*Electronic Telegraph*, 10 March 1998).[1]

The British government's justification for not censuring China was that dialogue was producing 'encouraging results' (*Electronic Telegraph*, 24 February 1998). China signed two key legal texts, the UN Covenants on Economic, Social and Cultural Rights and on Civil and Political Rights, adding credibility to this view. But at the end of 1998 and in the first half of 1999, the US State Department reported a sharp deterioration in the Chinese government's human rights record, in particular regarding the detention of political dissenters and the brutal suppression of Tibetan culture (*Electronic Telegraph*, 1 March 1999). China's blatant disregard for the provisions of the two Covenants is illustrated by the massive clampdown on human rights activists that followed President Clinton's trip in late 1998 (*Electronic Telegraph*, 18 October 1999).

In October 1999, the Chinese president, Jiang Zemin, visited Britain, providing the government with a golden opportunity to communicate to the Chinese leadership at the highest level that the results of the dialogue were far from satisfactory. Blair was under pressure from human rights groups to make a public statement condemning China's human rights record, but he declined to take this opportunity. It was reported that Downing Street wanted to 'play down human rights, insisting that it was

---

[1] Other human rights organisations also expressed disappointment. Jean-Paul Barthoz, of Human Rights Watch, called the collective decision of the fifteen EU foreign ministers 'a major step backwards' (*Electronic Telegraph*, 24 February 1998).

not the issue by which relations should be defined' (*Electronic Telegraph*, 22 October 1999). Cook did raise two names in discussion with his opposite number, but when questioned on Britain's low-profile approach to human rights, he referred to a list that officials in the Foreign and Commonwealth Office had handed over the previous month to their Chinese counterparts. This approach to human rights issues was little different from the one pursued by their predecessors, and it supports Hurd's claim that the government has altered the compass by no more than a few degrees.

Although it was widely reported in the press that the Labour government's reticence on human rights reflected its desire to secure new business contracts in the lucrative Chinese market, two other key reasons constrained the pursuit of tougher strategies for promoting human rights. The first concerns Britain's obligations to the people of Hong Kong. In Cook's testimony to the House of Commons Foreign Affairs Committee, he argued that 'the prime consideration of British foreign policy in relation to China must be . . . a duty of care to the six million residents of Hong Kong' (Cook, 1998: 53).

The second constraint is that Britain has vital security interests both in Asia-Pacific stability and in the broader need for Chinese participation in multilateral security institutions. And, given Indian and Pakistani nuclear weapons tests, China's support will be crucial to any future moves to strengthen the global non-proliferation regime. The dilemma is that the West needs China if there is to be any enforcement of international rules outside China, but this precludes the possibility of enforcing the rules *against* China for its violation of human rights on the inside.

Critics of Britain's China policy recognise that vital security interests are at stake but argue that they would not be jeopardised by a more assertive human rights policy. However, the charge that Blair and Cook are too timid in believing that there is no alternative to dialogue underestimates China's willingness to tolerate international condemnation and even the imposition of negative sanctions. The problem is that before the Chinese president's visit, the government defended its China policy on the grounds that it was delivering on human rights. This established a standard by which to hold it accountable and, given increasing repression inside China and growing criticism from domestic publics and human rights NGOs, it is incumbent upon the government to make the case that Britain's vital security interests would be undermined if the government adopted a more critical diplomacy of human rights. Otherwise, critics will rightly assert that New Labour has fallen into the traditional British habit of placing trade before human rights in the hierarchy of foreign policy principles.

One aspect of President Zemin's visit which cannot be justified in a democratic society is the government's handling of the peaceful demonstrations against the visit. The media were on hand to beam around the world pictures of the British police tearing up the banners of people campaigning for the right of Chinese people to conduct such demonstrations. In adopting such a tough line, not unlike the one adopted by the Chinese government when it kept Tiananmen Square empty on the tenth anniversary of the massacres there, the Blair government dealt a blow to democratic values and made a major miscalculation. It should have used the demonstrations to impress upon Jiang Zemin that Britain's China policy was constrained by the need to show progress on human rights. At the very least, this would have sent a different signal to the Chinese president than the one communicated by the summit that the Labour government's human rights talk was superfluous to the main issues of security and trade.

Indonesia, human rights and commercial interests

If Britain's relations with China pose a 'hard case' for the test of good international citizenship, relations with Indonesia do not concern vital security interests; the trade-off is between commercial considerations and human rights. Cook hoped that a dialogue with Indonesia could be an effective instrument for bringing about democratic reforms. 'Diplomatic pressure', he maintained, was 'important' (BBC Radio Four interview, 4 April 1998). This tactic was controversial given that Indonesia has one of the worst human rights records in the world.

The brutality of the Indonesian military was visible to all in the days following the 30 August election in East Timor. There is considerable evidence that the military were supplying the anti-independence militias with weapons and, in many cases, participating themselves in destroying the country (United Nations Mission in East Timor Press Release, 9 September 1999). It will be a while before the scale of the violence in August and September 1999 is documented, but the pattern since 1975 indicates a deliberate policy of mass executions on ethnic grounds. Only this time there was a UN presence on the island to record the horrors, aided by journalists and television crews.

When it became obvious that the Indonesian military were active in derailing the transition to democracy in East Timor, the British government broke with the policy of a quiet dialogue with Indonesia over human rights. Events demanded a tougher response, and the government can claim some credit for pressurising President Habibe to accept the deployment of UN peace enforcers in late 1999, although Clinton's threat of sanctions was the biggest single reason for their capitulation.

Just prior to travelling to the APEC summit in Auckland, Cook issued a strong statement condemning 'the appalling brutality' and demanding 'an urgent response from the international community' (Foreign and Commonwealth Office News, 7 September 1999). It would be a mistake to underestimate the important role played by Cook and the Foreign Office in supporting a 'coalition of the willing' to intervene (Britain contributed its Gurkha regiment to the multinational force) and, equally importantly, in drafting a Chapter Seven Security Council Resolution mandating the Australian-led force to restore peace and security in East Timor. This was a very different kind of response than Harold Wilson's government took in 1975 when Suharto's illegal annexation of the territory was thought by many in Whitehall to be in Britain's commercial interests (Pilger, *The Guardian*, 25 January 1999). In other words, the normative context which framed the present government's relations with Indonesia has changed considerably, in line with the wider transformation in the conduct of international relations after the Cold War.

What has not changed over the last two decades is the sale of armaments to Indonesia. In 1977, as reports of Suharto's genocidal policy were being widely publicised, David Owen, the foreign secretary, approved the sale of Hawk jets to the Indonesian government. In what will surely go down as the darkest hour of New Labour's ethical foreign policy, the government has continued to supply weapons to Suharto's successors, ranging from jets to rapid firing machine guns. The government's justification is woefully inadequate. Baroness Symons, the defence procurement minister, claimed that Indonesia has a right under the UN Charter to buy weapons for self-defence; but this is problematic given the overwhelming evidence that 'defence' forces have violently 'policed' a territory that has never been recognised as a *de jure* part of its sovereignty. Symons has not been the only member of the government to offer slippery explanations for arms exports to Jakarta. Even after nineteen days of state-sponsored anarchy in East Timor, the foreign secretary was standing by the unverifiable claim that '[t]his Government has refused to license any arms exports that might be used against the people of East Timor' (Cook, 1999a). We now *know* that the government of Indonesia had no control over the Indonesia military and security forces 'on the ground'. This suggests quite the opposite conclusion to the one reached by Cook. It is almost inconceivable that British-made hardware *has not been used* for the systematic 'internal repression' of the East Timorese.

The British government has to some extent acknowledged the contradiction that Indonesia exposes between the goals of a human-rights-centred foreign policy and the persistent export of arms. On 11 September 1999, Cook announced that the government had suspended the delivery of six Hawk 'trainer' jets equipped with sophisticated air-to-ground weapons. The foreign minister said that Britain will 'support an EU arms embargo and will take national action to suspend further arms exports' (Foreign and Commonwealth Office News, 11 September 1999). The problem is that this came far too late; what New Labour should have done on arrival in office was to cancel the order for the Hawks. While states have a right to self-defence, governments that are 'gross violators' of human rights should be denied arms irrespective of their declared usage. By linking external protection to good governance, strong incentives are created for states to act as guardians of human rights in the domestic sphere. The depressing conclusion is that Britain has failed to act as a good citizen in its relations with Indonesia because it has placed selfish economic advantage prior to human rights concerns. Perhaps the best description of the British government's Janus-faced policy towards Indonesia was offered – fittingly – by an East Timorese activist: 'There is a profound contradiction between pushing for a peaceful solution and arming the Indonesian armed forces which are orchestrating the militia death squads and preventing a peaceful solution in East Timor' (Budiardjo, *The Guardian*, 12 May 1999: 12).

NATO's humanitarian intervention in Kosovo

The good international citizen is committed to upholding the norms of international society, but how does a state committed to an ethical foreign policy act when these norms are in fundamental conflict? NATO's intervention in Kosovo in March 1999 exposed this dilemma at its starkest: on the one hand, the Milosević government was guilty of gross violations of international human rights standards; on the other hand, NATO acted without express authorisation from the UN Security Council and its use of force breached the UN Charter's prohibition on using force.

The Blair government argues that its use of force had a secure basis in international law. It accepts that military intervention lacked express Council authorisation, but claims to have been enforcing existing Security Council resolutions adopted under Chapter Seven that condemned Milosević's abuses of human rights. Moreover, the British government argues that there are precedents supporting the legality of NATO's action in Kosovo. Baroness Symons claimed that Western intervention in northern Iraq in 1991 to create 'safe havens' for the Kurds supports a new rule of humanitarian intervention under customary international law, a claim that is highly contentious (Wheeler, 2000).

The foreign secretary also defended the legality of the action. He reported to the Foreign Affairs Select Committee that 'all the legal advisers to the 19 member states in NATO' concluded that the action was legal (Cook, 1999b). Yet this view was not widely shared within the alliance, let alone outside it. For example, in late 1998 the then German Foreign Minister Klaus Kinkel was worried that the position taken by Russia and China in the Security Council made it difficult to argue that existing Security Council resolutions authorised NATO's use of force (Guicherd, 1999: 26–7). On this point, the German foreign minister was correct. Russia and China argued that NATO was setting a dangerous precedent by acting outside the authority of the UN Charter. Their view, shared by other non-Western states, is that these 'new rules' conflict with the 'old rules' that protect states from unwarranted interference in their affairs. By analogy, one could ask how NATO states would respond if a coalition of Arab countries were to use force against Israel without the Security Council's authorisation but with a host of condemnatory resolutions as their cover.

NATO is on weak grounds in claiming that there is a right of humanitarian intervention in customary international law, but alliance governments have raised an important issue concerning the relationship between legality and legitimacy. Underlying the justifications of Cook and Blair is the argument that the lack of explicit Security Council authorisation should not prevent humanitarian rescue. Given that the UN Charter is built upon the foundation of 'we the peoples', those opposing the action on legal grounds have to answer the question whether the threat or use of the veto should be allowed to block nineteen states from upholding minimum standards of common humanity. This issue of authority is a deep and complex one that it is not possible to address fully here. What we can say is that the position taken by the British government has at least advanced the argument that international legitimacy does not reside solely with the Security Council. In this context, whilst there is little enthusiasm in the society of states to recognise a new legal right of humanitarian intervention without Council authorisation, NATO's action was received favourably by the majority of states. And by raising new humanitarian claims to justify the use of force, New Labour might have set a precedent that others will follow in future cases where the Council is prevented from acting to stop or – where there is convincing evidence that mass killings are being planned – prevent crimes against humanity. In this sense, the Labour government could be said to have been acting as a 'norm entrepreneur' (Finnemore and Sikkink, 1998).

If a practice of humanitarian intervention outside Council authorisation develops on an *ad hoc* basis in the future, it will be open to the risk of abuse. To minimise but not eliminate this danger, it will be necessary to reach a consensus on the substantive criteria that should define a legitimate humanitarian intervention. This will not prevent disagreement on whether the criteria have been met in specific cases, but it will provide the common reference points within which such an argument can take place. In our earlier contribution to the debate, we argued that the government had not given any thought to the principles that should govern the use of force in defence of humanitarian values. The experience of trying to reverse the FRY's policy of ethnic cleansing prompted the Labour leadership to reflect seriously on the criteria for legitimate humanitarian intervention. As the air war against Yugoslavia was under way, Prime Minister Blair outlined a checklist of 'new rules' that should govern the resort to – and conduct of – so-called humanitarian wars. In his words, 'the most pressing foreign policy problem we face is to identify the circumstances in which we should get actively involved in other people's conflicts' (Blair, 1999). These rules constitute important criteria by which the good international citizen should decide whether to intervene to end gross violations of human rights, but we argue below that they need modifying in key respects. The remainder of the section will examine Blair's five rules in the light of the Kosovo case to see whether the action met his standard for judging the legitimacy of humanitarian intervention.

The first requirement that the prime minister laid down is that force can only be considered when 'we are sure of our case'. There is no doubt that Blair did not waver in his belief that NATO's military action was justified. It was, in his words, a 'just war based not on any territorial ambitions but on values'. He believed that Britain would have forfeited the right to call itself a member of a civilised international community if it had not tried to end Milosević's ethnic cleansing in Kosovo. To be 'sure of our case', Blair argued, intervention must be motivated by humanitarian goals. This leaves open the question whether humanitarian impulses should be the primary determinant of action, or is it sufficient that they play some role in the decision-making calculus? In contrast to some critics of NATO's Balkan policy, we do not claim that the humanitarian rationale must be the sole, or even the over-riding, motive. What must be ruled out is the invocation of 'just cause' to cover over the pursuit of self-interest. Moreover, any non-humanitarian reasons behind the action must not contradict the humanitarian purpose of the mission. In the case of Kosovo, the non-humanitarian (and publicly declared) reasons of preventing the conflict spreading and maintaining alliance credibility did not contradict the humanitarian aims of 'Operation Allied Force'.

The second criterion is that all 'diplomatic solutions' must have been exhausted before force is resorted to. 'We should always give peace every chance', Blair claimed, 'as we have in the case of Kosovo.' Some critics argue that the alliance foreclosed on diplomacy too early, whilst others go further and assert that the United States and United Kingdom adopted an unacceptably hard line negotiating position in order to legitimate the recourse to force (Booth, 1999, Chomsky, 1999 and Herring, 2000). This is a damning indictment of NATO strategy but it does not address the obvious rejoinder that had NATO *not* acted, Milosević and his generals would have been able to implement their policy of ethnic cleansing with impunity. The ink was not even dry on the 'October Agreement' negotiated between the FRY and NATO before the Milosević regime began implementing its plan for depopulating Kosovo of its Albanian population. Consequently, when peace talks broke down at Rambouillet in February, the alliance faced the choice of becoming militarily engaged or standing by and allowing the ethnic cleansing.

The third principle guiding humanitarian intervention should be whether there are military operations 'we can sensibly and prudently undertake'. What happened in East Timor after the election on 30 August 1999 was a deliberate policy of systematic expulsion and killing. If we take international humanitarian norms as our guide, then a humanitarian war against Indonesia could have been justified. But would it have been prudent? There must be serious doubts whether a multinational 'coalition of the willing' could have defeated Indonesia militarily; going to war against the world's fourth largest country would have entailed huge risks to the intervening forces, and would probably have further destabilised regional peace and security. Consequently, it is important when evaluating the ethical credentials of a state's foreign policy to distinguish between cases where the selective tolerance of human rights abuses is motivated by selfish considerations, and those where prudence dictates a cautious response. However, caution does not mean inaction, and it is incumbent upon the good international citizen to justify why it is refraining from taking tougher action against governments that violate minimum standards of common humanity.

Was military action prudent in Kosovo? NATO had an awesome military capability available, even if it was held back for the first month (it took NATO 12 days to fly the same number of combat operations that it flew in the first 12 hours of the Gulf War in 1991). Military resistance from the FRY was virtually non-existent. Whether air power was a 'sensible' strategy remains hotly debated. Those who believe it worked resort to the argument that before 24 March, diplomacy had failed, and eleven weeks later, Kosovar Albanians were returning to their homes (*Electronic Telegraph*, 6 June 1999). Those who believe it was a disaster point to the fact that the stated aim of 'averting a humanitarian catastrophe' was exacerbated by the bombing. As Ken Booth argues, while NATO was not to blame for the ethnic cleansing, 'it can be held responsible though for creating the cover of war for the ethnic cleansers, and for inflaming the latter's desire to extract revenge against the defenceless Albanians they despised' (Booth, 1999: 6).

Blair's rules also need to be broadened to consider the Just War requirement that the use of force must be proportionate. Did the level of force employed in Kosovo exceed the harm that it was designed to prevent, as some human rights groups and international lawyers allege? Is NATO guilty of breaching international humanitarian law in the way that it conducted the bombing campaign? Although the alliance never targeted civilians deliberately, as the pressure for a 'result' grew, NATO defined 'military related targets' to include bridges, factories, the television station and electricity grids, producing significant civilian casualties.

Were there other military options that were 'prudent' and potentially better suited to protecting the Kosovars? Preventing the acceleration of the ethnic cleansing after the start of NATO's bombing campaign would have required a ground intervention, but there was no political consensus in the alliance to risk soldiers' lives to save Kosovar strangers. Consequently, NATO had to make do with an air strategy that was ill suited to the rescue mission that it had embarked upon. Once it became clear that NATO's use of air power had actually exacerbated the ethnic cleansing, the air strategy changed from preventing a humanitarian catastrophe to reversing it, so that the refugees could return safely to their homes. Any ethical audit of the war has to consider whether the human costs would have been less had NATO accepted that saving civilian lives required risking allied ones. And even if all the diplomatic routes had been exhausted, the same cannot be said for *all non-violent strategies* for ending the repression of the Kosovars. Would the imposition of severe international sanctions on the FRY whilst offering economic incentives 'for a changed polity in Kosovo' have achieved a humanitarian outcome at less cost and risk than the use of force (Booth, 1999: 10)? The problem with this approach is twofold: first, mandatory economic sanctions had been imposed since 1992 in response to Milosević's aggression in Bosnia, and they had produced no change in behaviour; and second, how many Kosovars had to be killed and expelled before the international community decided that 'something must be done'?

The fourth element in Blair's criteria is that the intervening force must be 'prepared for the long term'. Given the commitment in money and manpower to the peacebuilding process in Kosovo, the government can make a case that it has met this aim. Set against this, the NATO led intervention force (KFOR) that entered Kosovo on 12 June after Milosević had capitulated failed to stop the Albanians from exacting revenge against the Serbs, and fear of reprisals led the vast majority of the pre-war Serbian population to leave Kosovo. Could the United Kingdom and NATO have done more to protect the Serbs? The human rights situation for the Serbian minority left in Kosovo continues to be very perilous, and it remains to be seen whether the United Kingdom and the wider international community has the will to police the inter-communal conflict in Kosovo over the next few years or perhaps even decades.

The final criterion outlined by the prime minister is whether or not national interests are involved. Blair hints that it made a difference that the human rights violations were taking place 'in such a combustible part of Europe'. His hope – and it is central to the ethos of good international citizenship – is that 'mutual self-interest and moral purpose' are compatible. But what if there are no national interests at stake? Would New Labour justify using force for humanitarian reasons *in the absence* of any claims to advance the national interest? This begs the question of whether Blair and Cook would have stood aside and watched Rwanda burn. Or would they have argued that intervention was a duty given that genocidal slaughter was taking place? The Kosovo experience suggests that Britain would have been more energetic in trying to mobilise a multinational response; whether it would have been prepared to lead such a force in the absence of American participation is highly questionable.

What did Blair omit from his criteria? The most obvious silence concerns the question of authorisation. The closest he came to addressing this was in asserting that 'new rules' will require reformed institutions. He argued that 'we need to find a new way to make the United Nations and its Security Council work if we are not to return to the deadlock that undermined the effectiveness of the Security Council during the Cold War'. To further this debate, Britain has submitted to the UN Secretary General a set of 'guidelines' for humanitarian intervention. On the specific question of authorisation, the foreign secretary has stated that 'the use of force must be collective and only in exceptional circumstances should it be undertaken without the express authority of the Security Council' (Cook and Campbell, Foreign and Commonwealth Office News, 4 September 2000). Despite the controversy triggered by NATO's bypassing the Security Council over Kosovo, the government wants to keep the door open to the possibility that it might have to put humanitarian principles before established legal procedures for the use of force.

Conclusion

The concept of good international citizenship provides a moral compass for governments committed to strengthening human rights in the society of states. The good international citizen seeks to achieve the following goals: strengthening international support for universal human rights standards; obeying the rules of international society; acting multi-laterally and with UN authorisation where possible; and recognising that a sustainable ethical foreign policy requires the deepening of civil rights and constitutional reform 'at home'.

It is important to bear in mind the difficulties inherent in being a good international citizen. The institutions of international society are often weak and divided, and the rules are frequently contested. Blair and Cook have underestimated these constraints, and over-stated the extent to which the government has the capacity to respond effectively to the many injustices around the world. There is nothing new here; successive post-war British governments have suffered from delusions of great power status and influence. Cook can instruct his diplomats to 'demand' that others uphold the values *we* cherish, but there is little that Britain can do on its own if they choose not to listen.

Nevertheless, we still need to ask how well the Labour government has implemented its new foreign policy. We saw that the much-heralded diplomacy of human rights produced little in the way of discernible achievements in China. But given the wider national and international security issues at stake, the government had a very weak hand to play in its China policy. The same cannot be said for its relations with Indonesia. Here the government's reluctance to halt arms sales to Indonesia – until it was too late – has done considerable damage to the credibility of Cook's 'ethical dimension'. Images of British weapons being used against the East Timorese independence movement prompted respected insiders, such as Martin O'Neill MP (chair of the Commons Trade and Industry Select Committee), to ask 'what an ethical foreign policy amounts to, and how different it is from that followed by the previous government, because it is not very clear' (*Electronic Telegraph*, 16 September 1999). What makes this failure more difficult to understand is that in economic terms, our interests are *so small*. In fact, British citizens are subsidising the export of weapons to Indonesia. A government committed to promoting international human rights norms must cease selling arms to those who do not share these values. The complicity of the Indonesian army in the East Timor tragedy tells us that 'assurances' from human rights viola-tors that weapons will not be turned against their civilian population are worthless.

Perhaps the biggest challenge for the Labour government in its remain-ing years of office is to eliminate British arms exports to countries with poor human rights records. The register set up to monitor Britain's ex-ports has clearly failed, as has the EU code based on the same principles.

On this issue, governments should listen to the NGOs like Oxfam, Saferworld and Amnesty International. These organisations see the dark underside of the arms trade, and the misery that results from the availability of weapons to the enemies of democracy. They are telling governments that the arms trade must be controlled by an international code that restricts transfers to states that flout international human rights standards.

The government's critics cite Britain's participation in NATO's war against the FRY as the nadir of its ethical foreign policy. They charge that wars fought for humanitarian reasons always lead to greater violence, and that non-violent alternatives would have caused less suffering and destruction in Kosovo. However, good international citizens are morally required to use force in exceptional cases where it is judged that all credible peaceful alternatives have been exhausted, where delay in acting will lead to large numbers of civilians being killed, and where there is a reasonable prospect of success. Blair maintains that the United Nations and the rule of law should be at the heart of any doctrine of international community, but Britain was right to justify its intervention in Kosovo on humanitarian grounds even though it lacked express Security Council authorisation. The government's legal advisors privately knew that there was no uncontested right of humanitarian intervention in international law, but at the same time they needed a credible legal defence to present to domestic and international audiences. Consequently, they found themselves in the difficult position of having to claim a customary right of humanitarian intervention when what they were effectively doing was advancing a new legal claim that challenged existing UN norms with regard to the use of force. For Russia, China and India, this set a dangerous precedent that undermined the rule of law, but we would argue that New Labour was acting as an ethical state in arguing that the veto power of Russia and China should not be allowed to block the defence of human rights.

Establishing a right of humanitarian intervention is an important step in defending human rights, but this does not guarantee that intervention will take place unless governments recognise it as a duty. In discharging this duty, the good international citizen should be constrained by the following requirements: first, there is no realistic alternative to using force; second, the means employed are proportionate; third, there is a reasonable chance of success; and fourth, there must be a significant humanitarian motivation and any non-humanitarian reasons must not contradict the humanitarian aims of the intervention. Evidence that New Labour recognises a duty to intervene can be seen in Cook's contention during the Kosovo crisis that failure to act to save the Kosovars would have made Britain complicit in the ethnic cleansing. However, as our examination of the Kosovo case illustrated, the determination of the Blair government to participate only in a casualty free humanitarian war undermined the ethical credentials of the intervention. In killing to defend human rights, the good international citizen must be prepared to ask its soldiers to risk and, if necessary, lose their lives to stop crimes against humanity.

In the cases considered above, we have argued that the Labour government has sought to advance the ethical dimension in foreign policy with ambiguous results. But it is important to bear in mind that while they have not played their hand as well as the criteria for good international citizenship demands, the government is not the *only* player in the game of global ethics. What critics often disregard is the responsibility that falls on the shoulders of non-governmental actors – such as ordinary citizens, corporations, civil society and the media – to live up to the principles of the UN Charter. An ethical audit of these actors would also produce mixed results. We could all do more to live up to the moral standards embodied in the human rights regime. But more directly, civil society in Britain needs to recognise that an ethical foreign policy is too important to be left to politicians, soldiers and diplomats. This requires a robust human rights culture at home that will hold ministers accountable for the priority accorded to human rights in foreign policy. Such a culture is not only essential to shame governments into humanitarian intervention, but it will also make it more difficult for governments to evade their declaratory commitment to human rights when this conflicts with arms exports. Britain has an arms industry worth around £5 billion a year, and this creates a powerful lobby on ministers. To balance this, a vociferous human rights movement must make its voice heard in the corridors of the Ministries of Defence and Trade and Industry.

What is new about the Labour government's foreign policy, and what represents more than a slight resetting of the compass, is that, unlike previous governments, it has created the context for the development of this human rights culture. It has established human rights standards by which it wants to be judged, and whilst it has failed to live up to these on many occasions, it is only possible to point to this deficiency because it had the courage to strive for an 'ethical dimension' to its foreign policy.

11 The EU, human rights and relations with third countries: 'foreign policy' with an ethical dimension?

Karen E. Smith

This chapter will consider to what extent the European Union (EU) conducts foreign policy 'with an ethical dimension'. Several of the EU's member states have declared that ethical considerations will influence their foreign and development policies; if there is no attempt to introduce ethical considerations into collective policy-making at the EU level, then the commitment to foreign policy with an ethical dimension must be doubted. But the EU may also 'add value': member states can push for EU action on ethical issues, thus augmenting their own policies, and reluctant member states could come under pressure to take ethical considerations into account. That an EU position represents the positions of fifteen member states and the institutions of the world's largest trading bloc also adds value: the 'politics of scale' increases the international impact of an ethical dimension.[1]

Of course, the first question to ask is whether the EU conducts 'foreign policy' at all, with or without an ethical dimension. The answer is a qualified yes. The EU does not have a foreign policy. Its foreign policy competences are divided or shared with the member states. And the member states must generally agree unanimously to act collectively in international affairs – which does not happen all the time. An effective common foreign policy also requires consistency between the different decision-making frameworks or 'pillars' (for trade and development policy, and foreign policy).

On occasion the EU does conduct foreign policy – the member states agree on policy objectives and use collective and/or national means to pursue them. The Union carries out extensive relations with many third countries, which can involve political dialogue, trade and development aid. Increasingly, political considerations shape those relations. In fact,

I would like to thank Christopher Hill, Margot Light, Helene Sjursen and the participants of workshops at the London School of Economics and the 1999 UACES Research Conference for their helpful comments on this chapter.

[1] Roy Ginsberg (1989) used the term 'politics of scale' to describe the benefits of collective action over unilateral action.

the use of economic and other policy instruments in support of human rights is about as close to an integrated, consistent foreign policy as the EU could come: political objectives would guide the use of economic and other instruments, bridging the divide between the EU's separate decision-making pillars. But the way the EU makes foreign policy is still a key obstacle to a consistent EU approach to human rights.

The ethical dimension considered here is limited to the objective of enhancing respect for human rights in third countries. The EU has *not* declared that it is conducting foreign policy with an ethical dimension, but it *has* repeatedly stressed that respect for human rights is an important objective of its relations with third countries.[2] The chapter will first explore why the EU has embraced human rights as a foreign policy aim, and how it pursues that objective. In the second section, the consistency of the EU's policy will be considered. Is the EU a 'good international citizen'? It concludes that the EU's approach to human rights is inconsistent, and explores the reasons why.

Human rights and the EU's external relations

Until the late 1980s, human rights were promoted largely by the declaratory diplomacy of European Political Cooperation (EPC). EPC démarches and declarations frequently emphasised the importance of human rights, and condemned third countries for abuses. But using European Community (EC) trade agreements or development aid to punish human rights abuses was not acceptable. The Commission, for example, continuously rebuffed the proposal of the European Parliament (EP) to draft agreements so that sanctions could be imposed if human rights were violated. The Community's development aid was supposed to be non-political, its relations with the 'Third World' free of the vestiges of colonialism and distinct from the superpowers (Grilli, 1993: 102).[3] Relations would not be affected by the domestic politics of developing countries, including their human rights records. The Community's image as a 'civilian power' stems partly from its reluctance to use coercive foreign policy instruments.

The situation began to change in the second half of the 1980s, partly because of EP criticism. The EP used its new assent power under the 1987 Single European Act to press for consideration of human rights: in 1987

---

[2] This chapter concentrates solely on the external dimension of the EU's human rights policy, although internal policies are also important: the EU's increasingly tight asylum policy, for example, could harm people fleeing human rights violations.

[3] An exception was made for Idi Amin's Uganda: in June 1977, the Council stated that EC development aid to Uganda would not reinforce or prolong the deprivation of fundamental rights there (*EC Bulletin*, no. 6, 1977, point 2.2.59).

and 1988, it refused to assent to financial protocols with Turkey and Israel because of human rights concerns. The foreign ministers on 21 July 1986 reaffirmed 'their commitment to promote and protect human rights and fundamental freedoms' (Council, 1986). But they did not declare how they would carry out that commitment, beyond declaratory diplomacy. The Community did, however, impose limited negative measures on South Africa in 1985 and 1986, and an arms embargo and some diplomatic and economic sanctions on China following the Tiananmen Square events of June 1989: two cases that would have been difficult to ignore, given public pressure for action.

The Cold War ends

The significant impetus for using a wider range of policy instruments to promote human rights arose from the fall of the Iron Curtain in Europe and the desires of Central and East European countries (CEEC) to 'rejoin Europe', by which they meant eventual accession to the Community. From 1988, the Community hoped to encourage its eastern neighbours to carry out political and economic reforms by making trade and cooperation agreements, aid, association agreements, and finally EU membership conditional on satisfying certain criteria, including democracy, the rule of law, human rights and respect for and protection of minorities. The EU considered reforms to be necessary to ensure stability and security in Europe, a traditional liberal internationalist view (and one that reflects the West European experience), and it was willing to use both carrots and sticks to achieve these goals.

This effectively set a precedent for relations with other third countries. In June 1991, the Luxembourg European Council reaffirmed that '[t]he Community and its Member States undertake to pursue their policy of promoting and safeguarding human rights and fundamental freedoms throughout the world.' It also indicated how human rights could be promoted: economic and cooperation agreements with third countries could include clauses on human rights (European Council, 1991). The Maastricht Treaty, signed in February 1992, reflected this change. Its provisions on development cooperation (article 130u) and on the Common Foreign and Security Policy (article J.1) include the objective of developing and consolidating democracy, the rule of law and respect for human rights and fundamental freedoms.[4]

There are, of course, other reasons for incorporating human rights considerations into relations with developing countries. Human rights were

---

[4] With the Maastricht Treaty, the CFSP replaced EPC, and became the second 'pillar' of the European Union. The CFSP is more 'intergovernmental' than the first pillar, the EC.

no longer held hostage to Cold War exigencies, states did not have to turn a blind eye to abuses in allies or friends. There seemed to be greater public pressure for 'milieu goals' – protection of the environment, relief of poverty and starvation, promotion of human rights – or at least, there was greater space for such concerns to be expressed and addressed. There was also, however, a need to raise public support for foreign assistance programmes. Aid would go to 'deserving' recipients, thus providing a rationale for continued giving. This was backed up by World Bank findings in November 1989 that the failure of reforms in Sub-Saharan Africa was due partly to bad governance (Crawford, 1996: 32–3). The new wave of democratisation – in Latin America, Central and Eastern Europe, Africa – reinforced the view that respect for human rights and democratic principles was not an exclusively Western phenomenon and could and should be promoted abroad. Several member states (including the United Kingdom, France and Germany) announced in 1990–91 that respect for human rights and democratic principles would be a condition for receiving development aid.

Of course, as realists would maintain, considerations of human rights may simply mask other interests.[5] As aid budgets decrease, violations of human rights (however defined) could provide an excuse to cut off aid to strategically or commercially unimportant states. Or considerations of human rights and democratic principles could merely mask the objective of forcing states to undertake economic and good governance reforms, which would benefit Western investors. Unpacking the reasons for adopting human rights considerations thus requires analysing how human rights records affect relations with different states, both important and unimportant.

How does the EU pursue its human rights objective?

The EU promotes respect for human rights in a variety of ways: through the application of positive and negative conditionality, the provision of aid for human rights programmes, and the use of diplomatic instruments such as démarches and political dialogue.

Political conditionality[6]

Political conditionality entails a state or international organisation linking perceived benefits to another state (such as aid), to the fulfilment of

[5] E. H. Carr (1946: 87) argued that so-called universal principles are really the 'unconscious reflexions of national policy based on a particular interpretation of national interest at a particular time'.
[6] This section builds on Smith, 1998.

conditions relating to the protection of human rights and the advancement of democratic principles. Positive conditionality promises benefits to a state if it fulfils the conditions; negative conditionality involves reducing, suspending or terminating those benefits if the state violates the conditions (Storey, 1995: 134; Stokke, 1995: 11–13).

The offer of trade and association agreements, technical and development assistance, political dialogue and other instruments is now usually made conditional on respect for human rights and democratic principles. If a country contravenes those principles, negotiations on, or the conclusion of, an agreement can be suspended: for example, the conclusion of a partnership and cooperation agreement (PCA) with Belarus has been suspended since 1997 over the government's lack of democracy and respect for civil and political rights.

Recently, the EU has also agreed that approval of licenses for arms exports will be conditional on respect for human rights. In May 1998, the Council agreed on a Code of Conduct on Arms Exports, following an initiative by the 1998 British presidency, which had picked up a campaign by several hundred NGOs for a Code (General Affairs Council, 1998b; Davis, 1998: 217; McLean and Piza-Lopez, 1998). The British initiative was part of its foreign policy with an ethical dimension, but there were also self-interested reasons: ensuring that the British arms industry did not suffer as other EU countries scooped up trade that it had relinquished for human rights reasons.

The non-binding Code consists of eight criteria that are to govern the member states' arms exports. Under one of these, member states should not issue export licenses if there is a clear risk that the arms could be used for internal repression, and they should exercise special caution in issuing licenses for exports to countries where serious violations of human rights have been ascertained. Despite pressure to strengthen the Code, this has yet to take place (*European Voice*, 18–24 February 1999; General Affairs Council, 1999).

The most significant example of the EU's adoption of conditionality is the 'human rights clause', which is supposed to be included in all cooperation and association agreements. In May 1992, the Council decided that all cooperation and association agreements concluded with other European states should contain a clause permitting the suspension of the agreements if human rights and democratic principles are not respected. However, including human rights clauses in external agreements with non-European countries was still controversial; only in May 1995 did the Council agree to do so. Since 1995, over twenty agreements have been signed that contain the human rights clause, including the revised Lomé convention (see Arts, 2000), as well as EC regulations on aid (Council of the European Union, 1999, point 4.2.5; European Commission, 1995a and 1995b).

The Community could thus alter or suspend agreements with third countries that violate human rights and democratic principles.[7] In practice, no agreement has been suspended or denounced because of the human rights clause, although aid has been reduced or suspended in several cases (see table 11.1).

There is a clear preference for a positive approach. The Commission (1994: 11) has declared that the focus is to be on providing incentives for the promotion of human rights; sanctions 'should be considered only if all other means have failed'. The human rights clause states that the priority is to keep agreements operational wherever possible, and a consultation procedure is to be followed before taking action. Furthermore, the Union tries to avoid penalising the population: aid can be channelled through NGOs rather than through the government, and humanitarian and emergency aid always continues. The Union will also consider increasing its support for countries in which positive changes have taken place (see Council, 1998).

However, although this promise of extra support has been made several times, there is scant evidence of additional assistance to countries where things are improving. The EU has extended assistance to countries that received little or no EC aid before they undertook reforms – such as South Africa and the CEEC – but there are no reporting mechanisms for evaluating aid recipients, and no systematic procedures for redirecting aid to countries with good human rights records.

Aid for Human Rights and Democratisation

Since 1990, the EC has given aid to third countries to help them improve their human rights records and institute democratic reforms. The funds for what became the European Initiative for Democracy and the Protection of Human Rights steadily increased from ECU 59.1 million in 1994, to Euro 98 million in 1999. In 1998, the European Court of Justice (ECJ) ruled that the EC's human rights programmes were not properly legally based. Two new regulations were approved in April 1999

---

[7] There have been calls by the European Parliament, the Economic and Social Committee, and outside experts to include social rights in the clause. See Economic and Social Committee, 1997 and Comité des Sages, 1998. Under the Generalised System of Preferences (GSP), additional preferences will be given to countries that apply ILO conventions on freedom of association and child labour; preferences can be withdrawn for states that allow forced labour or the export of goods made with prison labour. Regulation no. 3281/94, in OJ L348 (31 December 1994). In March 1997, the Council suspended GSP for Burma because of its widespread use of forced labour.

to provide funding to promote human rights, democratisation and conflict prevention measures in third countries. But the amount agreed for funding between 1999 and 2004 is Euro 410 million, with an annual total of only Euro 82 million – less than the 1999 budget.[8] In the grand scheme of things, this is not much money: it is a small percentage of external funding, which itself is a small percentage (less than 6 per cent) of the EU's budget. There are familiar problems with the programmes (a top-down approach, little connections between programmes, inadequate programme management leading to lengthy delays in disbursements, and so on).[9] However, external reviewers have generally evaluated the EU's human rights and democratisation programmes positively, finding that in many places they have effectively contributed to an improvement (Heinz, Lingenau and Waller, 1995; ISA Consult, Sussex University European Institute and GJW Europe, 1997; and Karkutli and Butzler, 1997).

The EU has also sent election observers to third countries to help ensure free and fair elections. But it lacks a coherent strategy, clear legal framework and decision-making process, and a clear financing source for extending such assistance. For example, some decisions to send observers (to Russia, 1993) have been taken in the CFSP pillar; others (Russia, 1995 and 1996) have been taken in the Community pillar (see European Commission, 2000).

Diplomatic instruments

Every year, the EU, through the CFSP, makes numerous declarations about the human rights situation in third countries, and delivers démarches expressing concern about particular cases. Martine Fouwels argues that they can be effective, especially in individual cases of human rights violations (Fouwels, 1997: 309). Diplomatic sanctions (suspending high-level contacts and withdrawing ambassadors) and arms embargoes have been imposed on third countries over their human rights records. For example, diplomatic sanctions on Nigeria were tightened in 1995, following the execution of writer Ken Saro-Wiwa. In October 1996, diplomatic sanctions on Burma/Myanmar were strengthened, due to lack of progress towards democratisation and human rights violations.

Human rights issues are supposed to be raised regularly in political dialogue meetings. And conducting a 'critical dialogue' on human rights is a way for the EU to express its displeasure with a particular situation. Between 1992 and 1997, the Union was engaged in a critical dialogue

---

[8] Regulations no. 975/1999 and 976/1999 in OJ L120, 8 May 1999.
[9] The European Court of Auditors (2000) found numerous weaknesses in the planning and implementation of the programmes.

with Iran. In 1995, the EU entered into a human rights dialogue with China. The troika[10] and Chinese representatives meet twice a year to address the EU's concerns about the human rights situation in China (Council General Secretariat, 1994: 9; Council, 1999, point 4.2.3).

Human rights considerations also play a role in the EU's regional cooperation initiatives and dialogues (Council 1999, point 4.2.6). The 1994–95 Stability Pact for Central and Eastern Europe was an attempt to encourage the CEECs to reach agreements on minority rights; this approach has been replicated in the current Stability Pact for South Eastern Europe. Human rights are a key issue in the Euro–Mediterranean dialogue, and have been an item for discussion in the Asia-Europe Meeting (ASEM), within the framework of the San José process (with Central American countries), at the June 1999 summit with Latin American and Caribbean states, and at the April 2000 summit with African states.

The negative measures that the EU could take to punish human rights violations do not yet include the use of force. The EU's defence dimension is still 'under construction'. Whether the EU *should* intervene militarily, in defence of human rights or otherwise, is another matter.[11]

EU policy evaluated

Beyond doubt, the EU has incorporated human rights considerations into its relations with third countries. Its external human rights 'policy' is far-reaching and innovative: the human rights clause is a powerful instrument considering demand by third countries for agreements with the EU. Moreover, the EU does add value – all the member states are at least obliged to consider human rights in their collective policy. Human rights are on the agenda, where they are difficult to ignore, and they have become an important part of the EU's international identity.

But the EU's human rights policy has been criticised. In October 1998, for example, four high-level human rights practitioners (the Comité des Sages) called for change in the EU's human rights policy, charging that 'the strong rhetoric of the Union is not matched by the reality. There is

---

[10] This includes the current and future Council presidencies, the High Representative for the CFSP, and the Commission.

[11] Nicholas Wheeler and Tim Dunne maintain that a 'good international citizen' has 'a duty to use force in order to maintain international peace and security, and to prevent or stop genocide and mass murder' (Wheeler and Dunne, 1998: 869). One could instead argue that the EU should remain true to its civilian power roots, and renounce the potential to use force, just as this potential has effectively been eliminated among its member states. Humanitarian intervention could be carried out through other organisations (such as the UN).

an urgent need for a human rights policy which is coherent, balanced, substantive and professional' (Comité des Sages, 1998: 2).[12]

How consistent has the EU been in incorporating human rights considerations into its relations with third countries? Is it a 'good international citizen' (Dunne and Wheeler, 1998: 855); does it forsake commercial and political advantages where they conflict with human rights?

Inconsistency in EU policy

The EU is guilty of inconsistency, since third countries are treated differently, even though their human rights (and democratic) records are similar. This is a familiar dilemma: considerations of human rights compete with political, security and commercial considerations in foreign policy-making and states ignore human rights violations in 'friendly' or 'important' countries.

Inconsistency can undermine the very inclusion of human rights considerations in foreign policy. R. J. Vincent (1989: 58) noted:

[F]inding its place in the empire of circumstance is more damaging to human rights policy than it might be to other items of foreign policy, because it can be argued that it is on the substance and appearance of even-handedness that a successful human rights policy depends.

Inconsistency raises doubts about the extent to which human rights are a genuine concern in foreign policy. They could mask other interests (to reduce aid budgets, for example). If the incorporation of human rights into foreign policies is seen as a cynical attempt to re-order a country's foreign relations, then the influence of human rights demands will plummet. An external human rights policy will have little impact if it is glaringly inconsistent.

There is considerable evidence of external inconsistency in the EU's external relations. Poor, marginal states (often in Africa) of little importance to the EU or one of its member states tend to be subjected to negative conditionality (see table 11.1); these are the cases where it is also easiest to show that you are doing something about human rights.[13] Nigeria, which did suffer economic and diplomatic sanctions over its human rights and democracy record between 1993 and 1999, is the

[12] The four experts were Mary Robinson (UN High Commissioner for Human Rights), Catherine Lalumiere, MEP (former Secretary-General of the Council of Europe), Professor Peter Leuprecht and Judge Antonio Cassese.
[13] If conditionality is usually applied with respect to poor, marginal states, then it cannot be seen as an attempt to force third countries to adopt market economic reforms. Economic operators are unlikely to be keen about investing in or trading with marginal countries, so there would be little pressure to apply conditionality.

Table 11.1 *Cases of aid suspension/interruption for violation of human rights and democratic principles*

Country	Action taken	Reason
Belarus	1997: technical aid programmes halted	Violations of human rights and democracy
Burma/Myanmar	1988: no aid	Suspension of democracy
Burundi	1996: no new programmes launched; Commission delegation staff withdrawn	*Coup d'état*; security situation
Cambodia	1997: aid suspended	Suspension of democracy
Comores	1995: cooperation slowed until 1996 elections; 1999: cooperation reviewed	*Coup d'état* (1995 and 1999)
Croatia	1995: suspended from PHARE aid programme; relations strengthened in 2000 following elections	Violations of human rights and democracy, peace agreements
Equatorial Guinea	1992: no significant cooperation operation implemented	Violations of human rights
Gambia	1994: cooperation maintained only if meets basic needs; since 1997: aid being resumed following transition to democratic civilian rule	*Coup d'état*
Guatemala	1993: no further decisions on aid to be taken	Suspension of constitutional regime
Guinea Bissau	1999: cooperation reviewed	Interruption of democratisation process
Haiti	1991: cooperation suspended; 1994: resumed following elections; 1997: cooperation slowdown	*Coup d'état* (1991); lack of political agreement (1997)
Kenya	1991: aid suspended; 1993: aid resumed, but no aid for structural adjustment	Lack of progress in political field
Malawi	1992: almost total aid freeze; 1993: aid resumed after referendum	No progress in political field
Niger	Jan. 1996: aid suspended for 6 months; 1999: cooperation reviewed	*Coup d'état* (1996 and 1999)

Table 11.1 (cont.)

Country	Action taken	Reason
Nigeria	1993: review new aid programmes on case-by-case basis; Nov. 1995: cooperation suspended; 1998/1999: cooperation resumed (and sanctions lifted) with return to civilian democratic rule	Lack of democracy; execution of Ken Saro-Wiwa
Russia	2000: TACIS aid only for democracy and human rights projects, for 6 months	Use of force against civilians in Chechnya
Serbia	1992: sanctions; 1999: no PHARE aid, no reconstruction aid	War (1992); violations of human rights in Kosovo (1999)
Sierra Leone	1997: existing aid programmes discontinued	*Coup d'état*
Sudan	1990: new aid projects suspended	Civil war; human rights violations
Tajikistan	1997: TACIS aid programme suspended	Violations of democracy and human rights
Togo	1992: new programmes frozen; 1995: aid gradually resumed; 1999: aid suspended	Interruption of democratisation process (1992 and 1999)
Zaire (Democratic Republic of Congo)	1992: cooperation suspended (aid in 1994 for Rwandan refugees); some aid resumed in 1997	Setbacks in democratisation process

exception, but even here, the sanctions did not include oil. Other important third states, such as Algeria, have been the object only of démarches and declarations. Although elections were cancelled in Algeria in January 1992, the Community and member states expressed concern about the developments, but took no punitive action (partly because a victory for the Islamic Salvation Front was seen as the greater of two evils). The October 1999 *coup d'état* in Pakistan did not lead to the suspension of aid. The EU has found itself in a dilemma with respect to Russia's intervention in Chechnya. Even though Russia is bound by a human rights clause in its PCA, suspending the agreement has not been seriously considered (although aid was redirected to democracy and human rights projects for six months in 2000).

Three reasons can be adduced for the inconsistencies: one or more member states blocks the use of negative measures on certain third countries because they would harm their commercial interests; one or more member states blocks the use of negative measures because the country is politically or strategically too important to antagonise; and doubts about the effectiveness of negative measures in general affect policy-making. All three reasons can also be collective, in that the EU may share commercial or political interests that would block the use of negative measures, and it may be widely felt within the EU that negative measures would be ineffective.

It should be reiterated that these dilemmas also affect national policy-making, but they are compounded by the nature of the EU. Implementing negative measures requires consensus among the member states, and it is difficult to overcome what Stanley Hoffmann (1966: 881–2) called the 'logic of diversity', the centripetal effects of the different international interests of the member states. Even where qualified majority voting can be used (to suspend aid), it is difficult in practice to take measures if a member state is strongly opposed, even though member states could take advantage of the 'shield effect',[14] hiding behind the collective decision, disclaiming responsibility and citing the exigencies of going along with everyone else. Thus, where negative measures are imposed, no member state has strongly opposed their use. But even where agreement can be reached, it may only result in a decision based on the 'lowest common denominator', which could entail the watering down of negative measures.

Commercial interests are certainly behind the decisions to exclude oil from sanctions on Nigeria. They are also one reason why sanctions against China have not been reconsidered since 1990. In April 1997, several EU member states refused to support a resolution condemning China in the UN Commission on Human Rights, which had been jointly supported by the member states every year since 1989. They were apparently interested in smoothing relations with China so that important commercial deals could be concluded (Fouwels, 1997: 318–21). The human rights dialogue with China helps to justify this.[15] In February 1998, the General Affairs Council declared that the dialogue had had 'encouraging results' and thus member states should not table or co-sponsor a draft resolution at the Commission on Human Rights (General Affairs Council, 1998a). Although human rights in China were of 'growing concern' a year later, the Council reiterated this stance (*Agence Europe*, 24 March 1999). The EU's critical dialogue with Iran left the member states free to import

[14] This is Joseph Weiler's term, cited in Fouwels, 1997: 310.
[15] For a similarly sceptical view of constructive engagement, see Chapter 6.

Iranian oil, illustrating again that dialogue with third countries can provide a cover for non-action.

The inclusion of the human rights clause in external agreements is also inconsistent. Angela Ward has demonstrated that the EU's most important trading partners are not subject to the clause (Ward 1998: 508–28). It is not included in 'sectoral agreements', so that if a trading relationship (as with the United States) has evolved on the basis of sectoral agreements rather than on a more formal, wide-ranging agreement, the third country is not held to the same human rights standards as other countries. Cooperation agreements concluded before 1995 with important trading partners (Canada, China, ASEAN) have not been renegotiated to include the human rights clause.[16] And in 1997, the EU and Australia halted negotiations on a Framework Cooperation agreement because Australia refused to agree to the human rights clause. Instead, the two sides signed a less formal joint declaration. This was also the case with New Zealand. In February 1999, both sides signed a political declaration rather than a formal treaty because New Zealand opposed the inclusion of a human rights clause (*European Voice*, 4–10 February 1999).

Nonetheless, EU insistence on human rights has led to tensions with major trading partners. The replacement declarations with Australia and New Zealand do not provide for as strong a partnership as the trade agreements would have. The EU's relations with ASEAN have been tense: the EU postponed a meeting of the foreign ministers for three years until 2000 because it would not tolerate participation by the Burmese junta. Its recent insistence on abolishing the death penalty has caused friction with the United States and China, when the EU sponsored a resolution banning executions worldwide, which was carried overwhelmingly by the UN Commission on Human Rights, although the United States and China abstained. However, the EU clearly does not envisage taking sanctions against these major trading partners over human rights issues.

There are also, of course, political and strategic reasons for treating China lightly: its support for international action in Kosovo is needed in the UN Security Council, and its cooperation in enforcing non-proliferation norms is crucial, to cite just two examples. Isolating Russia by imposing negative measures is considered inexpedient for similar reasons; there is the additional perceived risk that pushing Russia too far might lead to a backlash against Western-encouraged reforms. The EU position on Algeria partly reflects concern to avoid instability, so as to prevent mass migration towards Europe (and France, in particular).

---

[16] Portugal, however, blocked the renegotiation of the accord with ASEAN in protest at the Indonesian occupation of East Timor.

The Pakistani coup seems to have been tolerated because the prior situation was so unsatisfactory, but also because punishing Pakistan could destabilise relations between India and Pakistan. Such considerations are important and do present genuine challenges to policy-makers in terms of striking the balance between human rights and other considerations.

Member states can also block the imposition of strong measures against countries considered to fall within their spheres of influence. France has blocked sanctions on Cameroon and Niger, for example, despite violations of human rights and democratic principles (Olsen, 1998: 27).

There are also genuine doubts that negative measures *should* be taken. Which measures will improve the situation is not always obvious – quite apart from the issue of whether outsiders can indeed contribute to change. It could be more effective to strengthen economic and political links with the country concerned, thus engendering a process of internal change. Cutting off development aid to poor countries might worsen the situation, and would not address the root causes of violations. This is essentially a dilemma between strategies of 'asphyxiation' (blocking economic flows inhibits or halts bad behaviour) and 'oxygen' (economic activity leads to positive political consequences) (Lavin, 1996). There is some opposition within the EU to applying negative conditionality because it would isolate those states that most need aid and ties with the EU and generate instability. Integration, dialogue and trade – not sanctions – should be used to promote human rights. The EU also cannot exercise influence if it has no ties to the country concerned. Such concerns have affected relations with countries such as Turkey and Russia: there is agreement that negative conditionality would be ineffective. The target of sanctions may also not be clear – particularly in civil war situations, as in Algeria or the Democratic Republic of Congo.

The arguments against using sanctions crop up in national foreign policy-making as well, but within the EU there seems to be a strong tradition against coercive measures. This dates back to the Community's experience during the Cold War. A reluctance to use negative measures, however, opens the EU to charges of appeasement and complicity. At times, sending a negative message is necessary to maintain consistency, if nothing else. But it will not always be clear when this should be the case.

Overcoming inconsistency

Jack Donnelly (1982: 591) believes that the problem of inconsistency can be overstated: '[T]here need be no real inconsistency in treating similar violations differently . . . A blind demand that violation *x* produce response *y* is simplistic and silly. If the problems differ substantially, then so must the (immediate) aims and instruments of policy.' However, he maintains that 'if variations in the treatment of human rights violators are to be part of a consistent policy, human rights concerns need to be explicitly and coherently integrated into the broader framework of foreign policy'. This requires ordering foreign policy goals and values, which could justify principled trade-offs (Donnelly, 1982: 591–2). Trade-offs between objectives are to be expected – human rights promotion cannot possibly come first all the time. But where it does not come first, the reason must be explained, otherwise inconsistency will undermine the EU's foreign policy with an ethical dimension.

Whether the EU is capable of producing such a coherent approach has to be doubted. It has simply not yet developed the capacity to conduct strategic policy consistently; the system is evolving from one that aimed solely at reaching common positions on some international issues, but it has not yet evolved into one permitting such rational policy-making. In the EU's foreign policy-making system a balance between the collective and national levels must be reached on a case-by-case basis. Where the balance lies – closer to the collective or to the national levels – depends on the case. This is not conducive to strategic policy-making. In other words, the problems facing the EU in formulating and implementing a consistent foreign policy with an ethical dimension lie in the fundamental problem of making *foreign policy* in the EU.

The EU has articulated general policy objectives, but, with a few exceptions, it has not prioritised them, either generally, or with respect to specific countries or situations. 'Common strategies', as invented by the Amsterdam Treaty, are a step in this direction. But the common strategies on Russia, Ukraine and the Mediterranean have not ordered the wide variety of objectives listed (including the promotion of human rights, although this objective was not very prominently stated in the strategies). CFSP common positions and joint actions also set out the EU's objectives with respect to particular countries, but again these tend not to be systematically prioritised.

There is no list of the specific human rights that the Union seeks to promote, much less a 'ranking' of the rights. There are numerous references to the fundamental rights listed in the Universal Declaration on Human Rights and the International Covenants, as well as to the indivisibility of human rights. It is not clear which human rights violations are considered to be most serious, however, or which should be promoted above all others. The EU has no criteria by which to judge the human rights (and democratic) records of its partners, nor does it have a central font of information about those records. Of course, setting hard and fast rules prevents consideration of the specifics of each case; it limits flexibility.

But consistency implies that countries in more or less the same situation are treated more or less similarly: the same standards apply to all, unless otherwise justified.

Violations of democratic principles seem to be spotted and punished more often than infringements of human rights – perhaps because they are more obvious: a *coup d'état* can be easily condemned, but judging the 'cut-off point' above which human rights violations should be punished is more problematic. Consultations under the human rights clause are usually opened after violations of democratic principles (see table 11.1). But it is difficult to know whether this is a conscious policy; it could signal that human rights matter less than democracy.

The EP has repeatedly called for clear and operational criteria for the suspension of cooperation with third countries (see *Agence Europe*, 19 December 1998). The Economic and Social Committee (1997, points 3.2.4 and 3.3.2) has also called for annual reports on the human rights situations in all states with which the EU has concluded or is about to conclude agreements, and stressed the need for adequate arrangements to monitor compliance with the human rights clause.

In October 1999, the EU Council published its first annual human rights report, following a December 1998 pledge to do so (Council, 1999). Unlike the US State Department reports, the EU's does not assess the situation country by country. It covers broadly major EU initiatives in the field of human rights, such as the inclusion of human rights clauses in agreements, aid for human rights programmes and EU action in international fora. It gives examples of countries where specific thematic concerns have been raised (torture, death penalty, freedom of expression and so on), but it is not a comprehensive account. The EU also does some collective human rights monitoring. The member states' Consuls General in Jerusalem and Heads of Mission in Tel Aviv publish a regular human rights watch report on the Middle East Peace Process ('Settlements Watch', 'Jerusalem Watch' and 'Occupied Territories Watch'), which recount recent events and problems regarding human rights.[17] These reports are a first step towards a more comprehensive and transparent reporting system, but still do not set out priorities and criteria for action.

The EU's pillar system generates its own set of obstacles to consistency. The inter-pillar tussle over electoral observation is one manifestation of this. Another is the lack of clarity about the relationship of the CFSP human rights working groups to other working groups (*Agence Europe*, 2 June 1999). This contributes to the marginalisation of human rights concerns in policy-making.

---

[17] The reports are available from the CFSP section of the Council's web site (http://ue.eu.int).

Consistency could suffer during the settling-in period of the new High Representative for the CFSP and the Policy Planning and Early Warning Unit.[18] It is not yet clear where human rights will fit in, and how responsibilities will be divided with the first pillar. Coordination *within* the first pillar is also a problem. When Jacques Santer was president of the Commission, the RELEX group of external relations commissioners was to coordinate activity, but there were still problems, and human rights had little space. DG1A had responsibility for overall coherence of external human rights policy, but the DGIA human rights unit was small, and was not always involved in decision-making. Romano Prodi's Commission contains commissioners responsible for different functions: external relations, development, trade and enlargement. All of the external human rights units have been brought together within the external relations directorate-general. This may improve coherence and coordination.

The Community's legal competence to promote human rights in third countries is also problematic. If part of an external agreement falls outside Community competence, then the EC lacks capacity to conclude it in its own right; the agreement is a 'mixed agreement', and must be concluded (ratified) by the member states as well. Angela Ward argues that as a result of two European Court of Justice (ECJ) rulings (Opinion 2/94 and Portugal *vs.* Council (1996)), the 'authority of the Community to include human rights as an "essential element" in external agreements is restricted to accords concerning development cooperation', and that other cooperation agreements containing the human rights clause may be challenged as a result (Ward, 1998: 528–33, quote on 531).[19] Furthermore, in ruling 196/96 (the UK *vs.* Commission), the ECJ ruled that the Commission had no power to spend money legally in the absence of an agreed legal basis; this hit the human rights programmes in particular. Two new regulations had to be approved in April 1999 to provide a legal basis for human rights spending.

Thus, the place of human rights in the Union's foreign policy machinery is shaky: issues of human rights are marginalised, and there are still grounds for questioning the legality of action on human rights. To remedy this, the Comité des Sages recommended that a new office be created in the Council to work with the High Representative for CFSP. The EP has called for the creation of a European Human Rights Forum, consisting

---

[18] The High Representative is the EU's spokesman and interlocutor with third countries. The post was created by the 1999 Amsterdam Treaty, to remedy the inconsistencies of having a rotating Council presidency represent the EU internationally.

[19] However, other EU law specialists argue that the ECJ has only ruled that a human rights policy must not extend beyond the field of EC law; areas regulated by the EC can thus be subject to its human rights policy, on the basis of Amsterdam Treaty article 308 (Alston and Weiler, 1999: 22–7).

of representatives from the EP, Council and Commission, which would evaluate the Union's activities in this area and make policy recommendations (*Agence Europe*, 19 December 1998). There have been many calls for the creation of a human rights commissioner, but they have yet to be answered (*Agence Europe*, 19 December 1998; Comité des Sages, 1999).

In a December 1998 declaration celebrating the 50th anniversary of the Universal Declaration of Human Rights, the EU agreed that its human rights policies 'must be continued and, where necessary, strengthened and improved'. But the measures to be considered seem inadequate: assessment capabilities will be enhanced by publishing the annual human rights report (whose limitations are discussed above); funding for a Human Rights Masters programme will continue; a human rights discussion forum will meet; a roster of experts will be set up for human rights field operations; the legal basis for aid programmes will be provided (in the new Regulations); and 'all means to achieve the coherent realisation of these goals, including through the consideration of strengthening relevant EU structures' will be ensured (European Council, 1998: 111–13). The German presidency reported on the progress made in implementing these recommendations to the June 1999 Cologne European Council. On EU structures, it noted that 'the question of the sphere of competence of the CFSP Human Rights Working Group and its cooperation with other working groups is still on the agenda' (*Agence Europe*, 2 June 1999). Strengthening EU structures was still on the agenda at the following European Council in December 1999. Coordination will remain a problem for the foreseeable future.

Conclusion

Compared to the situation at the start of the 1990s, the place of human rights considerations in the EU's external relations has radically changed. A decade ago, they were hardly an issue; now they form an important part of the EU's international identity. To the extent that the EU conducts foreign policy, it does have a distinct ethical dimension, although it does not declare that this is its aim.

The challenge now is to improve the ways in which the EU promotes human rights. This involves institutional reforms, but it also depends on the further evolution of the member states' willingness to formulate common foreign policy, to define and prioritise their common goals, in which the place of human rights is clear. Institutional tinkering might help to improve the consistency with which the EU pursues an external human rights policy, but double standards are likely to persist for some time. And even if the EU can agree to take measures in given situations, their effectiveness could be reduced because of the necessity of reaching agreement among so many different member states. An implicit or formal need for unanimity in decision-making is still likely to produce watered-down decisions in response to human rights violations. The EU will be judged on how effective its human rights policy is – and here the limits of collective decision-making are apparent.

Nonetheless, the EU's human rights activities are significant. Human rights could be an issue around which the member states converge; agreement on the importance of human rights could spark movement towards more collective policy-making, precisely because of the benefits of the politics of scale and the extent to which respect for human rights is already felt to form part of the EU's international identity. By incorporating human rights into foreign policy, international actors like the EU are shaping the international environment. The requirements of membership in international society are evolving: the recognition of legitimate sovereignty now appears to include consideration of the protection of human rights (Barkin, 1998). The EU is one of the forces behind the evolution; it is at the forefront of efforts to make it illegitimate to violate human rights.

References

Adams, Francis 1998, 'USAID's Democracy Initiative: Recipient Needs or Donor Interests?', *International Studies Notes* 23 (3).

Addams, Jane 1976, in Allen Davis (ed.), *Jane Addams on Peace, War and International Understanding 1899–1932*, New York: Garland Publishing.

Adler, Emanuel 1997, 'Seizing the Middle Ground: Constructivism in World Politics', *European Journal of International Relations* 3 (3).

Albright, Madeleine (US Permanent Representative to the UN) 1994, Hearings before Sub-Committee on International Security, International Organisation and Human Rights (Committee on Foreign Relations, House of Representatives, 103rd Congress, 17 May).

Alston, Philip and J. H. H. Weiler 1999, 'An "Ever Closer Union" in Need of a Human Rights Policy: The European Union and Human Rights', in Philip Alston (ed.), *The EU and Human Rights*, Oxford: Oxford University Press.

Anscombe, G. E. M. 1958, 'Modern Moral Philosophy', *Philosophy* 33.
    1981, 'The Justice of the Present War Examined', in *The Collected Philosophical Papers of G. E. M. Anscombe, vol. 3: Ethics, Religion and Politics*, Oxford: Blackwell.

Arendt, Hannah 1986, 'Communicative Power', in Steven Lukes (ed.), *Power*, New York University Press.

Arts, Karin 2000, *Integrating Human Rights into Development Cooperation: The Case of the Lomé Convention*, The Hague: Kluwer Law International.

'Aziz, Tariq 1997, 'News Conference by Iraqi Deputy Prime Minister', *Iraq Television Network*, 7 November (FBIS-NES-97-315).
    1998, 'Interview with Iraqi Deputy Prime Minister', *Baghdad Iraq Television Network*, 24 February (FBIS-NES-98-055).

Barkin, J. Samuel 1998, 'The Evolution of the Constitution of Sovereignty and the Emergence of Human Rights Norms', *Millennium* 27 (2).

Barry, Brian 1995, *Justice as Impartiality*, Oxford University Press.

Baudot, Jacques forthcoming, 'Moral Power of the United Nations', in Barbara Sundburgh Baudot (ed.), *Ideas for an Ethical and Spiritual Renaissance*, London: Macmillan.

Baudrillard, Jean 1990, *Fatal Strategies*, New York: Semiotext(e).
    1998, *The Illusion of the End*, Cambridge: Polity Press.

Beck, Ulrich 1997, *The Risk Society: Towards a New Modernity*, London: Sage.
    1998, *Democracy without Enemies*, Cambridge: Polity Press.

Beigbeder, Yves 1999, *Judging War Criminals: The Politics of International Justice*, Basingstoke: Macmillan.

Beitz, Charles 1979, *Political Theory and International Relations*, Princeton, NJ: Princeton University Press.

Benedetti, Fanny and John Washburn 1999, 'Drafting the International Criminal Court Treaty: Two Years to Rome and an Afterword on the Rome Diplomatic Conference', *Global Governance* 5.

Beresford, Meg 1983, 'An Open Letter to the Soviet Peace Committee', *New Statesman*, 21 January.

Berlin, Isaiah 1969, *Four Essays on Liberty*, Oxford: Oxford University Press.

Best, Geoffrey 1984, *Nuremberg and After: The Continuing History of War Crimes and Crimes against Humanity*, Reading: University of Reading Press.

Bird, Graham and John E. Smith 1963, *The Spirit of American Philosophy*, Oxford: Oxford University Press.

Blair, Tony 1999, 'Doctrine of the International Community', Speech given at Hilton Hotel, Chicago, 22 April, <http://www.number-10.gov.uk/news.asp? NewsId=363> (retrieved 19 October 2000).

Booth, Ken 1999, 'The Kosovo Tragedy: Epilogue to Another "Low and Dishonest Decade"', Keynote Address to the South African Political Science Association Biennial Congress, Saldanha Military Academy, 29 June.

Brown, Archie 1999, 'Russia and Democratization', *Problems of Post-Communism* 46 (5).

Brown, Chris 1992a, *International Relations Theory: New Normative Approaches*, Hemel Hempstead: Harvester Wheatsheaf.

1992b, 'Marxism and International Ethics', in Terry Nardin and D. Mapel (eds.), *Traditions of International Ethics*, Cambridge: Cambridge University Press.

1999, 'Universal Human Rights: A Critique', in Dunne and Wheeler (eds.).

2000, 'Cultural Diversity and International Political Theory: From the Requirement to Mutual Respect?', *Review of International Studies* 26 (2).

Brown, Michael E., Sean M. Lynn-Jones and Steven E. Miller (eds) 1996, *Debating the Democratic Peace*, Cambridge, Mass: MIT Press.

Calvocoressi, Peter 1982, *World Politics since 1945*, 4th edition, London and New York: Longman.

Campbell, David 1993. *Politics Without Principle: Sovereignty, Ethics, and the Narratives of the Gulf War.* Boulder: Lynne Rienner.

1998. *Writing Security: United States Foreign Policy and the Politics of Identity*, revised edition. Minneapolis: University of Minnesota Press.

Carr, E. H. 1964, *The Twenty Years Crisis 1919–1939: An Introduction to the Study of International Relations*, London: Macmillan.

Carrington, Lord 1983, 'Lack of Consistent Political Strategy: A Cause of Friction,' *NATO Review* 31 (2).

Cassin, Rene 1995, 'The Charter of Human Rights, 1968', extracts in Marek Tree (ed.), *Peace! by the Nobel Peace Prize Laureates: An Anthology*, Paris: UNESCO.

China 1998, 'CCTV Interviews Iraq's 'Aziz in Baghdad', *Beijing Central Television Programme One Network*, 25 February 1998 (FBIS-CHI-98-056).

Chomsky, Noam 1999, *The New Military Humanism: Lessons from Kosovo*, London: Pluto Press.

Clapham, Andrew 1991, *Human Rights and the European Community: A Critical Overview*, Baden-Baden: Nomos Verlagsgesellschaft.

Clausewitz, Carl von 1993, *On War*, ed. Michael Howard and Peter Paret, London: Everyman.

Coalition for an International Criminal Court 1998, 'Press Room Overview', <www.igc.org/icc/html> (retrieved 25 October 1999).

Comité des Sages 1998, 'Leading by Example: A Human Rights Agenda for the European Union for the Year 2000', reprinted in Philip Alston (ed.) 1999, *The EU and Human Rights*, Oxford: Oxford University Press.

Conrad, Joseph 1990, *Nostromo*, London: Penguin.

Cook, Robin 1998, 'Foreign Policy and Human Rights', House of Commons Foreign Affairs Committee, 6 January.

1999a, 'Britain is Ready to Pursue Justice in East Timor', *The Observer*, 19 September.

1999b, House of Commons Committee on Foreign Affairs, 'Examination of Witnesses, Rt Hon. Robin Cook MP and Mr Peter Ricketts', 14 April, Question 154.

Cook, Robin and Menzies Campbell 2000, 'Article by the Foreign Secretary, Robin Cook, and Liberal Democrat Foreign Affairs Spokesman, Menzies Campbell, in the Financial Times, 4 September 2000', Foreign and Commonwealth Office, <www.fco.gov.uk>.

Coomans, Fons, Fred Grünfeld, Ingrid Westendorp and Jan Willems (eds.) 2000, *Rendering Justice to the Vulnerable: Liber Amicorum in Honour of Theo van Boven*, The Hague: Kluwer Academic Publishers.

Cooper, Robert 1996, *Post-Modern State and the World Order*, London: Demos.

Council of the European Community and Foreign Ministers Meeting within the EPC Framework 1986, 'Declaration on Human Rights', *European Political Cooperation Documentation Bulletin* 2 (2).

Council of the European Community 1991, 'Resolution of the Council and of the Member States Meeting in the Council on Human Rights, Democracy and Development', *EC Bulletin* 11.

Council of the European Union 1998, 'Common Position on Human Rights, Democratic Principles, the Rule of Law and Good Governance in Africa', Document no. 98/078, *European Foreign Policy Bulletin online* (<http://www.iue.it/EFPB/Welcome.html>), European University Institute, Florence, Italy.

1999, 'Draft Annual Report on Human Rights', Document no. 11350/99, Brussels, 1 October.

Council of the European Union, General Secretariat 1995, '1994 Memorandum to the European Parliament on the Activities of the European Union in the Field of Human Rights', Document no. 4404/95, Brussels, 24 January.

Cox, Robert W. 1986, 'Social Forces, States, and World Orders: Beyond International Relations Theory', in Robert O. Keohane (ed.), *Neorealism and its Critics*, New York: Columbia University Press.

Crawford, Gordon 1996, *Promoting Democracy, Human Rights and Good Governance Through Development Aid: A Comparative Study of the Policies of Four Northern Donors*, Working Paper on Democratization no. 1, Leeds: University of Leeds, Centre for Democratization Studies.

Crisp Roger (ed.) 1996, *How Should One Live? Essays on the Virtues*, Oxford: Oxford University Press.

Critchley, Simon 1992, *The Ethics of Deconstruction: Derrida and Lévinas*, Oxford: Blackwell.

Dahl, Robert A. 1956, *A Preface to Democratic Theory*, Chicago, IL: University of Chicago Press.

1989, *Democracy and its Critics*, New Haven, CT and London: Yale University Press.

Davis, Allen 1973, *American Heroine: The Life and Legend of Jane Addams*, Oxford: Oxford University Press.

Davis, Ian 1998, 'European Integration and the Arms Trade: Creating a New Moral Imperative?', in Bill McSweeney (ed.), *Moral Issues in International Affairs: Problems of European Integration*, London: Macmillan.

DeLillo, Don 1988, *Libra*, New York: Viking.

Der Derian, James 1992, *Anti-Diplomacy: Spies, Terrors, Speed and War*, Oxford: Blackwell.

Dewey, John 1922, *Human Nature and Conduct*, in Jo Ann Boydston (ed.), *The Middle Works of John Dewey, 1899–1924*, Volume 14, Carbondale, IL: Southern Illinois University Press.

1929, *Characters and Events: Popular Essays in Social and Political Philosophy*, Volume II, London: George Allen and Unwin.

1939, 'No Matter What Happens – Stay Out', in Jo Ann Boydston (ed.), *The Late Works of John Dewey, 1939–1941*, Volume 14, Carbondale, IL: Southern Illinois University Press.

1948, *Reconstruction in Philosophy*, Boston, MA: Beacon Press.

Di Palma, Giuseppe 1990, *To Craft Democracies: An Essay on Democratic Transitions*, Berkeley, CA: University of California Press.

Donnelly, Jack 1982, 'Human Rights and Foreign Policy', *World Politics* 34 (4).

1994, 'International Human Rights After the Cold War', in M. Klare and D. C. Thomas (eds.), *World Security: Challenges for a New Century*, 2nd edn, New York: St. Martin's Press.

1998, *International Human Rights*, 2nd edn, Boulder, CO: Westview Press.

Doyle, Michael 1983a, 'Kant, Liberal Legacies, and Foreign Affairs, Part 1', *Philosophy and Public Affairs* 12 (3).

1983b, 'Kant, Liberal Legacies, and Foreign Affairs, Part 2', *Philosophy and Public Affairs* 12 (4).

Dunne, Tim and Nicholas J. Wheeler (eds.) 1999, *Human Rights in Global Politics*, Cambridge: Cambridge University Press.

Eco, Umberto 1997, *Scritti Morali*, Milan: Bompianni.

Economic and Social Committee of the European Community 1997, 'The European Union and the External Dimension of Human Rights Policy', *Official Journal of the European Communities* C series, 206.

END Appeal 1982, 'A Nuclear Free Europe', *END Bulletin* 1.

Ethics, Special Issue 1988, 'Duties Beyond Borders', 98 (4).

European Commission 1994, 'On the Implementation in 1993 of the Resolution of the Council and of the Member States Meeting in the Council on Human Rights, Democracy and Development, adopted on 28 November 1991', COM (94) 42 final, 23 February.

1995a, 'On the Inclusion of Respect for Democratic Principles and Human Rights in Agreements between the Community and Third Countries', COM (95) 216 final, 23 May.

1995b, 'The European Union and the External Dimension of Human Rights Policy: From Rome to Maastricht and Beyond', COM (95) 567 final, 22 November.

1998, Final Report: Evaluation of the Phare and Tacis Democracy Programme (1992–97), <http://europa.eu.int/comm/scr/evaluation/reports/phare/951432.pdf> (retrieved 19 October 2000).

2000, 'Communication from the Commission on EU Election Assistance and Observation', COM (2000) 191 final, 11 April.

European Council, Luxembourg 1991, 'Declaration on Human Rights', *EC Bulletin* 6.

European Council, Vienna 1998, 'Statement on Human Rights', *EU Bulletin* 12.

European Court of Auditors 2000, 'Special Report no. 12/2000 on the Management of the Commission of European Union Support for the Development of Human Rights and Democracy in Third Countries', Luxembourg.

Evans, Gareth 1989, 'Making Australian Foreign Policy', *Australian Fabian Society*, Pamphlet 50.

Fierke, K. M. 1998, *Changing Games, Changing Strategies: Critical Investigations in Security*, Manchester: Manchester University Press and St. Martin's Press.

1999, 'Besting the West: Russia's Machiavella Strategy,' *International Feminist Journal of Politics* 1 (3).

2000, 'Logics of Force and Dialogue: The Iraq–UNSCOM Case as Social Interaction', *European Journal of International Relations* 5 (3).

Finnemore, Martha and Katherine Sikkink 1998, 'International Norm Dynamics and Political Change', *International Organization* 52 (4).

Foot, Philippa (ed.) 1967, *Theories of Ethics*, Oxford: Oxford University Press.

Forbes, Ian and Mark Hoffman 1993, *Political Theory, International Relations and the Ethics of Intervention*, London: Macmillan.

Foreign and Commonwealth Office 1997a, *Mission Statement for the Foreign and Commonwealth Office* <http://www.fco.gov.uk/> (retrieved 20 September 1999).

1997b, 'British Foreign Policy', Opening Statement by the Foreign Secretary, Mr Robin Cook, at a Press Conference on the FCO Mission Statement, London, *Daily Bulletin*, 12 May <http://www.fco.gov.uk/news/speechtext.asp?892> (retrieved 20 September 1999).

1997c, 'Speech by the Foreign Secretary: Human Rights into a New Century', *Daily Bulletin*, 17 July.

Foreign and Commonwealth Office and Department for International Development [FCO and DFID] 1998, *Human Rights Annual Report 1998*, London: HMSO.

1999, *Human Rights Annual Report 1999*, London: HMSO.

Forster, E. M. 1965, *Two Cheers for Democracy*, Harmondsworth: Penguin.

Fouwels, Martine 1997, 'The European Union's Common Foreign and Security Policy and Human Rights', *Netherlands Quarterly of Human Rights* 15 (3).

Freedom House 1997–98, *Freedom in the World: The Annual Survey of Political Rights and Civil Liberties, 1997–98*, New York: Freedom House.

Frost, Mervyn 1996, *Ethics in International Relations*, Cambridge: Cambridge University Press.

1997, 'Pitfalls on the Moral Highground: Ethics and South African Foreign Policy', in Walter Carlsnaes and Marie Muller (eds.), *Change and South Africa's External Relations*, Halfway House, South Africa: International Thompson Publishing.

1999, 'Putting the World to Rights: Britain's Ethical Foreign Policy', *Cambridge Review of International Affairs* 7 (2).

Fulbright, William 1967, *The Arrogance of Power*, London: Jonathan Cape.

Gardner, Lloyd G. 1986, *A Covenant with Power: America and World Order from Wilson to Reagan*, Oxford: Oxford University Press.

Gauthier, David 1986, *Morals by Agreement*, Oxford: Clarendon Press.

General Affairs Council 1998a, 'Conclusions of 23 February 1998 Meeting', Document no. 98/032, *European Foreign Policy Bulletin online* (<http://www.iue.it/EFPB/Welcome.html>).

1998b, 'Conclusions of 25 May 1998 Meeting', Document no. 98/079, *European Foreign Policy Bulletin online* (<http://www.iue.it/EFPB/Welcome.html>).

1999, 'Conclusions of 25 January 1999 Meeting', Document no. 99/017, *European Foreign Policy Bulletin online* (<http://www.iue.it/EFPB/Welcome.html>).

Giddens, Anthony 1998, *The Third Way*, Cambridge: Polity Press.

Ginsberg, Roy 1989, *Foreign Policy Actions of the European Community: The Politics of Scale*, Boulder, CO: Lynne Rienner.

Ginsburgs, George and V. N. Kudriavtsev (eds.) 1990, *The Nuremberg Trial and International Law*, Dordrecht: Martinus Nijhoff.

Goldstone, R. J. 1996, *Prosecuting War Criminals*, London: The David Davies Memorial Institute of International Studies.

Gorbachev, Mikhail 1987, 'Gorbachev Talks to Moscow Peace Forum', *Current Digest of the Soviet Press* 39 (7).

Grant, Stephanie 2000, 'The United States and the International Human Rights Treaty System: For Export Only?', in Philip Alston and James Crawford (eds.), *The Future of UN Human Rights Treaty Monitoring*, Cambridge: Cambridge University Press.

Grilli, Enzo 1993, *The European Community and the Developing Countries*, Cambridge: Cambridge University Press.

Guicherd, Catherine 1999, 'International Law and the War in Kosovo', *Survival* 41 (2).

Hampson, F. J. 1993, *Violation of Fundamental Human Rights in the Former Yugoslavia: The Case for a War Crimes Tribunal*, London: The David Davies Memorial Institute of International Studies.

Hanson, Marianne 1999, 'Australia and Nuclear Arms Control as "Good International Citizenship"', Working Paper No. 1999/2, Research School of Pacific and Asian Studies, ANU (Canberra).

Heidigger, Martin 1972, *On Time and Being*, New York: Harper & Rowe.

Heinz, Wolfgang, Hildegard Lingenau and Peter Waller 1995, 'Evaluation of EC Positive Measures in Favour of Human Rights and Democracy (1991–1993)', Berlin: German Development Institute.

Held, David (ed.) 1993, *Prospects for Democracy*, Cambridge: Polity.

Held, Virginia 1995, *Justice and Care: Essential Readings in Feminist Ethics*, Boulder, CO: Westview.

Herring, Eric 2000/01, 'From Rambouillet to the Kosovo Accords: NATO's War Against Serbia and its Aftermath', *International Journal of Human Rights* 4 (3/4).

Hersch, Jeanne 1968, 'Ends or Means' in 'Human Rights and Responsibilities: A Guide to Reinterpretation of Intellectual, Moral and Social Values', International Federation of University Women, XVIth Conference, Karlsruhe.

Hoffman, Mark 1994, 'Normative International Theory: Approaches and Issues', in A. J. R. Groom and Margot Light (eds.), *Contemporary International Relations: A Guide to Theory*, London: Pinter Publishers.

Hoffmann, Stanley 1966, 'Obstinate or Obsolete? The Fate of the Nation-State and the Case of Western Europe', *Daedalus* 95 (3).

1997–98, 'The Hell of Good Intentions', *Foreign Policy* 29.

Hofmann, W. 1984, 'Is NATO's Defense Policy Facing a Crisis?', *NATO Review* 32 (2).

Holbrooke, Richard 1998. *To End a War*. New York: The Modern Library.

Hughes, James 2000, 'Transition Models and Democratisation in Russia', in Mike Bowker and Cameron Ross (eds.), *Russia after the Cold War*, London: Longman.

Huntington, Samuel P. 1991, *The Third Wave: Democratization in the late Twentieth Century*, Norman, OK and London: University of Oklahoma Press.

Hurd, Lord Douglas 1997, 'Foreign Policy and Human Rights', Testimony before the House of Commons Foreign Affairs Committee, 16 December.

Ikenberry, G. John 1999, 'Why Export Democracy?: The "Hidden Grand Strategy" of American Foreign Policy', *The Wilson Quarterly* 23 (2).

International Criminal Tribunal for the Former Yugoslavia (ICTY) 1996, *The Path to the Hague: Selected Documents on the Origins of the ICTY*, New York: ICTY.

International Institute of Strategic Studies 1997, *The Military Balance* 1997/8, London: IISS.

'Iran Fully Supports UN–Iraq Agreement', 23 February 1998 (FBIS-NES-98-054).

Iraqi Leadership 1998, 'Statement on UN Agreement', *Tehran IRNA*, 23 February (FBIS-NES-98-054).

Iriye, Akira 1985, 'War as Peace, Peace as War', in Philip Windsor, Akira Iriye, Nobutoshi Hagihara and George Nivat (eds.), *Experiencing the Twentieth Century*, Tokyo: University of Tokyo Press.

ISA Consult, Sussex University European Institute, and GJW Europe 1997, 'Draft Final Europe: Evaluation of the PHARE and TACIS Democracy Programme, 1991–1997', Brussels.

Isma'il, Mamdu 1998, 'Egypt Was, and Always Will Be, the Safety Valve of its Arab Nation', *Cairo Arab Republic of Egypt Radio Network*, 27 February (FBIS- NES-98-058).

Jones, Lynne 1984, 'A Time for Change,' *END Journal* 28/29.

Kaldor, Mary 1984, 'Liberating Ourselves from Cold War Ideologies', *END Journal* 10.

Kaplan, Sidney 1956, 'Social Engineers as Saviors: Effects of World War I on Some American Liberals', *Journal of the History of Ideas* 17.

Karkutli, Nadim and Dirk Butzler 1997, 'Final Report: Evaluation of the MEDA Democracy Programme 1996–1998', European Commission, Brussels, <http://www.euromed.net/MEDA/evaluation/MDP/final-report-meda-96-98-16.htm> (retrieved 01 September 1999).

Katzenstein, Peter 1996, *The Culture of National Security*, New York: Columbia University Press.

Katzenstein, Peter, Robert Keohane and Stephen D. Krasner 1998, 'International Organization and the Study of World Politics', *International Organization* 52 (4).

Keal, Paul (ed.) 1992, *Ethics and Foreign Policy*, St Leonards, Australia: Allen and Unwin.

Keck, Margaret and Katherine Sikkink 1998, *Activists Beyond Borders: Advocacy Networks in International Politics*, Ithaca, NY: Cornell University Press.

Kelman, Herman and V. Lee Hamilton 1989, *Crimes of Obedience: Toward a Social Psychology of Authority and Responsibility*, New Haven, CT: Yale University Press.

King, Martin Luther [1967] 1972, 'Where Do We Go from Here?' presidential address to the Southern Christian Leadership Conference, published under the title 'New Sense of Direction', *Worldview* 15.

Kissinger, Henry 1977, *American Foreign Policy*, 2nd edn, New York: W. W. Norton.

Klinghoffer, Arthur Jay 1998, *The International Dimension of Genocide in Rwanda*, New York: New York University Press.

Kratochwil, Friedrich V. 1989, *Rules, Norms and Decisions: On the Conditions of Practical and Legal Reasoning in International Relations and Domestic Affairs*, Cambridge: Cambridge University Press.

Krauthammer, Charles 1999, 'Humanitarian War', *The National Interest* 57.

Krugman, Paul 1996, *Pop Internationalism*, Cambridge, MA: MIT Press.

Labour Focus on Eastern Europe 1980, Statements nos. 1 and 2 of the Interfactory Strike Committee 4 (1–3).

Laidi, Zaki 1998, *A World Without Meaning: The Crisis of Meaning within International Relations*, London: Routledge.

Lake, Anthony 1995, 'Remarks on the Occasion of the 10th Anniversary of the Center for Democracy', Washington, DC, 26 September, <http://www.whitehouse.gov/WH/EOP/NSC/html/speeches/tlcfd.html> (retrieved 19 October 2000).

Lauterpacht, Sir Hersch 1945, *An International Bill of the Rights of Man*, New York: Columbia University Press.

1950, *International Law and Human Rights*, London: Stevens & Sons Limited.

Lavin, Franklin L. 1996, 'Asphyxiation or Oxygen? The Sanctions Dilemma', *Foreign Policy* 104.

Lawler, Peter 1994, 'Constitute the "Good State"', in Paul James (ed.), *Critical Politics*, Melbourne: Arena Publications.

1999, 'The Good Citizen Britain? Tradition, Ethics and British Foreign Policy' (unpublished paper, September).

Ledeneva, Alena V. 1998, *Russia's Economy of Favours*, Cambridge: Cambridge University Press.

Lijphart, Arend 1984, *Democracies: Patterns of Majoritarian and Consensus Government in Twenty-One Countries*, New Haven, CT and London: Yale University Press.

Linklater, Andrew 1992, 'What is a Good International Citizen?', in Paul Keal (ed.), *Ethics and Foreign Policy*, Canberra: Allen and Unwin.

1996, 'The Achievements of Critical Theory', in Steve Smith, Ken Booth and Marysia Zalewski (eds.), *International Theory: Positivism and Beyond*, Cambridge: Cambridge University Press.

Linn, James 1935, *Jane Addams: A Biography*, New York: Greenwood Press.

Linz, Juan J. and Arturo Valenzuela (eds.) 1994, *The Failure of Presidential Democracy: Comparative Perspectives*, Vol. 1, Baltimore, and London: The Johns Hopkins University Press.

Lippmann, Walter 1943, *US Foreign Policy: Shield of the Republic*, Boston, MA: Little, Brown and Co.

Lipschutz, Ronnie 1992, 'Reconstructing World Politics: The Emergence of Global Civil Society', *Millennium* 21 (3).

Little, Richard and Mark Wickham-Jones (eds.) 2000, *New Labour's Foreign Policy: a new moral crusade?*, Manchester: Manchester University Press.

Lowenthal, Abraham F. (ed.) 1991, *Exporting Democracy: The United States and Latin America*, Baltimore, MD and London: John Hopkins University Press.

Lukacs, John 1976, *The Last European War*, London: Routledge and Kegan Paul.

Lukes, Steven 1985, *Marxism and Morality*, Oxford: Clarendon Press.

Luong, Pauline Jones and Erika Weinthal 1999, 'The NGO Paradox: Democratic Goals and Non-democratic Outcomes in Kazakhstan', *Europe-Asia Studies* 51 (7).

Lyotard, Jean-François 1984, *The Post-Modern Condition: A Report on Knowledge*, Manchester: Manchester University Press.

MacGinty, Roger 1997, 'Bill Clinton and the Northern Ireland Peace Process', *Aussenpolitik* 111.

MacIntyre, Alasdair 1981, *After Virtue*, Notre Dame, IN: Notre Dame University Press.

McLean, Andy and Eugenia Pia-Lopez 1998, 'Europe Begins to Tackle the Spread of Arms', *Conflict Prevention Newsletter* (published by the European Platform for Conflict Prevention and Transformation) 1 (3).

McManners, John 1966, *Lectures on European History: 1789–1914*, Oxford: Blackwell.

Mailer, Norman 1948, *The Naked and the Dead*, New York: Reinehart & Co.

Mansfield, E. D. and J. Snyder 1995, 'Democratization and War', *Foreign Affairs* 74 (3).

Marrus, Michael 1997, *The Nuremberg War Crimes Trial 1945–1946: A Documentary History*, Boston, MA: Bedford Books.

Marshall, George 1947 [1976], 'Speech at Harvard University, 5 June 1947', in *Post-War Integration in Europe*, compiled Richard Vaughan, London: Edward Arnold.

Mayall, James 2000, 'Democracy and International Society', *International Affairs* 76 (1).

Mearsheimer, John 1994/95, 'The False Promise of International Institutions', *International Security* 15 (1).

Medvedkov, Y. 1983, 'Independent Soviet Groups: "Our Aim is to Build Trust"', *END Journal 2*.

Meron, Theodor 1997, 'Answering for War Crimes: Lessons from the Balkans', *Foreign Affairs* 76 (1).

1998, *War Crimes Law Comes of Age*, Oxford: Clarendon Press.

Michnik, Adam 1981, 'What We Want to Do and What We Can Do', *Telos* 47.

Minear, Richard H. 1971, *Victors' Justice: The Tokyo War Crimes Trial*, Princeton, NJ: Princeton University Press.

Mohamad, Goenawan 1995, 'Public Address to Australian Institute of International Affairs', Brisbane, 12 October.

Morgenthau, Hans J. 1985, *Politics Among Nations: The Struggle for Power and Peace*, New York: Alfred Knopf.

Murray, A. 1997, *Reconstructing Realism: Between Power Politics and Cosmopolitan Ethics*, Edinburgh: Keele University Press.

NATO 1975–80, *Texts of Final Communiques*, Vol. II, issued by the Ministerial Session of the North Atlantic Council, the Defence Planning Committee and the Nuclear Planning Group, Brussels: NATO Information Service.

Nietzsche, Friedrich 1966, *Beyond Good and Evil*, New York: Vintage.

1990, *Twilight of the Idols*, London: Penguin.

Norman, R. 1983, *The Moral Philosophers*, Oxford: Clarendon Press.

Oberdorfer, Don 1992 [1991], *The Turn, How the Cold War Came to an End: The United States and the Soviet Union, 1983-1990*, London: Jonathan Cape.

O'Donnell, Guillermo and Philippe C. Schmitter 1986, *Transitions from Authoritarian Rule: Tentative Conclusions about Uncertain Democracies*, Baltimore, MD and London: The Johns Hopkins University Press.

Olsen, Gorm Rye 1998, 'The European Union and the Export of Democracy: Ad hoc Policy with Low Priority', Paper prepared for the ECPR-ISA Joint Conference, Vienna, 16–19 September.

Onuf, Nicholas 1989, *World of Our Making: Rules and Rule in Social Theory and International Relations*, Columbia, SC: University of South Carolina Press.

Organisation for Security and Co-operation in Europe 1999, 'Charter for European Security', Istanbul, November, <http://www.osce.org/docs/english/1990-1999/summits/istachart99e.htm> (retrieved 19 October 2000).

Orwell, George 1968, 'Politics and the English Language', April 1946, *Collected Essays*, Vol. IV, London: Secker & Warburg.

Pitken, H. F. 1972, *Wittgenstein and Justice: On the Significance of Ludwig Wittgenstein for Social and Political Thought*, Berkeley, CA: University of California Press.

Plumb, J. H. 1969, *The Death of the Past*, London: Penguin.

Putnam, Robert D. 1993, *Making Democracy Work: Civic Traditions in Modern Italy*, Princeton, NJ: Princeton University Press.

Reagan, Ronald 1983, 'Arms Control: A Plea for Patience', *Vital Speeches of the Day* 49 (13).

1985, 'The Geneva Summit', *Current Policy* 766.

Risse, Thomas, Stephen C. Ropp and Kathryn Sikkink (eds.) 1999, *The Power of Human Rights: International Norms and Domestic Change*, Cambridge: Cambridge University Press.

Rockefeller, Steven 1991, *John Dewey: Religious Faith and Democratic Humanism*, New York: Columbia University Press.

Röling, Bernard V. A. and Antonio Cassese 1993, *The Tokyo Trial and Beyond*, Cambridge: Polity Press.

Rorty, Richard 1989, *Contingency, Irony and Solidarity*, Cambridge: Cambridge University Press.

Rosenthal, Joel 1991, *Righteous Realists*, Baton Rouge, LA: University of Louisiana Press.

Rothman, Jay 1992, *From Confrontation to Cooperation: Resolving Ethnic and Regional Conflict*. London: Sage.

Ruth, Hilary and Anna Putnam 1989, 'William James' Ideas', *Raritan* VIII.

Safronchuk, Vasiliy 1998, 'What Will Fate of Annan–'Aziz Memorandum Be? Situation Still Edgy', *Moskow Sovetskaya Rossiya*, 28 February (FBIS-SOV-98-06).

Schatzki, Theodore 1996, *Social Practices*. Cambridge: Cambridge University Press.

Scheffler, Samuel (ed.) 1988, *Consequentialism and its Critics*, Oxford: Oxford University Press.

Schumpeter, Joseph A. 1975, *Capitalism, Socialism and Democracy*, New York: Harper.

Senior Nello, Susan and Karen E. Smith 1998, *The European Union and Central and Eastern Europe: The Implications of Enlargement in Stages*, Aldershot: Ashgate.

Short, Clare 1997, 'Poverty – A Challenge for the 21st Century', Statement at the House of Commons, 5 November, on the White Paper on International Development <http://www.dfid.gov.uk/public/news/news_frame.html> (retrieved 19 October 2000).

Smart, J. J. C and B. Williams 1973, *Utilitarianism: For and Against*, Cambridge: Cambridge University Press.

Smith, B. F. 1981, *The Road to Nuremberg*, London: Andre Deutsch.

Smith, Karen E. 1998, 'The Use of Political Conditionality in the EU's Relations with Third Countries: How Effective?', *European Foreign Affairs Review* 3 (2).

Smith, Tony 1994, *America's Mission: the United States and the Worldwide Struggle for Democracy in the Twentieth Century*, Princeton, NJ: Princeton University Press.

Soviet Peace Committee 1984, 'Dialogue I', 10–12 December, IKV Archives, no. 508, Amsterdam: Institute for Social History.

Spiro, Peter 1994, 'New Global Communities: Nongovernmental Organizations in International Decision-Making Institutions', *Washington Quarterly* 18.

Steel, Ronald 1980, *Walter Lippmann and the American Century*, Boston, MA: Little, Brown and Company.

Steiner, Hillel 1994, *An Essay on Rights*, Oxford: Blackwell.

Stiglitz, Joseph E. 1999, 'Whither Reform? Ten Years of the Transition', Keynote Address, World Bank Annual Conference on Development Economics, Washington, DC, 28–30 April, <http://www.worldbank.org/research/abcde/pdfs/stiglitz.pdf> (retrieved 19 October 2000).

Stokke, Olav 1995, 'Aid and Political Conditionality: Core Issues and State of the Art', in Olav Stokke (ed.), *Aid and Political Conditionality*, London: Frank Cass.

Storey, Hugo 1995, 'Human Rights and the New Europe: Experience and Experiment', in David Beetham (ed.), *Politics and Human Rights*, Oxford: Blackwell.

Talbott, Strobe 1996, 'Democracy and the National Interest', *Foreign Affairs* 75 (6).

Taylor, A. J. P. 1954, *The Struggle for Mastery in Europe*, Oxford: Clarendon Press.

Taylor, Telford 1992, *The Anatomy of the Nuremberg Trials*, Boston, MA: Little, Brown and Company.

Thayer, H. S. 1981, *Meaning and Action: A Critical History of Pragmatism*, Indianapolis, IN: Hackett.

Thompson, E. P. 1983, 'The Normalisation of Europe,' *Praxis International* 3 (1).

Tiruchelvam, Neelan 1993, 'Development and the Protection of Human Rights', in *Human Rights at the Dawn of the 21st Century*, Strasbourg: Council of Europe Press.

Tomaseveski, Katarina 1997, *Between Sanctions and Elections: Aid Donors and their Human Rights Performance*, London: Pinter.

Treaty on European Union 1997, Consolidated version incorporating the changes made by the Treaty of Amsterdam, signed on 2 October 1997, *Official Journal* C 340, 10 November.

Truman, Harry 1947, Address of the President of the United States: Recommendations for Assistance to Greece and Turkey, 12 March (Truman Doctrine), <http://www.whistlestop.org/study_collections/doctrine/large/folder 5/tde02-1.html> (retrieved 1 October 2000).

Tuchman, Barbara 1996, *The Proud Tower: A Portrait of the World Before the War 1890–1914*, New York: Ballantine Books.

United Nations Diplomatic Conference of Plenipotentiaries on the Establishment of an International Criminal Court 1998, 'The Rome Statute of the International Criminal Court', Document no. A/CONF.183/9, 17 July.

United Nations Secretary-General 1998, 'Technical Cooperation in the Field of Human Rights: Report of the Secretary-General, Commission on Human Rights', Fifty-fourth Session, Document number E/CN.4/1998/92, 3 March.

1999a, 'Report on the Work of the United Nations', <http://www.un.org/Overview/SG/index.html>.

1999b, 'Peace and Development – One Struggle, Two Fronts', Address to World Bank Staff, 19 October, <http://www.worldbank.org/html/extdr/extme/kasp101999.htm>.

United States Agency for International Development 1990, *The Democracy Initiative*, Washington, DC: USAID.

1997, *Agency Performance Report 1996*, Washington, DC: USAID.

1998, USAID FY 1998 Congressional Presentation, <http://www.usaid.gov/pubs/cp98/> (retrieved 19 October 2000).

United States State Department 1999, *Country Reports on Human Rights Practices 1998* <http://www.state.gov/www.global/human_rights/hrp_reprts_mainhp.html>.

van Aardt, Maxi 1996, 'A Foreign Policy to Die For: South Africa's Response to the Nigerian Crisis', *Africa Insight* 26 (2).

Villas-Boas, J. M. P. 1984, 'Public Perceptions and Nuclear Morality', *NATO Review* 32 (2).

Vincent, R. J. 1991 [1986], *Human Rights and International Relations*, Cambridge: Cambridge University Press.

1989, 'Human Rights and Foreign Policy', in Dilys Hill (ed.), *Human Rights and Foreign Policy: Principles and Practice*, London: Macmillan.

1990, 'The Place of Human Rights in Foreign Policy and the Strengthening of International Accountability', Ditchley Conference Report, D90/6.

Virilio, Paul 1997, *Pure War*, New York: Semiotext(e).

Voute, C. 1987, 'Letter to Dr. Horvath Istvan, Minister of Home Affairs of the Hungarian People's Republic', 15 August 1983, IKV Archives, Institute for Social History, Amsterdam.

Waltz, Kenneth 1959, *Man, The State and War*, New York: Columbia University Press.

Wapner, Paul 1995, 'Politics Beyond the State: Environmental Activism and World Civic Politics', *World Politics* 47.

Ward, Angela 1998, 'Frameworks for Cooperation between the European Union and Third States: A Viable Matrix for Uniform Human Rights Standards?', *European Foreign Affairs Review* 3 (3).

Washington, James M. (ed.) 1986, *A Testament of Hope: The Essential Writings and Speeches of Martin Luther King, Jr.*, New York: HarperCollins Publishers.

Watson, Adam 1982, *Diplomacy – The Dialogue Between States*, London: Eyre Methuen.

Wedel, Janine R. 1998, *Collision and Collusion: The Strange Case of Western Aid to Eastern Europe 1989–1998*, Basingstoke: Macmillan.

1999, 'Rigging the U.S.–Russian Relationship: Harvard, Chubais and the Transidentity Game', *Demokratizatsiya: The Journal of Post-Soviet Demokratizatsiya* 7 (4).

Wendt, Alexander 1992, 'Anarchy is What States Make of It: The Social Construction of Power Politics', *International Organization* 46 (2).

Weschler, Lawrence 1982, *Solidarity: Poland in the Season of its Passion*, New York: Simon and Schuster.

West, Cornel 1989, *The American Evasion of Philosophy: A Genealogy of Pragmatism*, Madison, WI: University of Wisconsin Press.

Westbrook, Robert 1991, *John Dewey and American Democracy*, Ithaca, NY: Cornell University Press.

Wheeler, Nicholas J. 2000, *Saving Strangers: Humanitarian Intervention in International Society*, Oxford: Oxford University Press.

Wheeler, Nicholas J. and Tim Dunne 1998, 'Good International Citizenship: A Third Way for British Foreign Policy', *International Affairs* 74 (4).

White, Robert E. 1999, 'Rethinking Foreign Policy Lessons from Latin America', International Policy Report of the Center for International Policy, July.

Wight, Martin 1966, 'Western Values in International Relations', in H. Butterfield and Martin Wight (eds.), *Diplomatic Investigations*, London: George Allen and Unwin.

Wills, Gary 1992, 'Total War', in Christopher Ricks and William L. Vance (eds.), *The Faber Book of America*, London: Faber and Faber.

Wilson, Peter 1998, 'The Myth of the "First Great Debate"', *Review of International Studies* 24 (Special Issue).

Wittgenstein, Ludwig 1958, *Philosophical Investigations*, Oxford: Basil Blackwell.

Wohlforth, William (ed.) 1996, *Witnesses to the End of the Cold War*, Baltimore, MD: Johns Hopkins Press.

Zalaquett, Jose 1981/3, 'The Human Rights Issue and the Human Rights Movement', Background Information Paper of the Commission of the Churches on International Affairs.

Zehfuss, Maja 2001, "Constructivism in International Relations: Wendt, Onuf and Kratochwil, in K. M. Fierke and Knud Erik Jorgensen (eds.), *Constructing International Relations: The Next Generation*, Armonk, NY: M. E. Sharpe.

Index

Acheson, Dean, 153
Adams, Gerry, 138
Addams, Jane, 7, 55, 57, 59, 65–71
Afghanistan, 16, 43, 164
  see also Kabul
Africa, 95, 98, 188, 192, 193
Algeria, 43, 45, 195, 197, 198
Amnesty International, 29, 102,
  107, 183
Annan, Kofi, 138, 144
  see also United Nations
  Secretary-General
Anscombe, G. E. M., 23
Anti-Imperialist League, 55–6
Arab League, 118
Arendt, Hannah, 131
arms
  EU Code of Conduct on Arms Exports,
    1, 182, 189
  exports, 18, 98, 175, 176, 182, 184
  sales, 1, 2, 3, 5, 16, 31, 37, 98,
    143, 144, 168, 182
  trade, 19, 104, 106
Asia, 80, 81, 98, 107, 148, 171, 173, 192
'Asian values', 4, 28, 81, 107
Association of South-East Asian Nations
  (ASEAN), 197
asylum seekers, 99, 160, 186 n. 2
Australia, 5, 102, 169, 170, 175, 197
Austria, 84
Azerbaijan, 76
'Aziz, Tariq, 138

Baghdad, 138, 159
Baudrillard, Jean, 162, 163–4
Beck, Ullrich, 154, 159, 160
Belarus, 189, 194
Belgrade, 148, 149, 158
Berlin, Isaish, 155
Blair, Tony, 15, 30–1, 83, 84, 135, 168,
  170, 172, 173, 174, 176, 177,
  178, 180, 181, 182, 183

Booth, Ken, 179–80
Bosnia, 2, 33, 112, 118, 124, 139, 140,
  180
Britain
  see United Kingdom
Burma (Myanmar), 43, 45, 190 n. 7, 191,
  194, 197
Burundi, 43, 194
Bush, George, Senior, 96, 97, 148

Callaghan, James, 15
Cambodia, 112, 194
Cameroon, 198
Canada, 96, 118, 170, 197
Carr, E. H., 56–7, 68, 69, 131
Carrington, Lord, 131
Carter, Jimmy, 79, 96, 169
Cassin, Rene, 111
Central and East European countries
  (CEECs), 187, 188, 190, 192
Chechnya, 195
China, 10, 61, 105, 114, 118, 139, 147,
  148, 168, 171–4, 177, 182, 183,
  187, 192, 196, 197
Chomsky, Noam, 27
Churchill, Winston, 77, 113
Clarke, Kenneth, 31
Clausewitz, Carl von, 156, 160, 162, 163
Clinton, Bill, 1, 10, 84, 85, 97, 112, 135,
  148, 149, 150, 163, 174
Clinton Doctrine, 158
commercial interests, 98, 174,
  175, 195–6
Commonwealth, 30, 32, 78
communitarianism, 4
Comoros, 197
conditionality, 86, 110, 188–90, 193, 198
  see also democratic conditionality
Conference on Security and Cooperation
  in Europe (CSCE), 78–9
constructive engagement, 86, 100, 103
  see also critical dialogue

Cook, Robin, 1, 15, 16, 17, 18, 28, 29, 112, 135, 139, 167, 169, 170, 171, 172, 173, 174, 175, 177, 181, 182, 183
Cooper, Robert, 163
cosmopolitanism, 4, 27, 170
Council of Europe, 83
crimes against humanity, 1–2, 112, 113, 115, 117, 118, 120, 121, 184
critical dialogue, 191–2, 196
    see also constructive engagement
Croatia, 158, 194
Cuba, 55, 100
Czechoslovakia, 25

Dahl, Robert, 80, 81, 82
debt, 94, 98, 104
democracy, 1, 5, 7–8, 11, 16, 17, 18, 28, 34, 53, 56, 58, 60, 62, 64, 67, 69, 75–92, 96, 97, 99, 100, 103, 147, 150, 151, 157, 167, 170, 174, 183, 190–1, 193, 195, 200
    conditionality, 83–4, 86–7, 187, 188, 189–90, 194–5, 200
    definition, 77–8, 79–83, 89–90
    and economic development, 75–6, 85–6
    and economic reform, 75–6, 83, 88
    electoralist fallacy, 89
democratic peace proposition, 84–5
Der Derian, James, 161
Dewey, John, 7, 55–6, 57, 58, 59–60, 62–5, 66, 67, 68, 69, 70, 71, 152
dialogical analysis/statecraft, 9, 141–3, 171–4
dialogue, 6, 9, 10, 130, 134–5, 138, 140, 142, 143, 144, 168, 174, 191–2, 196, 198
    see also critical dialogue
Doctrine of the International Community, 30
    criteria, 178–81
Donnelly, Jack, 198–9

East Timor, 2, 33, 34, 105, 112, 143, 165, 169, 174, 175, 176, 179, 182
Eastern Europe, 30, 79, 83, 95, 131, 133, 137, 138, 188, 192
    see also Central and East European countries
Eco, Umberto, 162
El Salvador, 95
ethnic cleansing, 118, 149, 158, 165, 178, 179, 180, 183
Equatorial Guinea, 194
European Community (EC), 15, 98, 186

European Union (EU), 1, 4, 5, 10, 11, 17, 30, 32, 84, 86, 98, 112, 176, 185–203
    Code of Conduct on Arms Exports, 1, 182, 189
    Common Foreign and Security Policy (CFSP), 187, 191, 199, 200, 201, 202
    Copenhagen membership criteria, 84
    Economic and Social Committee, 200
    European Commission, 108, 109, 186, 190, 201
    European Court of Justice (ECJ), 190, 201
    European Parliament (EP), 186–7, 200, 201
    European Political Cooperation (EPC), 186
    Lomé convention, 86, 189
    Maastricht Treaty, 187
    PHARE aid programme, 83, 194, 195
    TACIS aid programme, 83, 195
Evans, Gareth, 169–70

First World War, 3, 57, 60, 62, 64, 65, 76, 86
Forster, E. M., 75, 161
France, 23, 30, 61, 78, 119, 120, 188, 197, 198

Gambia, 194
genocide, 112, 115, 117–18, 120–1, 149
    Convention on the Prevention and Punishment of the Crime of Genocide, 115
Germany, 61, 84, 118, 120, 134, 151, 152, 165, 188, 202
good international citizen, 10–11, 30, 168, 169, 170, 171, 178, 181–2, 183, 184, 186, 193
Gorbachev, Mikhail, 79, 132, 138, 142
Great Britain
    see United Kingdom
Greece, 77, 78
Guatemala, 194
Guinea-Bissau, 194
Gulf War, 22, 97, 144, 147, 155, 159, 162, 179

Habibe, B. J., 174
Haider, Jorg, 84
Haiti, 33, 159, 194
Heidegger, Martin, 156
Helsinki Final Act, 79, 130, 131, 148
Hoffmann, Stanely, 169, 196

Holbrooke, Richard, 139
Hong Kong, 173
human rights, 1, 4, 5, 6, 8, 10, 11, 16, 17,
    18, 21, 25, 26, 27, 28, 29, 30, 33,
    35, 37, 43, 44, 45, 46, 48, 49–50,
    53, 75, 77, 80, 93–111, 112, 132,
    149, 167, 168, 170, 171–6, 179,
    180, 181, 183, 184, 186, 187, 188,
    189, 190, 191, 192, 193, 197, 198,
    199–203
  and the Conference on Security and
    Cooperation in Europe, 78–9, 131,
    148
  and economic reform, 98, 100
  International Convenant on Economic,
    Social and Cultural Rights, 94 n. 1,
    96, 172, 199
  International Convenant on Political and
    Civil Rights, 94 n. 1, 96, 97, 172,
    199
  Universal Declaration of Human Rights,
    94, 95, 102, 103, 106, 107, 108,
    111, 113, 115, 199, 202
humanitarian intervention/war, 1, 6–7, 10,
    11, 25, 26, 33–54, 75, 91, 98, 112,
    148, 149, 157, 158, 176, 178–83,
    184
  legality of, 169, 177–8, 181, 183
'humanitarianism', 10, 149, 157–8, 166
Hume, John, 138
Hurd, Douglas, 31, 87 n. 7, 168, 173
Hussein, Saddam, 9, 22, 139, 159, 163,
    166

Idealism, 3, 57, 68, 78
India, 78, 119, 121, 122, 123, 136, 163,
    173, 183, 198
Indonesia, 10, 18, 43, 45, 101, 102, 143,
    168, 174–6, 179, 182, 197 n. 16
International Criminal Court (ICC), 1,
    70–71, 93, 113, 115, 116, 119–28
  statute of, 117–18
International Criminal Tribunal for former
    Yugoslavia (ICTY), 113, 114, 115,
    127
International Criminal Tribunal for
    Rwanda (ICTR), 113, 114,
    115, 127
international law, 6, 9, 17, 22, 24, 25, 30,
    32, 33, 38, 41, 51, 62, 95, 96, 105,
    112, 113, 114, 116, 117, 121, 122,
    125, 127, 147, 165, 176, 177,
    180, 183
  international humanitarian law, 113,
    114, 116, 127, 128, 180

International Law Commission (ILC),
    115, 116, 117
international society, 6, 10, 24, 25, 26, 30,
    32, 151, 170, 171, 176, 182, 203
Iran, 22, 191, 196
Iraq, 2, 10, 17, 22, 26, 31, 33, 43, 45, 100,
    135, 138, 139, 144, 147, 148, 149,
    160, 163, 176
Irish Republican Army (IRA), 138, 140
Israel, 43, 118, 119, 138, 177, 187

James, William, 55–6, 57, 60, 152–3
Jingsheng, Wei, 172
Just War, 23, 52, 180

Kabul, 165
Kant, Immanuel, 20, 23
Kellogg–Briand Pact, 63
Kennan, George, 24, 59, 77, 78
Kenya, 194
Khartoum, 165
  see also Sudan
King, Martin Luther, 136, 140
Kinkel, Klaus, 177
Kissinger, Henry, 78, 131
Klestil, Thomas, 84
Kosovo, 2, 10–11, 30, 31, 33, 53 ns. 19
    and 20, 93, 112, 135, 139, 143,
    144, 147, 148, 149, 158, 159, 165,
    169, 176, 178, 179, 180, 181, 183,
    195, 197
  see also Belgrade, Serbia, Yugoslavia
Kurds, 26, 149, 176
Kuwait, 22, 112, 144, 147, 165

Laden, Osama bin, 164
Laidi, Zaki, 157–8
Lake, Anthony, 85
Latin America, 76, 77, 95, 96, 103, 104,
    118, 188, 192
Lauterpacht, Sir Hersch, 94, 95, 107–8
League of Nations, 60, 61, 62, 63, 64, 71,
    77
Libya, 161–2
Lijphart, Arend, 81–2
Lindberg, Mary, 153
Linklater, Andrew, 134–5, 171
Lippmann, Walter, 7, 57, 59–63, 65, 67,
    69
Luce, Henry, 151

Mailer, Norman, 150, 151
Major, John, 31, 32
Malawi, 194
Mandela, Nelson, 95

Marshall Plan, 77, 86
Mearsheimer, John, 24, 25
Mediterranean, 192, 199
Michnik, Adam, 133, 134
Middle East, 95, 135, 138, 148, 200
Milosević, Slobodan, 9, 124, 135, 139,
    144, 160, 166, 176, 178, 179, 180
Mitterrand, François, 87 n. 7
Mobuto Sese Seko, 25
Mohamad, Goenawan, 101–2, 111
moral principle, 19, 20, 22, 23, 24, 26, 58,
    71, 94, 143
Morgenthau, Hans, 24, 59

Namibia, 95
Napoleon Bonaparte, 160, 161
national interest, 2, 15, 17, 18, 32, 52, 56,
    78, 122, 128, 144, 170, 171, 181,
    188 n. 5
Netherlands, 96
New Zealand, 197
Nicaragua, 25
Nietzsche, Friedrich, 155–6
Niger, 194, 198
Nigeria, 191, 193, 195, 196
non-governmental organisations (NGOs),
    4, 7, 8, 33, 56, 70, 71, 93, 95, 96,
    97, 98, 99, 101, 107, 108, 109, 110,
    111, 121, 124, 126, 138, 140, 173,
    183, 189, 190
non-intervention, 6–7, 25, 26, 32, 38, 42,
    43–4, 45, 46, 47, 48, 49, 50–1,
    121, 167
North Atlantic Treaty Organisation
    (NATO), 11, 17, 30, 42, 106, 119,
    130, 137, 138, 140, 142, 149, 160
    role in Kosovo conflict, 26, 93, 98, 139,
    158, 160, 169, 176–81, 183
Northern Ireland, 135, 138
Nuremberg Trials (International Military
    Tribunal at Nuremberg), 113, 114,
    117, 121

O'Neill, Nartin, 182
Operation Allied Force, 178
Operation Desert Fox, 159
Operation Desert Storm, 22
Organisation of American States (OAS),
    83–4, 96
Organisation of Security and Cooperation
    in Europe (OSCE), 85
Outlawry of War movement, 57, 60, 62,
    63, 67
Owen, David, 175
Oxfam, 101, 183

Pakistan, 43, 119, 163, 174, 195, 198
Palestinian Liberation Organisation
    (PLO), 140
Peirce, Charles, 55, 57, 152
Philippines, 55, 60, 95
Pilger, John, 27, 168
Pinochet, Augusto, 93, 116, 127
Plumb, J. H., 154
Poland, 136
Portugal, 17
pragmatism, 7, 55, 56, 57, 58, 59, 60, 62,
    62, 68, 69, 70, 71, 72, 152
Prodi, Romano, 201

Qichen, Qian, 172

Reagan, Ronald, 79, 96, 97, 132, 137,
    138, 192
Realism, 2, 3, 4–5, 22, 23–4, 57, 69, 85,
    129, 141, 169
'pop realism', 17, 24, 25, 27
Red Cross, 102
Reynolds, Albert, 138
Rifkind, Malcolm, 31
Roosevelt, Franklin D., 113
Rorty, Richard, 155
Rusk, Dean, 157
Russia, 87, 88, 90, 130, 139, 147, 177,
    183, 191, 195, 197, 198, 199
Rwanda, 2, 33, 43, 105, 181

Saferworld, 183
sanctions, 11, 17, 148, 173, 174, 180, 186,
    187, 190, 191, 193, 195, 196, 197,
    198
Santer, Jacques, 201
Sarajevo, 149
Save the Children, 107
Scandinavia, 5, 96
Schroder, Gerhard, 84
Schumpeter, Joseph, 80, 81
Second World War, 61, 65, 68, 77, 86, 91,
    93, 94, 113, 151, 153
Serbia, 10, 76, 98, 147, 158, 159,
    160, 196
see also Belgrade, Kosovo, Yugoslavia
Short, Clare, 29
Sierra Leone, 33, 195
Somalia, 42, 43, 112, 147, 158, 159
South Africa, 5, 48, 49, 50, 51 n. 16, 78,
    95, 118, 135, 187, 190
sovereignty, 3, 38, 41, 57, 120, 122, 126,
    127, 128, 167, 175, 203
Soviet Union, 39, 42, 61, 78, 79, 95, 135,
    148, 151

Spain, 116
Spanish–American War, 55, 60, 76
Stalin, Joseph, 77, 90, 133
Steiner, Hillel, 17
Strategic Defence Initiative (SDI), 132,
    142
Sudan, 16, 31, 43, 141, 195
    see also Khartoum
Suharto, President, 175
Symons, Baroness, 175, 176

Tajikistan, 195
Thatcher, Margaret, 15, 32, 167
Thompson, E. P., 136
Tibet, 105
Tiruchelvam, Neelan, 107
Togo, 195
Tokyo Trials (International Military
    Tribunal of the Far East), 113, 114,
    117, 121
Trinidad and Tobago, 115, 125
Truman, Harry, 77
Truman Doctrine, 77
Turkey, 17, 187, 198

Uganda, 186 n. 3
Ukraine, 87, 199
Union of Soviet Socialist Republics
    (USSR)
    see Soviet Union
United Kingdom (UK), 1, 4, 5, 9, 10–11,
    15–18, 23, 27–8, 30–1, 41, 61, 78,
    98, 105, 112, 116, 119, 128, 139,
    141, 143, 144, 165, 167–84, 188,
    189, 201
    Department for International
        Development (DFID), 16, 93, 99
    Foreign and Commonwealth Office
        (FCO), 15, 19, 107, 173, 175
    Annual Report on Human Rights, 16,
        93, 99–100, 101, 106, 110
    Mission Statement, 15–16, 17, 18, 28,
        167, 168
    Labour government, 10–11, 15, 27, 31,
        32, 34, 85, 112, 130, 131, 132, 135,
        144, 167, 177, 182, 184
United Nations (UN), 7, 10, 11, 20, 25,
    30, 32, 71, 96, 98, 100, 109, 112,
    116, 138, 140, 174, 175, 183
    Charter, 22, 26, 71, 99, 102, 110, 114,
        121, 123, 175, 177, 184
    Commission on Human Rights, 172,
        196, 197
    Conference on the Environment and
        Development, 70

Conference on Population, 70
Convention against Torture, 116
Development Programme, 106
Economic and Social Council, 71
General Assembly, 117, 126
High Commissioner for Human Rights,
    99, 110
International Court of Justice, 125, 127
Secretary-General, 101, 181
Security Council, 30, 71, 98, 113, 114,
    121, 122, 123, 124, 125, 126, 176,
    181, 197
United States (US), 4, 5, 7, 9, 10, 16, 18,
    22, 31, 32, 55, 57, 60, 61, 62, 63,
    65, 67, 96, 103–4, 108, 109, 110,
    133, 134, 135, 138, 139, 141, 143,
    144, 147–62, 165–6, 179, 197
    Agency for International Development
        (USAID), 82, 83, 87
    and the International Criminal Court,
        119, 120, 121, 122, 123, 125, 126
    and the Nuremberg and Tokyo
        tribunals, 113–14
    and the promotion of democracy, 75,
        76, 77, 79
    State Department, 172, 200

Vietnam War, 10, 96, 104, 148, 149,
    153–4, 155, 156
Vincent, John, 131, 193
Virilio, Paul, 160

Wallace, Henry, 151
Waltz, Kenneth, 163
war crimes, 1, 112, 113, 115, 116, 117,
    118, 119, 120
    Geneva conventions, 115–16, 117, 118
Ward, Angela, 196–7, 201
'Washington consensus', 86, 88
Westerdorp, Carl, 139
Western Europe, 79, 95, 97, 102, 133, 160
Wilson, Harold, 15, 175
Wilson, Woodrow, 60, 76, 148, 152, 153
Wittgenstein, Ludwig, 132
Women's International League for Peace
    and Freedom (WILPF), 65, 67
World Bank, 106, 188

Yugoslavia, 26, 34, 42, 43, 45, 112, 118,
    158, 159, 169, 178, 179, 180, 183
    see also Belgrade, Kosovo, Serbia

Zaire (Democratic Republic of Congo),
    25, 195, 198
Zemin, Jiang, 105, 172, 174